Juvenile Justice

Juvenile Justice
Redeeming Our Children

Barry Krisberg
National Council on Crime and Delinquency

SAGE Publications
Thousand Oaks ▪ London ▪ New Delhi

For information:

Sage Publications, Inc.
2455 Teller Road
Thousand Oaks, California 91320
E-mail: order@sagepub.com

Sage Publications Ltd.
1 Oliver's Yard
55 City Road
London EC1Y 1SP
United Kingdom

Sage Publications India Pvt. Ltd.
B-42, Panchsheel Enclave
Post Box 4109
New Delhi 110 017 India

Library of Congress Cataloging-in-Publication Data

Krisberg, Barry.
Juvenile justice: redeeming our children / Barry Krisberg.
    p. cm.
Includes bibliographical references and index.
ISBN 0-7619-2500-7 (cloth: acid-free paper)—
ISBN 0-7619-2501-5 (pbk.: acid-free paper)
    1. Juvenile justice, Administration of—United States. 2. Juvenile justice, Administration of—United States—History. I. Title.
HV9104.K75 2005
364.36′0973—dc22

2004009991

Printed on acid-free paper in the United States of America.

04   05   06   07   08   09   10   9   8   7   6   5   4   3   2   1

Acquiring Editor:	Jerry Westby
Editorial Assistant:	Vonessa Vondera
Project Editor:	Tracy Alpern
Copy Editor:	Patricia Oman, Publication Services, Inc.
Typesetter:	C&M Digitals (P) Ltd.
Indexer:	Naomi Linzer
Cover Designer:	Michelle Kenny

Contents

Preface

More than 30 years ago I had the unique opportunity of spending almost every day for several months with about 20 young men who were leaders of juvenile gangs in Philadelphia. They introduced me to their fellow gang members and family members and allowed me to share part of their world. They generously shared their lives with me and profoundly changed my own.

To law enforcement officials and to many community residents, these young men were very dangerous offenders who had been arrested many times and had spent a fair amount of time in juvenile facilities and adult prisons, but to me, they were my teachers and mentors in settings that were very different from my experiences. First and foremost, these young men taught me to listen and to reflect on the life experiences of those less fortunate than myself. Much of my academic and professional career has been built on listening carefully to young people who are often very angry and bitter about their own lives. I have always tried to faithfully communicate what they told me to others in the worlds of public policy, the university community, professional groups, and students. Most recently, I found myself interviewing more than 150 young people who were confined in the California Youth Authority. They told me of everyday examples of abuse and maltreatment by those who were supposed to provide for their education and treatment. Retelling their stories to my fellow Californians is leading to a major reexamination of how the nation's most populous state is treating its troubled young people. I saw the reformative power of this approach in the early 1970s when Jerome Miller, then Commissioner of the Massachusetts Department of Youth Services, held press conferences across the state and simply asked his young clients to tell the media what was being done to them by a brutal and corrupt youth corrections system. One result of this effort was that Massachusetts closed its barbaric training schools and returned most youths to smaller, high-quality, community-based programs. Even today, the Miller reforms represent the "gold standard" for juvenile justice in the Bay State and across the nation.

My Philadelphia encounters with young gang members taught me to embrace the value of redemptive justice. It is what we all would want for ourselves and our family members—a justice system that offers the hope that people can improve and can restart their lives in a more positive direction. I believe that the concept of redemptive justice was central to what Jane Addams and other pioneers in juvenile justice were striving to achieve. Rather than killing off the idealistic vision of the juvenile court, we need to rediscover it.

This book attempts to assemble the research that supports this perspective. I hope to encourage students to think critically. Sometimes, the language used in this book is less than polite—but now is the time for plain talk and "speaking truth to power." My hope is that this book and the courses in which it will be utilized will be springboards to lead the current generation of idealistic young people into progressive action.

I have many debts to repay to those who helped me assemble this book. NCCD researchers Priscilla Aguirre, Jessica Craine, Sharan Dhanoa, Poonam Juneja, and Kelly Knight assisted in reviewing earlier drafts, running down key references, and suggesting ways to improve the overall effort. My appreciation goes to great colleagues such as Yitzhak Bakal, Frederick Mills, Richard Tillson, and Buddy Howell who were my sounding boards, patiently listening as I tried to work out some of my ideas. I owe a special debt to the University of California at Berkeley students who lived through a semester devoted to the materials in this book and showed me how to improve my presentation. To my own teachers and mentors, especially Marvin Wolfgang and Thorsten Sellin, I owe so much. They taught me that ideas could change the world for the better and that advances in enlightened social policy are the true measure of lasting intellectual contributions.

Jerry Westby of Sage Publications was a patient and very supportive editor. Susan Marchionna was the central person in pulling together this manuscript. She conducted complex research, forced me to write and think more clearly, and made sure that the final product was worthy of its goals. Without Susan's very hard work, this book would still be in progress.

Finally, I want to thank my two sons, Moshe and Zaid, who continue to keep me plugged into the world of young people, educating me about what is really important in life. My life partner, Karen McKie, is responsible for infusing a humanistic spirit into my scholarly work. Her "conceptual physics" helped me look at familiar topics with a fresh set of eyes. Most important, she has showed me what unconditional love and building community can accomplish in a less-than-perfect world. Her love and support make my world possible.

Sage Publications gratefully acknowledges the contributions of the following reviewers:

Franklin E. Zimring
University of California at
Berkeley

Yolander G. Hurst
Southern Illinois University

Charles E. Owens
University of North Florida

Patricia H. Jenkins
Temple University

Nancy Rodriguez
Arizona State University, West

Sesha Kethineni
Illinois State University

Morgan Peterson
Palomar College

Lee Ayers
Southern Oregon University

Charles L. Dreveskracht
Northeastern State University

Verna J. Henson
Texas State University–San Marcos

Martha Smithey
University of Texas at El Paso

Allison Ann Payne
College of New Jersey

Frances G. Pestello
University of Dayton

Ron Fagan
Pepperdine University

Jeffrey P. Rush
University of Tennessee at
Chattanooga

Terrance J. Taylor
Georgia State University

One

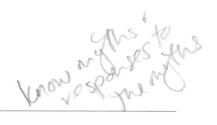

Juvenile Justice: Myths and Realities

perception → reaction

"I t's only me." These were the tragic words spoken by Charles "Andy" Williams as the San Diego Sheriff's Department SWAT team closed in on the frail high school sophomore who had just turned 15 years old. Williams had just shot a number of his classmates at Santana High School, killing 2 and wounding 13. This was another in a series of school shootings that shocked the nation; however, the young Mr. Williams did not fit the stereotype of the "super-predator" that has had an undue influence on juvenile justice policy for the past decade.

Juvenile justice policies have historically been built on a foundation of myths. From the "dangerous classes" of the 19th century to the super-predators of the late 20th century, government responses to juvenile crime have been dominated by fear of the young, anxiety about immigrants or racial minorities, and hatred of the poor (Platt, 1968; Wolfgang, Thornberry, & Figlio, 1987). Politicians have too often exploited these mythologies to garner electoral support or to push through funding for their pet projects. The general public has bought into these myths, as evidenced by numerous opinion polls illustrating the perception that juvenile crime rates are raging out of control (Dorfman & Schiraldi, 2001). Even during periods in which juvenile arrests were falling, the National Victimization Survey in 1998 reported that 62% of Americans felt that juvenile crime was rising. A 1996 California poll showed that 60% of the public believed that youths are responsible for most violent crime, although youngsters under age 18 years account for just 13% of arrests for violence offenses. Similarly, the

1

public perceives that school-based violence is far more common than the rates reflected in official statistics. Several observers feel that these misperceptions are, in part, created by distorted media coverage of juvenile crime (Dorfman & Schiraldi, 2001).

By far the most destructive myth about juvenile crime was the creation of the super-predator myth (Elikann, 1999). The myth began with predictions of future increases in youth violence made by James Q. Wilson (1995) and John DiIulio (1995a). Wilson claimed that by 2010 there would be 30,000 more juvenile "muggers, killers, and thieves." DiIulio predicted that the new wave of youth criminals would be upon us by 2000. Within a year, DiIulio's (1996) estimate for the growth in violent juveniles had escalated to 270,000 by 2010 (compared to 1990). Other criminologists such as Alfred Blumstein (1996) and James Fox (1996) suggested that the rise in violent arrests of juveniles in the early 1990s would combine with a growing youth population to produce an extended crime epidemic. Fox warned that our nation faces a future juvenile violence that may make today's epidemic pale in comparison (Fox, 1996). He urged urgent action. Not to be outdone in rhetoric, DiIulio referred to a "Crime Bomb" and painted the future horror that "fatherless, Godless, and jobless" juvenile "super-predators" would be "flooding the nation's streets" (DiIulio, 1996, p. 25).

All of these dire predictions proved inaccurate. Juvenile crime rates began a steady decline beginning in 1994, reaching low levels not seen since the late 1970s. In part, the myth was based on a misinterpretation of the research of Wolfgang, Figlio, and Sellin (1972), which found that a small number of juveniles accounted for a large number of juvenile arrests. DiIulio and his panicky friends applied this number to the entire growth in the youth population to manufacture their bogus trends. But, even worse, the academic purveyors of the super-predator myth used overheated rhetoric to scare the public.

Consider that the definition of a predator is an animal that eats other animals. Perhaps only the *Tyrannosaurus Rex* might truly qualify as a super-predator. The symbolism of the vicious youth criminal who preys on his victims is truly frightening. This is reminiscent of the Nazi propaganda that referred to Jews as vermin that spread disease and plague. Further, the imagery of the child without a conscience was reinforced by media accounts of a generation of babies born addicted to crack cocaine and afflicted with severe neurological problems. Interestingly, a recent review of medical studies of "crack babies" found no substantial evidence that in utero exposure to cocaine negatively affected the child's development more than traditional risk factors such as parental alcohol and tobacco consumption. Herrnstein and Murray (1994) completed the grotesque portrait of the super-predator by claiming to demonstrate a linkage between low intelligence and crime. They suggested that persons of low IQ would respond only to blunt punishments, rather than more subtle prevention or rehabilitation programs.

The media loved the dramatic story about the "barbarians at the gates," and the politicians soon jumped on the bandwagon. A major piece of federal juvenile crime legislation enacted in 1997 was titled The Violent and Repeat Juvenile Offender Act of 1997 (S-10).

At the state level, the super-predator myth played an important role in 47 states amending their laws on juvenile crime to get tougher on youthful criminals (Torbet et al., 1996). Legislators modified their state laws to permit younger children to be tried in adult criminal courts. More authority was given to prosecutors to file juvenile cases in adult courts. Judges were permitted to use "blended sentences" that subjected minors to a mixture of juvenile court and criminal court sanctions. Legislators also weakened protection of the confidentiality of minors tried in juvenile courts, allowing some juvenile court convictions to be counted later in adult proceedings to enhance penalties. State laws were amended to add punishment as an explicit objective of the juvenile court system and to give victims a more defined role in juvenile court hearings. Prior to these revisions, victims of juvenile crime had no formal participation in juvenile court proceedings. During the 1990s, rates of juvenile incarceration increased, and more minors were sentenced to adult prisons and jails. This social and legal policy shift and its consequences are discussed further later in this chapter.

The movement to treat ever younger offenders as adults was aided by other myths about juvenile justice. First, it was asserted that the juvenile court was too lenient and that the juvenile court could not appropriately sanction serious and violent youthful offenders. Second, it was argued that traditional juvenile court sanctions were ineffective and that treatment did not work for serious and chronic juvenile offenders. Neither of these myths is supported by empirical evidence.

An analysis of juvenile court data in 10 states found that juvenile courts responded severely to minors charged with homicide, robbery, violent sex crimes, and aggravated assaults (Butts & Connors-Beatty, 1993). This study found that juvenile courts sustained petitions (the juvenile court equivalent of a conviction) in 53% of homicide cases, 57% of robbery cases, 44% of serious assaults, and 55% of violent sex crimes. By contrast, a study by the Bureau of Justice Statistics of adult felony cases in state courts found that the odds of an arrested adult being convicted for violent offenses ranged from a low of 13% for aggravated assaults to a high of 55% for homicide (Langan & Solari, 1993). Figure 1.1 compares the

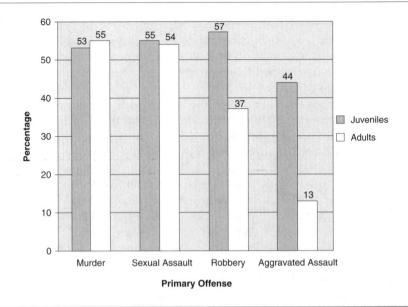

Figure 1.1   Odds of an Arrested Adult Being Convicted in Criminal Court vs.
Odds of Conviction for Delinquency Referrals in 10 States

SOURCE: Jones and Krisberg (1994, p. 25).

odds of conviction for a violent crime in criminal versus juvenile courts
(Jones & Krisberg, 1994). Other data also suggest that the sentencing of
juveniles is not more lenient in juvenile courts compared to criminal
courts. Data from California reveal that minors convicted and sentenced
for violent crimes actually serve longer periods of incarceration in the
California Youth Authority (CYA) than do adults who are sent to the state
prison system (Jones & Krisberg, 1994).

Another study compares the sentences of 16- and 17-year-olds in
New York and New Jersey. These two states have very different responses
to youthful offenders. Whereas New York prosecutes most 16- and
17-year-olds in its criminal courts, New Jersey handles the vast majority
of these youths in its juvenile courts. The researchers found that for
youngsters who were accused of burglary and robbery, there were little
differences in the severity of case dispositions in the juvenile courts of
New Jersey compared to the criminal court proceedings in New York.
Moreover, the study found that similar youths had lower rearrest rates
if they were handled in the juvenile system rather than the adult court
system (Fagan, 1991).

There is an impressive body of research that refutes the myth that nothing works with juvenile offenders. There are many studies showing the effectiveness of treatment responses for young offenders (Palmer, 1992). Gendreau and Ross (1987) have assembled an impressive array of studies showing the positive results of correctional interventions for juveniles. Others such as Greenwood and Zimring (1985) and Altschuler and Armstrong (1984) isolated the critical components of successful programs. More recently, Lipsey and his colleagues (1998) and the National Council on Crime and Delinquency (NCCD, 2000) have summarized the promising treatment responses for serious and violent juvenile offenders. More details about these successful interventions are reviewed in Chapter 8. For now, it is important to see how the myth that juvenile offenders cannot be rehabilitated misguides policy changes that restrict the jurisdiction of the juvenile court and that impose harsher penalties on children.

A related myth that dominates political discourse on youth crime is that longer mandatory penalties of incarceration would reduce juvenile crime. This recommendation rests on the notion that there are a small number of offenders who are responsible for the vast majority of violent crime. Thus, if we could lock away these "bad apples" for a long period of time, the immediate crime problem would be greatly reduced. This idea has some natural intuitive appeal, since incarcerated offenders cannot commit offenses in the community. However, incarceration does not guarantee cessation of delinquent behavior. Further, there are several studies that point to the "dangerous few"—the small number of chronic offenders, in particular, gang members, who contribute to a disproportionate amount of violent crime (Loeber & Farrington, 2001).

There are several flaws in the argument that longer, mandatory sentences would reduce violent youth crime. Presently the vast majority of youngsters who are incarcerated in juvenile and adult correctional facilities have been convicted of nonviolent offenses (Jones & Krisberg, 1994). Broad-based policies mandating longer periods of confinement are most likely to increase the extent of incarceration for property offenders, drug offenders, and youths who are chronic minor offenders. Further, high-risk juvenile offenders do not remain high-risk forever. Using incapacitation as a crime-control strategy assumes that criminal careers, once begun, will increase and include more violent behavior over time. Research studies on juvenile crime careers reveal a different picture. The prevalence of serious violent crime peaks between the ages of 16 and 17, and after age 20 the prevalence drops off sharply (Elliott, 1994). The likelihood that individuals will commit violent crimes during the ages of 21–27 is approximately the same as for children ages 12 and 13 (Elliott, 1994). Haapanen's (1988) long-term follow-up studies of youths released from the CYA show that longer sentences for youthful offenders would have little or no impact on overall societal rates of violent crime. In addition, the youth population is projected to increase substantially over the next 20 years. Thus, for every current juvenile offender that is taken out of circulation, there are increasing numbers entering their peak crime-committing years.

Juvenile justice professionals generally reject the notion that the incarcerative system by itself can exert a major effect on reducing crime rates (National Council on Crime and Delinquency, 1997). There is a growing body of knowledge that shows prevention and early intervention programs to be far more cost-effective than incapacitation in reducing rates of youth crime (Greenwood, Model, Rydell, & Chiesa, 1996). And, there is some evidence that secure confinement of youngsters at early ages actually increases their subsequent offending behavior (Krisberg, 1997).

These are just some of the major myths that continue to confuse and confound the process of rational policy development for the juvenile justice system. There are others that claim to offer "miracle cures" for juvenile delinquency. Citizens are fed a regular diet of these "miracle cures" by the entertainment media and local news broadcasts, politicians, and entrepreneurs. Many communities have implemented programs such as Scared Straight that claimed that brief, one-day visits by youngsters to prison to be yelled at by inmates can cure emotional and family problems— despite compelling research that the program was not effective (Finckenaur, Gavin, Hovland, & Storvoll, 1999). Juvenile justice officials quickly jumped on the bandwagon to start up boot camps with scant evidence that these efforts could reduce recidivism (MacKenzie, 2000). Programs such as Tough Love and Drug Abuse Resistance Education (D.A.R.E.) have garnered media attention and significant funding without possessing solid empirical foundations. Perhaps the most destructive "miracle cure" to surface in recent years has been the mistaken belief that placing youths in adult prisons would advance public safety (Howell, 1998; Krisberg, 1997).

To achieve the ideal goal of juvenile justice, which is to protect vulnerable children and, at the same time, help build safer communities, these myths must be debunked. If the emperor indeed has no clothes, we need to acknowledge this fact and move to sounder social policies. The following chapters will show how to assemble the evidence on which effective responses to youth crime can be built. We will review the best research-based knowledge on what works and what does not. There is a path out of the morass of failed juvenile justice policies, but we must look critically at current policy claims, and we must apply high standards of scientific evidence to seek new answers.

Chapter 3 gives an important historical context to the ongoing quest for the juvenile justice ideal. The history of juvenile justice has not been a straightforward march to the more enlightened care of troubled youths. There have been race, class, and gender biases that have marked some of the contours of this history. Learning how we have arrived at the current system of laws, policies, and practices is a crucial step in conceiving of alternatives to the status quo.

Summary

Sadly, too much of what passes for public policy on juvenile justice has been founded on misinformation and mythology. Throughout our history, fear of the young, concern about immigrants, gender bias, and racial and class antagonism have dominated the evolution of juvenile justice. The media and politicians exploit these prejudices and fears for their own purposes.

The most powerful myth in the mid-1990s was the alleged wave of young super-predators. Some suggested that America would face an unprecedented increase in juvenile violence at their hands. This myth fueled a moral panic that shaped many public policies designed to get tougher with juvenile offenders. There were a large number of new laws that made it easier to try children in criminal courts, and that increased the number of young people in prisons and jails. Critics of the juvenile court argued that it was too lenient in its sentencing practices, although there was little evidence backing these claims. Calls for longer periods of incarceration were also part of this moral panic. The research did not support the assertion that more incarceration would lead to lower juvenile crime rates.

Review Questions

1. What was the super-predator myth? How did its proponents support their claims? Did the predicted juvenile crime wave occur, and if not, what did affect juvenile crime trends in the late 1990s?

2. What unsubstantiated claims are used to support harsher sentencing for juveniles?

3. Does increased incarceration reduce rates of juvenile crime; how has this conclusion been reached?

Two

Data Sources

G etting the facts straight about juvenile crime and about the operation of the juvenile justice system is a challenging job. One confronts a range of statistical data sources that are not integrated and that offer only very partial information on the subject. Further, America's justice systems are radically decentralized. There are more than 10,000 separate law enforcement agencies and nearly 3,000 juvenile courts. These agencies administer laws that are determined by each of the 50 states. In addition, juvenile justice systems in the District of Columbia, Native American tribal areas, Puerto Rico, Guam, American Samoa, and American trust territories are governed by other legal structures administered by the federal government.

At the federal level, multiple agencies are responsible for collecting and analyzing statistical data on juvenile crime and juvenile justice. In various states and localities, sources of accurate data are even more diffuse and difficult to obtain. Much of the information about juvenile crime and the processing of young offenders is collected on an ongoing basis, but this information is rarely, if ever, utilized for local planning or evaluation purposes. In this age of information, the juvenile justice system continues to function and evolve based on anecdotes, subjective impressions, and the latest high-profile case that was reported on the evening news. This situation undoubtedly contributes to the ascendancy of myths in the formulation of juvenile justice policy and practice.

This chapter reviews available national sources of data and describes their strengths and weaknesses. Later, the chapter will discuss a range of current research methods to deepen our understanding of the contours of youth crime and the juvenile justice system. Serious students of juvenile justice are best advised to master a broad range of research techniques to help them gain a more holistic comprehension of the subject. Students are also advised to be skeptical of all statements of fact and to become critical consumers of juvenile justice statistics and research findings.

Understanding the Contours of Juvenile Crime

No one knows for sure how much crime is attributable to young people. The Department of Justice conducts an annual telephone survey to estimate the nature and extent of victimization, but these data do not tell us how much of this victimization is caused by young people. Moreover, the National Crime Victimization Survey (NCVS) does not collect data from children below the age of 12, because they believe that the results would be unreliable. This omission no doubt understates the extent of victimization that occurs in elementary schools, playgrounds, and in the home (Snyder & Sickmund, 1999). Indeed, even for older adolescents, other national surveys suggest that the NCVS underestimates the amount of criminal victimization experienced by teenagers (Wordes & Nuñez, 2002). Surveys of youths that are conducted in person, in homes, or at schools have produced estimates of teen victimization that are almost twice as high as the NCVS (Wordes & Nuñez, 2002).

Historically, citizens report only a fraction of their crime victimizations to the police. Teens are even less likely to report being victimized, especially for violent offenses. Further, police make arrests in a small percentage of the cases ranging from 50% of reported violent crimes to 20% of property crimes. In the case of drug offenses, there is rarely a victim who voluntarily comes forward, so there are no valid estimates of how many drug offenses result in arrests.

The drop-off from reported victimization in official reports to the police to someone being arrested for a specific offense is highly significant for the understanding of juvenile crime. We know the age (or sex or ethnicity) of the offender only when he or she is taken into police custody. Thus, our main statistics about youth crime are, at best, descriptive of the subset of offenders who get caught. The relationship of this subset to the general population of juvenile offenders is unknown, and perhaps unknowable. Because the arrested group can be a very small proportion of those who are actually committing crimes, the basic statistical data and the nature and distribution of juvenile crime, or trends over time, are hopelessly inadequate. Further, those who are arrested are not necessarily guilty of the crime. In many jurisdictions, more than half of police referrals to the juvenile court result in dropped charges (Synder & Sickmund, 1999). Being arrested is a measure of police practices, such as where police patrol or to which crimes they pay the closest attention, rather than a valid indicator of youth behavior. This discrepancy is especially true for crimes such as drug trafficking, in which both the offender and other crime participants may want to keep the matter low profile. Delbert Elliott and his associates have compared the numbers of crimes that were reported by juveniles in confidential surveys with the number of these offenses that resulted in an official arrest. They found that only about 1 in 7 very serious crimes that were admitted to in the surveys resulted in an arrest; for less serious crimes, the odds of getting caught were 1 in 50 (Huizinga & Elliott, 1987). This discrepancy casts serious doubt on research and evaluation generalizations that are made using only police statistics. Later in this chapter we will discuss the utility and limitations of self-report surveys to advance our understanding of the contours of youth crime.

National data on juvenile arrests are assembled by the Federal Bureau of Investigation from reports submitted by thousands of local law enforcement agencies through the Uniform Crime Reporting System (UCR). From year to year the number of participating agencies varies, making analyses of trends extremely problematic. For example, for several years in the 1990s, the Chicago Police Department did not report data on juvenile arrests to the Illinois Criminal Justice Authority, which compiles statewide crime statistics. The omission of Chicago data created an obvious distortion in statistics pertaining to Cook County (where Chicago is one of a number of cities) and for overall Illinois juvenile crime data (Krisberg, Noya, Jones, & Wallen, 2001). Law enforcement reporting is more consistent for the most serious offenses—including homicide, rape, robbery, burglary, larceny, auto theft, and arson—but the data from various jurisdictions are not at all uniform for minor assaults—vandalism, drug offenses, and status offenses such as truancy, running away, curfew violations, possession of alcohol, and incorrigibility. These latter offenses are among the most frequent crimes resulting in teenage arrests. Thus, juvenile crime data are extremely uneven and frustrate the ability to plan and evaluate responses to juvenile crime at the federal, state, and local levels.

Even less is known, in any systematic manner, about how the police handle youths once they are arrested. The annual UCR report, *Crime in the United States,* contains just one table that provides data on police dispositions of juvenile arrests. Whereas the information is broken down by the size of the jurisdiction, the data are not presented for specific cities or states. In general, it appears that law enforcement agencies refer about two thirds of arrests to the juvenile court. A very small fraction of juvenile arrests (roughly 7%) are directly referred to criminal courts. The remaining juvenile arrests are handled informally within the police department or referred to community welfare agencies. Local police practices are extremely diverse in terms of the methods used to informally process juvenile arrestees, ranging from giving the youth a referral card to more formal counseling or informal supervision programs operated within law enforcement agencies (sometimes in partnership with other community agencies). Some police agencies favor informal handling of juvenile cases, whereas others emphasize much more formal case processing through custody. This variability in police practices limits researchers' abilities to utilize police data to compare policies or programs between jurisdictions or within the same locale over a long time period.

Juvenile Court Statistics

Data on the operation of the juvenile court were first collected by the U.S. Children's Bureau in 1926. These data were in summary form, permitting very little in the way of detailed analyses. With support from the federal Office of Juvenile Justice and Delinquency Prevention (OJJDP), the quality and quantity of juvenile court statistics was greatly enhanced. Compiled by the National Center for Juvenile Justice (NCJJ), aggregate data are collected by more than 80% of the nation's juvenile court jurisdictions (Stahl, 1998). These data cover the total number of cases handled, a distribution of cases by gender, and whether each case was handled without a formal delinquency petition. Beginning in 1979, NCJJ began collecting individual-level data from 15 states or large jurisdictions with automated data systems. Today these individual-level data come from juvenile courts that represent 67% of the youth population and are referred to as the National Juvenile Court Data Archives.

As with police arrest statistics, juvenile court data analysis confronts a broad range of state laws and local practices that frustrate cross-jurisdictional comparisons. Further, since the NCJJ data are not based on a systematic sample of all jurisdictions (they include only the reporting courts), any national estimates or trends over time must be viewed with extreme caution. Still, some data are better than none, and the Juvenile Court Data Archives are a rich source of research material for students of the juvenile court.

There are no existing national or state data sources covering the practices of prosecutors in the juvenile court. Through the Juvenile Defendants in Criminal Court Program (JDCC), the Pretrial Services Resource Center does provide some prosecution data on juveniles tried in adult courts in approximately 40 of the nation's 75 most populous jurisdictions (Henry, Moffit, Robins, Earls, & Silva, 1993).

Juveniles Taken Into Custody

Data on juvenile corrections are more problematic. Beginning in the early 1970s, the U.S. Bureau of the Census administered a biannual survey to all public and private juvenile correctional facilities. Known popularly as the Children in Custody (CIC) survey, this was the primary source of information on children in confinement for a quarter of a century (Smith, 1998). There were always concerns that the survey did not adequately cover all types of juvenile facilities, and the growth of correctional programs operated by private agencies made this problem more difficult. The Bureau of the Census was able to get a near 100% return on surveys sent to public juvenile facilities. Like most national surveys, CIC was hampered by the same problems of differing legal codes that governed youth corrections in the states (Dedel, 1998). Data were reported to the Bureau of the Census based on aggregate counts, as opposed to individual residents, limiting the extent of data and policy analysis that could be accomplished. Though information based on a one-day snapshot of the incarcerated population seemed reasonably reliable, other data that included estimates of annual admissions or length of stay were far less credible.

There has been a variety of attempts to supplement the CIC. In 2000 the Bureau of Justice launched an in-depth survey of a random sample of youths in secure facilities (Beck, Kline, & Greenfield, 1988) that is currently being replicated by Westat. This Survey of Youth in Custody provides a more intensive view of the kinds of youth in secure facilities and the personal issues that they have confronted in their lives. The current Westat replication will cover far more topics, including the conditions of confinement.

In the 1990s, the NCCD field-tested and then implemented a data-collection effort designed to gather basic information on youths who were admitted annually to state-operated commitment facilities. These data were individual-based, permitting richer policy analysis and allowing for more precise calculations of length of stay (DeComo, Tunis, Krisberg, & Herrera, 1993). More than 60,000 admissions were captured in 1996. The primary limitation of this NCCD effort was that not all states participated (similar to the National Juvenile Court Data Archives), and the data collection did not cover short-term detention facilities that are mostly run by units of local government, into which the vast majority of youths were taken into custody. The NCCD state-level data collection did capture the vast majority of very serious offenders in juvenile corrections, as well as those who were confined for the longest periods of time. This problem is quite similar to those encountered by researchers in the field of adult corrections. There are reasonably complete data on persons entering state prison systems, but we know far less about the attributes of the much larger pool of individuals sent to local jails.

After 1995, OJJDP retired both the traditional CIC survey and the NCCD effort to get admissions and releases from state juvenile facilities. Instead, OJJDP funded the Bureau of the Census to complete a one-day roster of all youths in facilities covered by the previous CIC survey. The roster approach was intended to collect individual-level data on youths in a wide variety of custodial settings (Moone, 1997). This approach failed to collect data on length of stay or estimates of admissions to juvenile facilities. The first roster was completed in 1997 and the second in 2000. Due to the fact that the data are not generally available in a public-access computer file and are only reported in a series of aggregate tables, it is still too early to assess the strengths and weaknesses of this new method of assembling juvenile custody data. The transition to the roster method does, however, allow us to track trends in juvenile custody and compare them with past patterns.

The growing practice of trying children in criminal courts requires that researchers and policymakers examine data sets on adult corrections to develop a complete portrait of juvenile incarceration. Very limited data are available on this key aspect of the justice system. For example, the National Jail Survey, conducted by the U.S. Bureau of Justice Statistics (BJS), provides periodic counts of the number of juveniles admitted to jails, as well as a one-day count of residents in these facilities. Another BJS data collection effort, the National Correctional Reporting Program (NCRP), has data from several states on the numbers of persons under age 18 who enter prisons in the reporting states. In both these statistical data sources, the definition of a juvenile is derived from the local jurisdiction, thus perpetuating the problem of wide variability in the sorts of data that are reported from differing locales.

Self-Reported Delinquency Surveys

The obvious limitations in official data sources have led a number of researchers to base their analyses of youth crime on surveys that are either conducted in school settings or in the homes of youths. These surveys ask young people to report about the incidence and prevalence of their misconduct. Such self-report surveys have been utilized since the mid-1970s. Increasingly, researchers examining the causes and correlates of delinquent behavior, drug use, and sexual behavior rely on self-report surveys as their primary source of information. Two of the most influential of these surveys are the National Youth Survey (Elliott & Ageton, 1980) and the Monitoring the Future Project (Johnson & Bechman, 1981). Sponsored by The National Institute of Mental Health, the National Youth Survey, begun in 1976, was designed to gain a better understanding of both conventional and deviant types of behavior by youths. It involved collecting information from a representative sample of young people in the United States. Seven waves of the survey were conducted— 1976, 1977, 1978, 1979, 1980, 1983, and 1987. The Monitoring the Future Project is an ongoing annual study of the behaviors, attitudes, and values of American secondary school students, college students, and young adults. Each year, approximately 50,000 8th, 10th, and 12th grade students are surveyed (12th graders since 1975, and 8th and 10th graders since 1991). In addition, annual follow-up questionnaires are mailed to a sample of each graduating class for a number of years after their initial participation.

In general, self-report surveys reveal that a much larger proportion of the youth population admits to engaging in law-breaking behavior—a far greater number of offenders than are apprehended by the police. Further, self-report surveys cast significant doubts on the facts about delinquency derived from studies of captured offenders. For example, the large differences among ethnic groups, age-specific rates of offending, or different crime patterns among boys and girls that are observed in police or court data often are diminished or change radically in the results of the self-report studies (Elliott, 1994).

Critics of self-report surveys have raised questions about the willingness of various groups of young people to honestly report on their criminal behavior. Some youngsters may fail to disclose their misconduct, whereas others will brag or exaggerate it. It is reasonable to assume that some behaviors, including sex offending, may be subject to underreporting. Concerns have also been expressed that self-report studies contain a large amount of very minor law violations, whereas official statistics may reflect more serious offenses. Another concern with self-report surveys is the dependency on English language skills that may lead to distorted data from youngsters for whom English is a second language.

Qualitative Data Sources

So far the discussion about data sources has mainly focused on quantitative and statistical information. These sorts of numerical data are very useful in understanding the contours of delinquent behavior and the operations of the juvenile justice system. But, quantitative data can provide only a narrow comprehension of the subject. Qualitative methods are needed to achieve a holistic understanding of the subject matter—what the great sociologist Max Weber called "Verstehen."

There are many potential sources of humanistic data on juvenile delinquency and juvenile justice. For example, the work of scholars at the University of Chicago during the 1920s provided some of the richest sources of data on urban life. Most notably, Frederick Thrasher's *The Gang* (1927) provided a crucial understanding of adolescent behavior that remains fresh and relevant today. Another famous Chicago sociologist, Clifford Shaw, employed the technique of a delinquent's own story, a kind of sociological biography, in such classics as *Brothers in Crime* (1938) and *The Jack-Roller: A Delinquent Boy's Own Story* (1930). Shaw provided vital descriptions of underworld life that fueled the growth of criminological theory in the 1930s and 1940s.

Social scientists employing the delinquent's own perspective to comprehend the world of youth crime continue to the present period. Peterson and Truzzi (1972) offer a splendid collection of edited interviews with offenders. Krisberg (1971) used observations and interviews with Philadelphia gang members to give us a glimpse of their world views. Other gang researchers, such as Moore and Hagedorn (1988) and Sanchez-Jankowski (1991), have offered very useful insights into juvenile delinquency through extensive interviews and their descriptions of hanging out with gang members. Katz, in *Seductions of Crime: Moral and Sensual Attractions in Doing Evil* (1988), uses qualitative methods to supplement quantitative data. Katz argues that traditional social science methods provide excellent views of the background of crime but that more humanistic data are needed to adequately describe the foreground, the proximate forces that propel individuals into criminal behavior.

In addition to the works of sociologists of the street corner, the student of juvenile delinquency can utilize a broad range of autobiographical materials that portray the lives of youthful offenders. These can take the form of both fiction and nonfiction such as Haley's *The Autobiography of Malcolm X* (1965), Claude Brown's *Manchild in the Promised Land* (1966), Piri Thomas's *Down These Mean Streets* (1967), or the more recent autobiography of a Los Angeles gang member, Sanyika Shakur's *Monster* (1993). Likewise, there are a number of theatrical productions and films that can offer a vivid picture of the lives of youthful offenders such as *Rebel Without a Cause* (1955), *The Education of Sonny Carson* (1974), *Boyz N the Hood* (1991), *American Me* (1992), or the classic *Angels with Dirty Faces* (1938). The student can also look to some lyrics from contemporary urban music such as hip-hop and rap for further understanding of the worlds of delinquent youths.

Qualitative methods are also very useful for theory-building about the juvenile justice system. Observations studies such as those conducted by Wilson (1968), Cicourel (1968), and Emerson (1969) provide very valuable analyses of the norms and operations of the juvenile justice system in a variety of communities. Autobiographical works beginning with Charles Loring Brace's *The Dangerous Classes of New York* (1872), Jane Addams's *Twenty Years at Hull-House* (1911), and Judge Ben Lindsey's *The Dangerous Life* (1931) offer very fascinating accounts of the evolution of the juvenile justice system in America. Later works by juvenile court judges such as Lois Forer (1970) and Lisa Richette (1969) offer a more contemporary view of the juvenile court. There are also a number of excellent accounts of juvenile justice systems by journalists (Hubner & Wolfson, 1996) that can deepen the student's learning about the workings of the justice system and fascinating personal accounts of reform campaigns such as Jerome Miller's important story of reforming juvenile corrections in Massachusetts, *The Last One Over the Wall* (1991).

Summary

There are several sources of data on juvenile offending. None of the available data is comprehensive, and they all have significant limitations. Information on juvenile crime can be gleaned from arrest statistics, juvenile court data, data on youth in custody, self-report surveys, and a range of qualitative sources. Much of the existing research is based on arrest statistics, but the proportion of those arrested is a small, and probably biased, sample of all those youngsters committing crimes. Moreover, the highly decentralized nature of the juvenile justice system, including significant differences in law and practice among communities, makes interpreting available official data quite challenging. Any conclusions drawn from existing statistical systems must be treated with some caution. Given limitations in each data source, researchers and policy makers are encouraged to utilize multiple sources to complement their view of juvenile crime.

Review Questions

1. What are some of the major obstacles to gaining an accurate statistical picture of juvenile crime and juvenile justice?

2. Compare and contract the relative strengths and weaknesses of self-report data, official arrest statistics, and qualitative data to guide our understanding of juvenile crime and juvenile justice.

Three

The Historical Legacy of Juvenile Justice

The first institution for the control of juvenile delinquency in the United States was the New York House of Refuge, founded in 1825, but specialized treatment of wayward youth has a much longer history—one tied to changes in the social structure of medieval Europe. These same changes prompted the colonization of the New World and led to attempts to control and exploit the labor of African, European, and Native American children.

Virtually all aspects of life were in a state of flux for the people of Europe in the later Middle Ages (16th and 17th centuries). The economy was being transformed from a feudal system based on sustenance agriculture to a capitalistic, trade-oriented system focusing on cash crops and the consolidation of large tracts of land. In religious matters, the turmoil could be amply witnessed in the intense struggles of the Reformation. Politically, power was increasingly concentrated in the hands of a few monarchs, who were fashioning strong centralized states. The growth of trade and exploration exposed Europeans to a variety of world cultures and peoples.

For the lower classes of European society, these were "the worst of times." The rising population density as well as primitive agricultural methods led to a virtual exhaustion of the land. Increasing urban populations created new demands for cheap grain, and landlords responded by

19

increasing the fees paid by peasants who worked the land. Large numbers of peasants were displaced from the land to permit the growth of a capitalist pasturage system. The standard of living of the European peasantry dropped sharply, and this new, displaced class streamed into the cities and towns in search of means of survival. The workers and artisans of the cities were deeply threatened by the prospect that this pauper class would drive down the general wage level. Most European towns experienced sharp rises in crime, rioting, and public disorder.

To control and defuse the threat of this new "dangerous class," the leaders of the towns enacted laws and other restrictions to discourage immigration and contain the movement of the impoverished peasantry. "Poor laws" were passed, preventing the new migrants from obtaining citizenship, restricting their membership in guilds, and often closing the city gates to them. Vagrancy laws were instituted to control and punish those who seemed a threat to the social order. Certain legislation, such as the Elizabethan Statute of Artificers (1562), restricted access into certain trades, forcing the rural young to remain in the countryside.

Urban migration continued despite most attempts to curtail it. The collective units of urban life, the guild and the family, began to weaken under the pressure of social change. Children often were abandoned or released from traditional community restraints. Countless observers from the period tell of bands of youths roaming the cities at night, engaging in thievery, begging, and other forms of misbehavior (Sanders, 1970).

At this time family control of children was the dominant model for disciplining wayward youth. The model of family government, with the father in the role of sovereign, was extended to those without families through a system of *binding out* the young to other families. Poor children, or those beyond parental control, were apprenticed to householders for a specified period of time. Unlike the apprenticeship system for the privileged classes, the binding-out system did not oblige the master to teach his ward a trade. Boys generally were assigned to farming tasks and girls were brought into domestic service.

As the problem of urban poverty increased, the traditional modes of dealing with delinquent or destitute children became strained. Some localities constructed institutions to control wayward youth. The Bridewell (1555) in London is generally considered the first institution specifically designed to control youthful beggars and vagrants. In 1576 the English Parliament passed a law establishing a similar institution in every English county. The most celebrated of these early institutions was the Amsterdam House of Corrections (1595), which was viewed as an innovative solution to the crime problem of the day.[1] The houses of correction combined the principles of the poorhouse, the workhouse, and the penal institution. The youthful inmates were forced to work within the institution and thus develop habits of industriousness. Upon release they were expected to enter the labor force, so house of correction inmates often were hired out to private contractors. Males rasped hardwoods used in the dyeing industry, and when textile manufacturing was introduced to the houses of correction, this became the special task of young woman inmates.

The early houses of correction, or so-called "Bridewells," accepted all types of children including the destitute, the infirm, and the needy. In some cases, parents placed their children in these institutions because they believed the regimen of work would have a reformative effect. Although it is debatable whether the houses of correction were economically efficient, the founders of such institutions clearly hoped to provide a cheap source of labor to local industries. The French institutions, called *hospitaux generaux*, experimented with technological improvements and different labor arrangements. This often brought charges of unfair competition from guilds, who feared the demise of their monopoly on labor, and businessmen, who felt threatened by price competition at the marketplace. Some authors stress the economic motive of these early penal institutions: "The institution of the houses of correction in such a society was not the result of brotherly love or of an official sense of obligation to the distressed. It was part of the development of capitalism" (Rusche & Kirchheimer, 1939, p. 50).

The enormous social, political, and economic dislocations taking place in Europe provided a major push toward colonization of the Americas. People emigrated for many reasons—some to get rich, some to escape political or religious oppression, and some because they simply had nothing to lose. Settlement patterns and the resulting forms of community life varied considerably. In the Massachusetts Bay Colony, for example, the Puritans attempted to establish a deeply religious community to serve God's will in the New World. The Puritans brought families with them and from the outset made provisions for the care and control of youths.

In contrast, the settlement of Virginia was more directly tied to economic considerations. There were persistent labor shortages, and the need for labor prompted orders for young people to be sent over from Europe. Some youths were sent over by "spirits," who were agents of merchants or shipowners. The spirits attempted to persuade young people to emigrate to America. They often promised that the New World would bring tremendous wealth and happiness to the youthful immigrants. The children typically agreed to work a specific term (usually 4 years) in compensation for passage across the Atlantic and for services rendered during the trip. These agreements of service were then sold to inhabitants of the new colonies, particularly in the South. One can imagine that this labor source must have been quite profitable for the plantations of the New World. Spirits were often accused of kidnapping, contractual fraud, and deception of a generally illiterate, destitute, and young clientele.

Other children coming to the New World were even more clearly coerced. For example, it became an integral part of penal practice in the early part of the 18th century to transport prisoners to colonial areas. Children held in the overcrowded Bridewells and poorhouses of England were brought to the Americas as indentured servants. After working a specified number of years as servants or laborers, the children were able to win their freedom. In 1619 the colony of Virginia regularized an agreement for the shipment of orphans and destitute children from England.

That same year, Africans, another group of coerced immigrants, made their first appearance in the Virginia Colony. The importation of African slaves eventually displaced the labor of youthful poor because of greater economic feasibility. The black chattels were physically able to perform strenuous labor under extreme weather conditions without adequate nutrition. These abilities would finally be used to describe them as beasts. Also, the high death rates experienced under these conditions did not have to be accounted for. The bondage of Africans was soon converted into lifetime enslavement, which passed on through generations. The southern plantation system, dependent on the labor of African slaves, produced tremendous wealth, further entrenching this inhuman system (Stamp, 1956; Yetman, 1970). Racism, deeply lodged in the English psyche, provided the rationale and excuse for daily atrocities and cruelties.[2]

Studies of slavery often overlook the fact that most slaves were children. Slave traders thought children would bring higher prices. Accounts of the slave trade emphasize the economic utility of small children, who could be jammed into the limited cargo space available on slave ships. Children were always a high proportion of the total slave population, because slave owners encouraged the birth of children to increase their capital. Little regard was paid by slave owners to keeping families together. African babies were a commodity to be exploited just as one might exploit the land or the natural resources of a plantation, and young slave women often were used strictly for breeding. A complete understanding of the social control of children must include a comparison of the institution of slavery to the conditions faced by children in other sections of the country.[3]

Another group of children who often are ignored in discussions of the history of treatment of youth in North America are Native Americans. In 1609 officials of the Virginia Company were authorized to kidnap Native American children and raise them as Christians. The stolen youths were to be trained in the religion, language, and customs of the colonists. The early European colonists spread the word of the Gospel to help rationalize their conquests of lands and peoples. But an equally important motivation was their interest in recruiting a group of friendly natives to assist in trade negotiations and pacification programs among the native peoples. The early Indian schools resembled penal institutions, with heavy emphasis on useful work, Bible study, and religious worship. Although a substantial amount of effort and money was invested in Indian schools, the results were considerably less than had been originally hoped:

> Missionaries could rarely bridge the chasm of mistrust and hostility that resulted from wars, massacres and broken promises. With so many colonists regarding the Indian as the chief threat to their security and the Indians looking upon the colonists as hypocrites, it is little wonder that attempts to win converts and to educate should fail. (Bremner, Barnard, Hareven, & Mennel, 1970, p. 72)

Unlike attempts to enslave children of African descent, early efforts with Native Americans were not successful. Relations between European colonists and Native Americans during this period centered around trading and the securing of land rights. These contrasting economic relationships resulted in divergent practices in areas such as education. Although there was general support for bringing "the blessings of Christian education" to the Native American children, there was intense disagreement about the merits of educating African slaves. Whereas some groups, such as the Society for the Propagation of the Gospel, argued that all "heathens" should be educated and converted, others feared that slaves who were baptized would claim the status of freemen. There was concern among whites that education of slaves would lead to insurrection and revolt. As a result, South Carolina and several other colonies proclaimed that conversion to Christianity would not affect the status of slaves (Bremner et al., 1970). Many southern colonies made it a crime to teach reading and writing to slaves. A middle-ground position evolved, calling for religious indoctrination without the more dangerous education in literacy (Bremner et al., 1970; Gossett, 1963).

In the early years of colonization, the family was the fundamental mode of juvenile social control, as well as the central unit of economic production. Even in situations where children were apprenticed or indentured, the family still served as the model for discipline and order. Several of the early colonies passed laws requiring single persons to live with families. The dominant form of poor relief at this time was placing the needy with other families in the community (Rothman, 1971). A tradition of family government evolved in which the father was empowered with absolute authority over all affairs of the family. Wives and children were expected to give complete and utter obedience to the father's wishes. This model complemented practices in political life, where absolute authority was thought to be crucial to the preservation of civilization.

Colonial laws supported and defended the primacy of family government. The earliest laws concerning youthful misbehavior prescribed the death penalty for children who disobeyed their parents. For example, part of the 1641 Massachusetts *Body of Liberties* reads as follows:

> If any child, or children, above sixteen years of age, and of sufficient understanding, shall CURSE or SMITE their natural FATHER or MOTHER, he or they shall be putt to death, unless it can be sufficiently testified that the Parents have been very unchristianly negligent in the education of such children: so provoked them by extreme and cruel correction, that they have been forced thereunto, to preserve themselves from death or maiming: *Exod* 21:17, *Lev* 20:9, *Exod* 21:15. (Hawes, 1971, p. 13)

Although there is little evidence that children were actually put to death for disobeying their parents, this same legal principle was used to justify the punishment of rebellious slave children in the southern colonies. Family discipline typically was maintained by corporal punishment. Not only were parents held legally responsible for providing moral education for their children, but a Massachusetts law of 1642 also mandated that parents should teach their children reading and writing. Later, in 1670, public officials called tithingmen were assigned to assist the selectmen (town councilmen) and constables in supervising family government. The tithingmen visited families who allegedly were ignoring the education and socialization of their children. Although there are records of parents brought to trial due to their neglect of parental duties, this manner of supervising family government was not very successful.

The family was the central economic unit of colonial North America. Home based industry, in which labor took place on the family farm or in a home workshop, continued until the end of the 18th century. Children were an important component of family production, and their labor was considered valuable and desirable. A major determinant of a child's future during this time was the father's choice of apprenticeship for his child. Ideally the apprenticeship system was to be the stepping stone into a skilled craft, but this happy result was certain only for children of the privileged classes. As a consequence, children of poor families might actually be *bound out* as indentured servants. The term of apprenticeship was generally seven years, and the child was expected to regard his master with the same obedience due natural parents. The master was responsible for the education and training of the young apprentice and he acted *in loco parentis,* assuming complete responsibility for the child's material and spiritual welfare. Although apprenticeships were voluntary for the wealthier citizens, for the wayward or destitute child they were unavoidable. The use of compulsory apprenticeships was an important form of social control exercised by town and religious officials upon youths perceived as troublesome (Bremner et al., 1970).

The industrial revolution in North America, beginning at the end of the 18th century, brought about the gradual transformation of the labor system of youth. The family-based productive unit gave way to an early factory system. Child labor in industrial settings supplanted the apprenticeship system. As early as the 1760s there were signs that the cotton industry in New England would transform the system of production, and by 1791 all stages in the manufacture of raw cotton into cloth were performed by factory machinery. The Samuel Slater factory in Providence, Rhode Island, employed 100 children aged 4–10 years in cotton manufacture. Here is a description of the workplace environment:

> They worked in one room where all the machinery was concentrated under the supervision of a foreman, spreading the cleaned cotton on the carding machine to be combed and passing it though the roving machine, which turned the cotton into loose rolls ready to be spun. Some of the children tended the spindles, removing and attaching bobbins. Small, quick fingers were admirably suited for picking up and knotting broken threads. To the delight of Tench Coxe, a champion of American industry, the children became "the little fingers . . . of the gigantic automatons of labor-saving machinery." (Bremner et al., 1970, p. 146)

During the next two decades, the use of children in New England industrial factories increased, and children composed 47%–55% of the labor force in the cotton mills. The proliferation of the factory system transformed the lives of many Americans. On one hand, enormous wealth began to accumulate in the hands of a few individuals. At the same time, the switch from a family-based economy to a factory system where workers sold their labor meant that many families were displaced from the land. A large class of permanently impoverished Americans evolved. The use of child labor permitted early industrialists to depress the general wage level. Moreover, companies provided temporary housing and supplies to workers at high prices, so that workers often incurred substantial debts rather than financial rewards.

Increased child labor also contributed to the weakening of family ties, because work days were long and often competed with family chores. Children were now responsible to two masters—their fathers and their factory supervisors. Work instruction became distinct from general education and spiritual guidance as the family ceased to be an independent economic unit. Conditions of poverty continued to spread, and the social control system predicated upon strong family government began to deteriorate. During the first decades of the 19th century, one could begin to observe a flow of Americans from rural areas to the urban centers. As increasing economic misery combined with a decline in traditional forms of social control, an ominous stage was being set. Some Americans began to fear deeply the growth of a "dangerous class" and attempted to develop new measures to control the wayward youth who epitomized this threat to social stability.

The Houses of Refuge (1825–1860)[4]

Severe economic downturns in the first two decades of the 19th century forced many Americans out of work. At the same time, increasing numbers of Irish immigrants arrived in the United States. These changes in the social structure, combined with the growth of the factory system, contributed to the founding of specialized institutions for the control and prevention of juvenile delinquency in the United States (Hawes, 1971; Mennel, 1973; Pickett, 1969).

As early as 1817, the more privileged Americans became concerned about the apparent connection between increased pauperism and the rise of delinquency. The Society for the Prevention of Pauperism was an early attempt to evaluate contemporary methods of dealing with the poor and to suggest policy changes. This group also led campaigns against taverns and theaters, which they felt contributed to the problem of poverty. The efforts of several members of this group led to the founding in New York City of the first House of Refuge in 1825. The group conducted investigations, drew up plans and legislation, and lobbied actively to gain acceptance of their ideas. In other Northeastern cities, such as Boston and Philadelphia, similar efforts were under way.

A number of historians have described these early 19th-century philanthropists as "conservative reformers" (Coben & Ratner, 1970; Mennel, 1973). These men were primarily from wealthy, established families and often were prosperous merchants or professionals. Ideologically, they were close to the thinking of the colonial elite and, later, to the Federalists. Popular democracy was anathema to them because they viewed themselves as God's elect and felt bound to accomplish His charitable objectives in the secular world. Leaders of the movement to establish the houses of refuge, such as John Griscom, Thomas Eddy, and John Pintard, viewed themselves as responsible for the moral health of the community, and they intended to regulate community morality through the example of their own proper behavior as well as through benevolent activities. The poor and the deviant were the objects of their concern and their moral stewardship.

Although early 19th-century philanthropists relied on religion to justify their good works, their primary motivation was the protection of their class privileges. Fear of social unrest and chaos dominated their thinking (Mennel, 1973). The rapid growth of a visible impoverished class, coupled with apparent increases in crime, disease, and immorality, worried those in power. The bitter class struggles of the French Revolution and periodic riots in urban areas of the United States signaled danger to the status quo. The philanthropy of this group was aimed at reestablishing social order, while preserving the existing property and status relationships. They were responsible for founding such organizations as the American Sunday School Union, the American Bible Society, the African Free School Society, and the Society for Alleviating the Miseries of Public Prisons. They often were appointed to positions on boards of managers for lunatic asylums, public hospitals, workhouses for the poor, and prisons.

The idea for houses of refuge was part of a series of reform concepts designed to reduce juvenile delinquency. Members of the Society for the Prevention of Pauperism were dissatisfied with the prevailing practice of placing children in adult jails and workhouses. Some reformers felt that exposing children to more seasoned offenders would increase the chances of such children becoming adult criminals. Another issue was the terrible condition of local jails. Others worried that, due to these abominable conditions, judges and juries would lean toward acquittal of youthful criminals to avoid sending them to such places. Reformers also objected that the punitive character of available penal institutions would not solve the basic problem of pauperism. The reformers envisioned an institution with educational facilities, set in the context of a prison. John Griscom called for "the erection of new prisons for juvenile offenders" (Mennel, 1973). A report of the Society for the Prevention of Pauperism suggested the following principles for such new prisons:

> These prisons should be rather schools for instruction, than places of punishment, like our present state prisons where the young and the old are confined indiscriminately. The youth confined there should be placed under a course of discipline, severe and unchanging, but alike calculated to subdue and conciliate. A system should be adopted that would provide a mental and moral regimen. (Mennel, 1973, p. 11)

By 1824 the society had adopted a state charter in New York under the name of the Society for the Reformation of Juvenile Delinquents and had begun a search for a location for the House of Refuge.

On New Year's Day, 1825, the New York House of Refuge opened with solemn pomp and circumstance. A year later the Boston House of Reformation was started, and in 1828 the Philadelphia House of Refuge began to admit wayward youth. These new institutions accepted both children convicted of crimes and destitute children. Because they were founded as preventive institutions, the early houses of refuge could accept children who "live an idle or dissolute life, whose parents are dead or if living, from drunkenness, or other vices, neglect to provide any suitable employment or exercise any salutary control over said children" (Bremner et al., 1970, p. 681). Thus, from the outset, the first special institutions for juveniles housed together delinquent, dependent, and neglected children— a practice still observed in most juvenile detention facilities today.[5]

The development of this new institution of social control necessitated changes in legal doctrines to justify the exercise of power by refuge officials. In *Commonwealth v. M'Keagy* (1831), the Pennsylvania courts had to rule on the legality of a proceeding whereby a child was committed to the Philadelphia House of Refuge on the weight of his father's evidence that the child was "an idle and disorderly person." The court affirmed the right of the state to take a child away from a parent in cases of vagrancy or crime, but because this child was not a vagrant, and the father was not poor, the court ruled that the child should not be committed. Judicial officials did not wish to confuse protection of children with punishment, because this might engender constitutional questions as to whether children committed to houses of refuge had received the protection of due process of law.

The related question of whether parental rights were violated by involuntary refuge commitments was put to a legal test in *Ex parte Crouse* (1838). The father of a child committed to the Philadelphia House of Refuge attempted to obtain her release through a writ of habeas corpus. The state supreme court denied the motion, holding that the right of parental control is a natural but not inalienable right:

> The object of the charity is reformation, by training the inmates to industry; by imbuing their minds with principles of morality and religion; by furnishing them with means to earn a living; and, above all, by separating them from the corrupting influence of improper associates. To this end, may not the natural parents, when unequal to the task of education, or unworthy of it, be superseded by the *parens patriae*, or common guardian of the community? The infant has been snatched from a course which must have ended in confirmed depravity; and, not only is the restraint of her person lawful, but it would have been an act of extreme cruelty to release her from it. (*Ex parte Crouse*, 1838)

The elaboration of the doctrine of *parens patriae* in the Crouse case was an important legal principle used to support the expanded legal powers of the juvenile court. It is important to recognize the significance of both social class and hostility toward Irish immigrants in the legal determination of the Crouse case.[6] Because Irish immigrants were viewed at this time as corrupt and unsuitable as parents, it is easy to see how anti-immigrant feelings could color judgments about the suitability of parental control. As a result, children of immigrants made up the majority of inmates of the houses of refuge.

The early houses of refuge either excluded blacks or housed them in segregated facilities. In 1849 the city of Philadelphia opened the House of Refuge for Colored Juvenile Delinquents. Racially segregated refuges were maintained in New York City and Boston only through the limited funds donated by antislavery societies. Because refuge managers viewed all young woman delinquents as sexually promiscuous with little hope for eventual reform, young women also received discriminatory treatment.[7]

The managers of houses of refuge concentrated on perfecting institutional regimens that would result in reformation of juveniles. Descriptions of daily activities stress regimentation, absolute subordination to authority, and monotonous repetition:

> At sunrise, the children are warned, by the ringing of a bell, to rise from their beds. Each child makes his own bed, and steps forth, on a signal, into the Hall. They then proceed, in perfect order, to the Wash Room. Thence they are marched to parade in the yard, and undergo an examination as to their dress and cleanliness; after which they attend morning prayer. The morning school then commences, where they are occupied in summer, until 7 o'clock. A short intermission is allowed, when the bell rings for breakfast; after which, they proceed to their respective workshops, where they labor until 12 o'clock, when they are called from work, and one hour allowed them for washing and eating their dinner. At one, they again commence work, and continue at it until five in the afternoon, when the labors of the day terminate. Half an hour is allowed for washing and eating their supper, and at half-past five, they are conducted to the school room, where they continue at their studies until 8 o'clock. Evening Prayer is performed by the Superintendent; after which, the children are conducted to their dormitories, which they enter, and are locked up for the night, when perfect silence reigns throughout the establishment. The foregoing is the history of a single day, and will answer for every day in the year, except Sundays, with slight variations during stormy weather, and the short days in winter. (Bremner et al., 1970, p. 688)[8]

Routines were enforced by corporal punishment as well as other forms of control. Houses of refuge experimented with primitive systems of classification based on the behavior of inmates. The Boston House of Reformation experimented with inmate self-government as a control technique. But, despite public declarations to the contrary, there is ample evidence of the use of solitary confinement, whipping, and other physical punishments.

Inmates of the houses of refuge labored in large workshops manufacturing shoes, producing brass nails, or caning chairs. Young woman delinquents often were put to work spinning cotton and doing laundry. It is estimated that income generated from labor sold to outside contractors supplied up to 40% of the operating expenses of the houses of refuge. The chief problem for refuge managers was that economic depressions could dry up the demand for labor, and there was not always sufficient work to keep the inmates occupied. Not only were there complaints that contractors abused children, but also that such employment prepared youngsters for only the most menial work.

Youths were committed to the houses of refuge for indeterminate periods of time until the legal age of majority. Release was generally obtained through an apprenticeship by the youths to some form of service. The system was akin to the binding-out practices of earlier times. Males typically were apprenticed on farms, on whaling boats, or in the merchant marine. Young women usually were placed into domestic service. Only rarely was a house-of-refuge child placed in a skilled trade. Apprenticeship decisions often were made to ensure that the child would not be reunited with his or her family, because this was presumed to be the root cause of the child's problems. As a result, there are many accounts of siblings and parents vainly attempting to locate their lost relatives.

The founders of the houses of refuge were quick to declare their own efforts successful. Prominent visitors to the institutions, such as Alexis de Tocqueville and Dorothea Dix, echoed the praise of the founders. Managers of the refuges produced glowing reports attesting to the positive results of the houses. Sharp disagreements over the severity of discipline required led to the replacement of directors who were perceived as too permissive. Elijah Devoe (1848), a house of refuge assistant superintendent, wrote poignantly of the cruelties and injustices in these institutions. There are accounts of violence within the institutions as well. Robert Mennel (1973) estimates that approximately 40% of the children escaped either from the institutions or from their apprenticeship placements. The problems that plagued the houses of refuge did not dampen the enthusiasm of the philanthropists, who assumed that the reformation process was a difficult and tenuous business at best.

Public relations efforts proclaiming the success of the houses of refuge helped lead to a rapid proliferation of similar institutions (Rothman, 1971). While special institutions for delinquent and destitute youth increased in numbers, the public perceived that delinquency was continuing to rise and become more serious. The founders of the houses of refuge argued that the solution to the delinquency problem lay in the perfection of better methods to deal with incarcerated children. Most of the literature of this period assumes the necessity of institutionalized treatment for children. The debates centered around whether to implement changes in architecture or in the institutional routines. Advocates of institutionalized care of delinquent and dependent youths continued to play the dominant role in formulating social policy for the next century.

The Growth of Institutionalization and the Child Savers (1850–1890)

In the second half of the 19th century, a group of reformers known as the Child Savers instituted new measures to prevent juvenile delinquency (Hawes, 1971; Mennel, 1973; Platt, 1968). Reformers including Lewis Pease, Samuel Gridley Howe, and Charles Loring Brace founded societies to save children from depraved and criminal lives. They created the Five Points Mission (1850), the Children's Aid Society (1853), and the New York Juvenile Asylum (1851). The ideology of this group of reformers differed from that of the founders of the houses of refuge only in that this group was more optimistic about the possibilities of reforming youths. Centers were established in urban areas to distribute food and clothing, provide temporary shelter for homeless youth, and introduce contract systems of shirt manufacture to destitute youth.

The Child Savers criticized the established churches for not doing more about the urban poor. They favored an activist clergy that would attempt to reach the children of the streets. Although this view was somewhat unorthodox, they viewed the urban masses as a potentially dangerous class that could rise up if misery and impoverishment were not alleviated. Charles Loring Brace observed, "Talk of heathen! All the pagans of Golconda would not hold a light to the ragged, cunning, forsaken, godless, keen devilish boys of Leonard Street and the Five Points . . . Our future voters, and President-makers, and citizens! Good Lord deliver us, and help them!" (quoted in Mennel, 1973, p. 34). Brace and his associates knew from firsthand experience in the city missions that the problems of poverty were widespread and growing more serious. Their chief objection to the houses of refuge was that long-term institutionalized care did not reach enough children. Moreover, the Child Savers held the traditional view that family life is superior to institutional routines for generating moral reform.

Brace and his Children's Aid Society believed that delinquency could be solved if vagrant and poor children were gathered up and "placed out" with farm families on the western frontier. Placing out as a delinquency prevention practice was based on the idealized notion of the U.S. farm family. Such families were supposed to be centers of warmth, compassion, and morality; they were "God's reformatories" for wayward youth. Members of the Children's Aid Society provided food, clothing, and sometimes shelter to street waifs and preached to them about the opportunities awaiting them if they migrated westward. Agents of the Children's Aid Society vigorously urged poor urban youngsters to allow themselves to be placed out with farm families. Many believed that western families provided both a practical and economical resource for reducing juvenile delinquency. The following passage from a Michigan newspaper gives a vivid picture of the placing out process:

> Our village has been astir for a few days. Saturday afternoon, Mr. C. C. Tracy arrived with a party of children from the Children's Aid Society in New York . . .
> Sabath day Mr. Tracy spoke day and evening, three times, in different church edifices to crowded and interested audiences. In the evening, the children were present in a body, and sang their "Westward Ho" song. Notice was given that applicants would find unappropriated children at the store of Carder and Ryder, at nine o'clock Monday morning. Before the hour arrived a great crowd assembled, and in two hours *every child was disposed of*, and more were wanted.
> We *Wolverines* will never forget Mr. Tracy's visit. It cost us some tears of sympathy, some dollars, and some smiles. We wish him a safe return to Gotham, a speedy one to us with the new company of destitute children, for whom good homes are even now prepared. (Mennel, 1973, p. 39)

Contrary to the benevolent image projected by this news story, there is ample evidence that the children were obliged to work hard for their keep and were rarely accepted as members of the family. The Boston Children's Aid Society purchased a home in 1864, which was used to help adjust street youth to their new life in the West. The children were introduced to farming skills and taught manners that might be expected of them in their new homes.

Another prevention experiment during the middle part of the 19th century was the result of the work of a Boston shoemaker, John Augustus. In 1841, Augustus began to put up bail for men charged with drunkenness, although he had no official connection with the court. Soon after, he extended his services to young people. Augustus supervised the youngsters while they were out on bail, provided clothing and shelter, was sometimes able to find them jobs, and often paid court costs to keep them out of jail. This early probation system was later instituted by local child-saving groups, who would find placements for the children. By 1869

Massachusetts had a system by which agents of the Board of State Charities took charge of delinquents before they appeared in court. The youths often were released on probation, subject to good behavior in the future.

These noninstitutional prevention methods were challenged by those who felt an initial period of confinement was important before children were placed out. Critics also argued that the Children's Aid Societies neither followed up on their clients nor administered more stringent discipline to those who needed it. One critic phrased it this way:

> The "vagabond boy" is like a blade of corn, coming up side by side with a thistle. You may transplant both together in fertile soil, but you will have the thistle still. . . . I would have you pluck out the vagabond first, and then let the boy be thus provided with "a home," and not before. (Mennel, 1973, p. 46)

Many Midwesterners were unsettled by the stream of "criminal children" flowing into their midst. Brace and his colleagues were accused of poisoning the West with the dregs of urban life. To combat charges that urban youths were responsible for the rising crime in the West, Brace conducted a survey of western prisons and almshouses to show that few of his children had gotten into further trouble in the West.

Resistance continued to grow against the efforts of the Children's Aid Societies. Brace, holding that asylum interests were behind the opposition, maintained that the longer a child remains in an asylum, the less likely he will reform. (The debate over the advantages and disadvantages of institutionalized care of delinquent youth continues to the present day.) Brace continued to be an active proponent of the placing out system. He appeared before early conventions of reform school managers to present his views and debate the opposition. As the struggle continued over an ideology to guide prevention efforts, the problem of delinquency continued to grow. During the 19th century, poverty, industrialization, and immigration, as well as the Civil War, helped swell the ranks of the "dangerous classes."[9]

Midway through the 19th century, state and municipal governments began taking over the administration of institutions for juvenile delinquents. Early efforts had been supported by private philanthropic groups with some state support. But the growing fear of class strife, coupled with increasing delinquency, demanded a more centralized administration. Many of the newer institutions were termed *reform schools* to imply a strong emphasis on formal schooling. In 1876, of the 51 refuges or reform schools in the United States, nearly three quarters were operated by state or local governments. By 1890, almost every state outside the South had a reform school, and many jurisdictions had separate facilities for male and female delinquents. These institutions varied considerably in their admissions criteria, their sources of referral, and the character of their inmates. Most of the children were sentenced to remain in reform schools until they reached the age of majority (18 years for girls and 21 for boys) or until they were reformed. The length of confinement, as well as the decision to transfer unmanageable youths to adult penitentiaries, was left to the discretion of reform school officials.

Partially in response to attacks by Brace and his followers, many institutions implemented a cottage or family system between 1857 and 1860. The cottage system involved dividing the youths into units of 40 or fewer, each with its own cottage and schedule. Although work was sometimes performed within the cottages, the use of large congregate workshops continued. The model for the system was derived from the practice of European correctional officials. There is evidence from this period of the development of a self-conscious attempt to refine techniques to mold, reshape, and reform wayward youth (Hawes, 1971).

During this period, a movement was initiated to locate institutions in rural areas, because it was felt that agricultural labor would facilitate reformative efforts. As a result, several urban houses of refuge were relocated in rural settings. Many rural institutions used the cottage system, as it was well suited to agricultural production. In addition, the cottage system gave managers the opportunity to segregate children according to age, sex, race, school achievement, or "hardness." Critics of the institutions, such as Mary Carpenter, pointed out that most of the presumed benefits of rural settings were artificial and that the vast majority of youths who spent time in these reform schools ultimately returned to crowded urban areas.

The Civil War deeply affected institutions for delinquent youth. Whereas prisons and county jails witnessed declines in population, the war brought even more youths into reform schools. Institutions were strained well beyond their capacities. Some historians believe that the participation of youths in the draft riots in northern cities produced an increase in incarcerated youths. Reform schools often released older youngsters to military service to make room for additional children. Due to the high inflation rates of the war, the amount of state funds available for institutional upkeep steadily declined. Many institutions were forced to resort to the contract labor system to increase reform school revenues to meet operating expenses during the war and in the postwar period.

Voices were raised in protest over the expansion of contract labor in juvenile institutions. Some charged that harnessing the labor of inmates, rather than the reformation of youthful delinquents, had become the raison d'être of these institutions. There were growing rumors of cruel and vicious exploitation of youth by work supervisors. An 1871 New York Commission on Prison Labor, headed by Enoch Wines, found that refuge boys were paid 30 cents per day for labor that would receive 4 dollars a day on the outside. In the Philadelphia House of Refuge, boys were paid 25 cents a day and were sent elsewhere if they failed to meet production quotas. Economic depressions throughout the 1870s increased pressure to end the contract system. Workingmen's associations protested against the contract system, because prison and reform school laborers created unfair competition. Organized workers claimed that refuge managers were making huge profits from the labor of their wards:

> From the institutional point of view, protests of workingmen had the more serious result of demythologizing the workshop routine. No longer was it believable for reform school officials to portray the ritual as primarily a beneficial aid in inculcating industrious habits or shaping youth for "usefulness." The violence and exploitation characteristic of reform school workshops gave the lie to this allegation. The havoc may have been no greater than that which occasionally wracked the early houses of refuge, but the association of conflict and the contract system in the minds of victims and outside labor interests made it now seem intolerable. (Mennel, 1973, p. 61)

The public became aware of stabbings, fighting, arson, and attacks upon staff of these institutions.

> All signs pointed toward a decline of authority within the institutions. The economic troubles of the reform schools continued to worsen. Additional controversy was generated by organized Catholic groups, who objected to Protestant control of juvenile institutions housing a majority of Catholics. This crisis in the juvenile institutions led to a series of investigations into reform school operations.[10] The authors of these reports proposed reforms to maximize efficiency of operation and increase government control over the functioning of institutions in their jurisdictions. One major result of these investigative efforts was the formation of Boards of State Charity. Members of these boards were appointed to inspect reform schools and make recommendations for improvements but were to avoid the evils of the patronage system. Board members, who were described as "gentlemen of public spirit and sufficient leisure," uncovered horrid institutional conditions and made efforts to transfer youngsters to more decent facilities. Men such as Frederick Wines, Franklin Sanborn, Hastings Hart, and William Pryor Letchworth were among the pioneers of this reform effort. (Mennel, 1973, p. 61)

Although it was hoped that the newly formed boards would find ways to reduce the proliferation of juvenile institutions, such facilities continued to grow, as did the number of wayward youths. These late-19th-century reformers looked toward the emerging scientific disciplines for solutions to the problems of delinquency and poverty. They also developed a system to discriminate among delinquents, so that "hardened offenders" would be sent to special institutions such as the Elmira Reformatory. It was generally recognized that new methods would have to be developed to restore order within the reform schools and to make some impact upon delinquency.

Juvenile institutions in the South and the far West developed much later than those in the North or the East, but did so essentially along the same lines. One reason for this was that delinquency was primarily a city problem, and the South and far West were less urbanized. Another reason was that in the South, black youths received radically different treatment from whites. Whereas there was toleration for the misdeeds of white youth, black children were controlled under the disciplinary systems of slavery. Even after Emancipation, the racism of southern whites prevented them from treating black children as fully human and worth reforming. The Civil War destroyed the prison system of the South. After the war, southern whites used the notorious Black Codes and often trumped up criminal charges to arrest thousands of impoverished former slaves, placing them into a legally justified forced labor system. Blacks were leased out on contract to railroad companies, mining interests, and manufacturers. Although many of these convicts were children, no special provisions were made because of age. Conditions under the southern convict lease system were miserable and rivaled the worst cruelties of slavery. Little in the way of specialized care for delinquent youth was accomplished in the South until well into the 20th century. The convict lease system was eventually replaced by county road gangs and prison farms, characterized by grossly inhumane conditions of confinement. These were systems of vicious exploitation of labor and savage racism (McKelvey, 1972).

Juvenile Delinquency and the Progressive Era

The period from 1880 to 1920, often referred to by historians as the Progressive Era, was a time of major social structural change in the United States. The nation was in the process of becoming increasingly urbanized, and unprecedented numbers of European immigrants were migrating to cities in the Northeast. The United States was becoming an imperialist power and was establishing worldwide military and economic relationships. Wealth was becoming concentrated in the hands of a few individuals who sought to dominate U.S. economic life. Labor violence was on the rise, and the country was in the grip of a racial hysteria affecting all peoples of color. The tremendous technological developments of the time reduced the need for labor (Weinstein, 1968; Williams, 1973).

During the Progressive Era, those in positions of economic power feared that the urban masses would destroy the world they had built. Internal struggles developing among the wealthy heightened the tension. From all sectors came demands that new action be taken to preserve social order and to protect private property and racial privilege (Gossett, 1963). Up to this time, those in positions of authority had assumed a laissez-faire stance, fearing that government intervention might extend to economic matters. Although there was general agreement on the need for law enforcement to maintain social order, there was profound skepticism about attempts to alleviate miserable social conditions or reform deviant individuals. Some suggested that if society consisted of a natural selection process in which the fittest would survive, then efforts to extend the life chances of the poor or "racially inferior" ran counter to the logic of nature.

Others during this era doubted the wisdom of a laissez-faire policy and stressed that the threat of revolution and social disorder demanded scientific and rational methods to restore social order. The times demanded reform, and before the Progressive Era ended, much of the modern welfare state and the criminal justice system were constructed. Out of the turmoil of this age came such innovations as widespread use of the indeterminate sentence, the public defender movement, the beginning of efforts to professionalize the police, extensive use of parole, the rise of mental and IQ testing, scientific study of crime, and ultimately the juvenile court.

Within correctional institutions at this time, there was optimism that more effective methods would be found to rehabilitate offenders. One innovation was to institute physical exercise training, along with special massage and nutritional regimens. Some believed that neglect of the body had a connection with delinquency and crime. Those who emphasized the importance of discipline in reform efforts pressed for the introduction of military drill within reform schools. There is no evidence that either of these treatment efforts had a reformative effect upon inmates, but it is easy to understand why programs designed to keep inmates busy and under strict discipline would be popular at a time of violence and disorder within prisons and reform schools. As institutions faced continual financial difficulties, the contract labor system came under increasing attack. Criticism of reform schools resulted in laws in some states to exclude children under the age of 12 from admission to reform schools. Several states abolished the contract labor system, and efforts were made to guarantee freedom of worship among inmates of institutions. Once again, pleas were made for community efforts to reduce delinquency, rather than society relying solely upon reform schools as a prevention strategy. The arguments put forth were reminiscent of those of Charles Loring Brace and the Child Savers. For example, Homer Folks, president of the Children's Aid Society of Pennsylvania, articulated these five major problems of reform schools in 1891:

1. The temptation it offers to parents and guardians to throw off their most sacred responsibilities . . .
2. The contaminating influence of association . . .
3. The enduring stigma . . . of having been committed . . .
4. . . . renders impossible the study and treatment of each child as an individual.
5. The great dissimilarity between life in an institution and life outside. (Mennel, 1973, p. 111)

One response was to promote the model of inmate self-government within the institution's walls. One such institution, the George Junior Republic, developed an elaborate system of inmate government in 1893, in which the institution became a microcosm of the outside world. Self-government was viewed as an effective control technique, because youths became enmeshed in the development and enforcement of rules, while guidelines for proper behavior continued to be set by the institutional staff. The inmates were free to construct a democracy, so long as it conformed to the wishes of the oligarchic staff (Hawes, 1971).

The populist governments of several southern states built reform schools, partly due to their opposition to the convict lease system. But, these institutions too were infused with the ethos of the Jim Crow laws, which attempted to permanently legislate an inferior role for black Americans in southern society. One observer described the reform school of Arkansas as a place "where White boys might be taught some useful occupation and the negro boys compelled to work and support the institution while it is being done" (Mennel, 1973, p. 12). Black citizens, obviously displeased with discrimination within southern reform schools, proposed that separate institutions for black children should be administered by the black community. A few such institutions were established, but the majority of black children continued to be sent to jail or to be the victims of lynch mobs.

Growing doubt about the success of reform schools in reducing delinquency led some to question the wisdom of applying an unlimited *parens patriae* doctrine to youth. In legal cases, such as *The People v. Turner* (1870), *State v. Ray* (1886), and *Ex parte Becknell* (1897), judges questioned the quasi-penal character of juvenile institutions and wondered whether there ought not to be some procedural safeguards for children entering court on delinquency charges.

The state of Illinois, which eventually became the first state to establish a juvenile court law, had almost no institutions for the care of juveniles. Most early institutions in Illinois had been destroyed in fires, and those that remained were regarded as essentially prisons for children. Illinois attempted a privately financed system of institutional care, but this also failed. As a result, progressive reformers in Chicago complained of large numbers of children languishing in the county jail and pointed out that children sometimes received undue leniency due to a lack of adequate facilities.

A new wave of Child Savers emerged, attempting to provide Chicago and the state of Illinois with a functioning system for handling wayward youth.[11] These reformers, members of the more wealthy and influential Chicago families, were spiritual heirs of Charles Loring Brace, in that they, too, feared that social unrest could destroy their authority. But through their approach, they hoped to alleviate some of the suffering of the impoverished and ultimately win the loyalty of the poor. Reformers such as Julia Lathrop, Jane Addams, and Lucy Flower mobilized the Chicago Women's Club on behalf of juvenile justice reform. Other philanthropic groups, aligning with the powerful Chicago Bar Association, helped promote a campaign leading to the eventual drafting of the first juvenile court law in the United States. Although previous efforts had been made in Massachusetts and Pennsylvania to initiate separate trials for juveniles, the Illinois law is generally regarded as the first comprehensive child welfare legislation in this country.

The Illinois law, passed in 1899, established a children's court that would hear cases of delinquent, dependent, and neglected children. The *parens patriae* philosophy, which had imbued the reform schools, now extended to the entire court process. The definition of delinquency was broad, so that a child would be adjudged delinquent if he or she violated any state law or any city or village ordinance. In addition, the court was given jurisdiction in cases of incorrigibility, truancy, and lack of proper parental supervision. The court had authority to institutionalize children, send them to orphanages or foster homes, or place them on probation. The law provided for unpaid probation officers, who would assist the judges and supervise youngsters. In addition, the law placed the institutions for dependent youth under the authority of the State Board of Charities and regulated the activities of agencies sending delinquent youth from the East into Illinois.

The juvenile court idea spread so rapidly that within 10 years of the passage of the Illinois law, 10 states had established children's courts.

By 1912, 22 states had juvenile court laws, and by 1925 all but two states had established specialized courts for children. Progressive reformers proclaimed the establishment of the juvenile court as the most significant reform of this period. The reformers celebrated what they believed to be a new age in the treatment of destitute and delinquent children. In *Commonwealth v. Fisher* (1905), the Pennsylvania Supreme Court defended the juvenile court ideal in terms reminiscent of the court opinion in the Crouse case of 1838:

> To save a child from becoming a criminal, or continuing in a career of crime, to end in maturer years in public punishment and disgrace, the legislatures surely may provide for the salvation of such a child, if its parents or guardians be unwilling or unable to do so, by bringing it into one of the courts of the state without any process at all, for the purpose of subjecting it to the state's guardianship and protection.

Critics, pointing to the large number of children who remained in jails and detention homes for long periods, expressed doubt that the court would achieve its goal. Some judges, including the famous Judge Ben Lindsey of Denver, decried the seemingly unlimited discretion of the court. With so much diversity among jurisdictions in the United States, it is difficult to describe the functioning of a typical court. As the volume of cases in the urban areas soon overwhelmed existing court resources, judges became unable to give the close personal attention to each case advocated by the reformers. As little as 10 minutes was devoted to each case as court calendars became increasingly crowded. Similarly, as caseloads soared, the quality of probationary supervision deteriorated and became perfunctory.

It is important to view the emergence of the juvenile court in the context of changes taking place in U.S. society at that time. Juvenile court drew support from a combination of optimistic social theorists, sincere social reformers, and the wealthy, who felt a need for social control. The juvenile court movement has been viewed as an attempt to stifle legal rights of children by creating a new adjudicatory process based on principles of equity law. This view misses the experimental spirit of the Progressive Era by assuming a purely conservative motivation on the part of the reformers.

Although most reformers of the period understood the relationship between poverty and delinquency, they responded with vastly different solutions. Some reformers supported large-scale experimentation with new social arrangements, such as the Cincinnati Social Unit Experiment, an early forerunner of the community organization strategy of the war on poverty of the 1960s (Shaffer, 1971). Other reformers looked to the emerging social science disciplines to provide a rational basis for managing social order. During the Progressive Era, there was growth in the profession of social work, whose members dealt directly with the poor.[12] Progressive reformers conducted social surveys to measure the amount of poverty, crime, and juvenile dependency in their communities. They supported social experiments to develop new behavior patterns among the lower classes to help them adjust to the emerging corporate economy. The development of mental testing became crucial in defining access to the channels of social mobility and for demonstrating, to the satisfaction of the white ruling class, their own racial superiority. Moreover, biological explanations of individual and social pathology rationalized the rise in crime and social disorder without questioning the justice or rationality of existing social arrangements.

The thrust of Progressive Era reforms was to found a more perfect control system to restore social stability while guaranteeing the continued hegemony of those with wealth and privilege. Reforms such as the juvenile court are ideologically significant, because they preserved the notion that social problems (in this case, delinquency, dependency, and neglect) could be dealt with on a case-by-case basis, rather than through broadbased efforts to redistribute wealth and power throughout society. The chief dilemma for advocates of the juvenile court was to develop an apparently apolitical or neutral system while preserving differential treatment for various groups of children. The juvenile court at first lacked a core of functionaries who could supply the rationale for individualized care for wayward youth, but soon these needs were answered by the emergence of psychiatry, psychology, and criminology, as well as by the expanding profession of social work.

The Child Guidance Clinic Movement

In 1907, Illinois modified its juvenile court law to provide for paid probation officers, and the Chicago Juvenile Court moved into new facilities with expanded detention space. The Juvenile Protective League, founded by women active in establishing the first juvenile court law, was intended to stimulate the study of the conditions leading to delinquency. The members of the Juvenile Protective League were especially troubled that large numbers of wayward youth repeatedly returned to juvenile court. Jane Addams, a major figure in U.S. philanthropy and social thought, observed, "At last it was apparent that many of the children were psychopathic cases and they and other borderline cases needed more skilled care than the most devoted probation officer could give them" (Hawes, 1971, p. 244).

But the new court facilities did provide an opportunity to examine and study all children coming into the court. The Juvenile Protective League promised to oversee this study of delinquency, and Ellen Sturges Dummer donated the necessary money to support the effort. Julia Lathrop was chosen to select a qualified psychologist to head the project. After consulting with William James, she selected one of his former students, William A. Healy. Healy proposed a 4- to 5-year study to compare some 500 juvenile court clients with patients in private practice. The investigation, according to Healy, "would have to involve all possible facts about heredity, environment, antenatal and postnatal history, etc." (Hawes, 1971, p. 250).

In 1909, the Juvenile Protective League established the Juvenile Psychopathic Institute, with Healy as its first director and Julia Lathrop, Jane Addams, and Judge Julian W. Mack on the executive committee.[13] The group, in its opening statement, expressed its plans

> to undertake . . . an inquiry into the health of delinquent children in order to ascertain as far as possible in what degrees delinquency is caused or influenced by mental or physical defect or abnormality and with the purpose of suggesting and applying remedies in individual cases whenever practicable as a concurrent part of the inquiry. (Hawes, 1971, pp. 250–251)

Jane Addams added her concern that the study investigate the conditions in which the children lived, as well as the mental and physical history of their ancestors.

Healy held an MD degree from the University of Chicago and had served as a physician at the Wisconsin State Hospital. He had taught university classes in neurology, mental illness, and gynecology; had studied at the great scientific centers of Europe; and was familiar with the work of Sigmund Freud and his disciples. The major tenet of Healy's scientific credo was that the individual was the most important unit for study. Healy argued that the individualization of treatment depended upon scientific study of individual delinquents.

Healy and his associates published *The Individual Delinquent: A Textbook of Diagnosis and Prognosis for All Concerned in Understanding Offenders* in 1915. This book, based on a study of 1,000 cases of repeat juvenile offenders, was intended as a practical handbook. The methodology involved a study of each offender from social, medical, and psychological viewpoints. Healy even did anthropometric measurements, suggested by Cesare Lombroso and his followers, although Healy doubted that delinquents formed a distinctive physical type.[14] However, Healy never was able to locate a limited set of causes for delinquency through empirical observation. He stressed the wide range of potential causes of delinquency, including the influence of bad companions, the love of adventure, early sexual experiences, and mental conflicts. At this stage, Healy adopted an eclectic explanation of delinquency: "Our main conclusion is that every case will always need study by itself. When it comes to arraying data for the purpose of generalization about relative values of causative factors we experience difficulty" (Mennel, 1973, p. 165). Despite exhaustive research, Healy and his associates could not find distinctive mental or physical traits to delineate delinquents from nondelinquents.

Later, in 1917, Healy advanced his theory of delinquency in *Mental Conflicts and Misconduct*. In this work, Healy stressed that although individuals may experience internal motivation toward misbehavior, this usually results in their merely feeling some anxiety. When mental conflict becomes more acute, the child may respond by engaging in misconduct. These ideas were heavily influenced by the work of Adolf Meyer, whose interpretation of Freud had a major influence on U.S. psychiatry. Healy agreed with Meyer that the family was a crucial factor in delinquency: "The basis for much prevention of mental conflict is to be found in close comfortable relations between parents and children" (Hawes, 1971, p. 255). Healy's emphasis on the family was well received by those in the delinquency prevention field who had traditionally viewed the family as God's reformatory.

The significance of Healy's work cannot be overemphasized, as it provided an ideological rationale to defend the juvenile court. Healy's work gave legitimacy to the flexible and discretionary operations of the court. Although some used Healy's emphasis on the individual to minimize the importance of social and economic injustice, there is evidence that Healy understood that delinquency was rooted in the nature of the social structure:

> If the roots of crime lie far back in the foundations of our social order, it may be that only a radical change can bring any large measure of cure. Less unjust social and economic conditions may be the only way out, and until a better social order exists, crime will probably continue to flourish and society continue to pay the price. (Healy, Bronner, & Shimberg, 1935, p. 211)

Healy's work also gave support to the concept of professionalism in delinquency prevention. Because juvenile delinquency was viewed as a complex problem with many possible causes, this rationale was used to explain the increased reliance on experts. In the process, the juvenile court became insulated from critical scrutiny by its clients and the community. If actions taken by the court did not appear valid to the layman, this was because of a higher logic, known only to the experts, which explained that course of action. Moreover, the failure of a specific treatment program often was attributed to the limits of scientific knowledge or to the failure of the court to follow scientific principles in its dispositions.

After his work in Chicago, Healy went to the Judge Harvey Baker Foundation in Boston to continue his research, where he began actual treatment of youths. Healy became a proselytizer for the child guidance clinic idea. Working with the Commonwealth Fund and the National Committee for Mental Hygiene, Healy aided the development of child guidance clinics across the nation. These efforts were so successful that by 1931, 232 such clinics were in operation. There is even a report of a traveling child guidance clinic that visited rural communities in the West to examine children. The child guidance clinic movement became an important part of a broader campaign to provide mental hygiene services to all young people. The clinics initially were set up in connection with local juvenile courts, but later some of them became affiliated with hospitals and other community agencies.

In Sheldon and Eleanor Glueck's classic delinquency research, they evaluated the success of Healy's Boston clinic. In *One Thousand Juvenile Delinquents: Their Treatment by Court and Clinic* (1934), the Gluecks found high rates of recidivism among children treated at the clinic. Healy, though deeply disappointed by the results, continued his efforts. The Gluecks continued, in a series of longitudinal studies, to search for the causes of delinquency and crime.[15] Like Healy, they maintained a focus on the individual, and they increased efforts to discover the factors behind repeated delinquency. The work of the Gluecks reflected a less optimistic attitude about the potential for treatment and rehabilitation than that found in Healy's work. They emphasized the importance of the family, often ignoring the impact of broader social and economic factors. It is ironic that the thrust of delinquency theories in the 1930s should be toward individual and family conflicts. As 20% of the American people were unemployed, the effects of the depression of the 1930s must have been apparent to the delinquents and their families, if not to the good doctors who studied them with such scientific rigor.

The Chicago Area Project

The Chicago Area Project of the early 1930s is generally considered the progenitor of large-scale, planned, community-based efforts with delinquent youth. The project differed from the dominant approaches of the time, which relied on institutional care and psychological explanations for delinquent behavior. The Chicago Area Project, conceived by University of Chicago sociologist Clifford Shaw, was an attempt to implement a sociological theory of delinquency in the delivery of preventive services. The theoretical heritage of the project is found in such works as *The Jack-Roller* (1930), *Brothers in Crime* (1938), and *Juvenile Delinquency and Urban Areas* (1942), all written by Shaw and his associates. They attributed variations in delinquency rates to demographic or socioeconomic conditions in different areas of cities. This environmental approach assumed that delinquency was symptomatic of social disorganization. The adjustment problems of recent immigrants, together with other problems of urban life, strained the influence on adolescents of traditional social control agencies such as family, church, and community. Delinquency was viewed as a problem of the modern city, which was characterized by the breakdown of spontaneous or natural forces of social control. Shaw contended that the rapid social change that migrant rural youths are subjected to when entering the city promotes alienation from accepted modes of behavior: "When growing boys are alienated from institutions of their parents and are confronted with a vital tradition of delinquency among their peers, they engage in delinquent activity as part of their groping for a place in the only social groups available to them" (Kobrin, 1970, p. 579). The Chicago Area Project thus viewed delinquency as "a reversible accident of the person's social experience" (Kobrin, 1970).

The project employed several basic operating assumptions. The first was that the delinquent is involved in a web of daily relationships. As a result, the project staff attempted to mobilize adults in the community, hoping to foster indigenous neighborhood leadership to carry out the programs with delinquent youth. The second assumption was that people participate only if they have meaningful roles; therefore, the staff attempted to share decision making with neighborhood residents. To maximize community participation, staff members had to resist the urge to direct the programs themselves. The final premise of the Area Project was that within a given community there are people who, when given proper training and guidance, can organize and administer local welfare programs. A worker from within the community, who has knowledge of local customs and can communicate easily with local residents, is more effective in dealing with delinquency problems. The project staff believed that placing community residents in responsible positions would demonstrate the staff's confidence in the ability of residents to solve their own problems.

The Area Project was overseen by a board of directors responsible for raising and distributing funds for research and community programs. In several years, 12 community committees developed in Chicago as "independent, self-governing, citizens' groups, operating under their own names and charters" (Sorrento, quoted in Sechrest, 1970, p. 6). The neighborhood groups were aided by the board in obtaining grants to match local funds. Personnel from the Institute for Juvenile Research at the University of

Chicago served as consultants to local groups. The various autonomous groups pursued such activities as the creation of recreation programs or community-improvement campaigns for schools, traffic safety, sanitation, and law enforcement. There were also programs aimed directly at delinquent youth, such as visitation privileges for incarcerated children, work with delinquent gangs, and volunteer assistance in parole and probation.

Most observers have concluded that the Chicago Area Project succeeded in fostering local community organizations to attack problems related to delinquency (Kobrin, 1970; Shaw & McKay, 1942). Evidence also shows that delinquency rates decreased slightly in areas affected by the project, but these results are not conclusive. Shaw explained the difficulty of measuring the impact of the project as follows:

> Conclusive statistical proof to sustain any conclusion regarding the effectiveness of this work in reducing the volume of delinquency is difficult to secure for many reasons. Trends in rates for delinquents for small areas are affected by variations in the definition of what constitutes delinquent behavior, changes in the composition of the population, and changes in the administrative procedures of law enforcement agencies. (Witmer & Tufts, 1954, p. 16)

The Illinois State Division of Youth Services took over all 35 staff positions of the Area Project in 1957. It appears that this vibrant and successful program was quickly transformed into "a rather staid, bureaucratic organization seeking to accommodate itself to the larger social structure, that is, to work on behalf of agencies who came into the community rather than for itself or for community residents" (Sechrest, 1970, p. 15).

The Chicago Area Project, with its grounding in sociological theory and its focus on citizen involvement, contrasts sharply with other delinquency prevention efforts of the 1930s. Its focus on prevention in the community raised questions about the continued expansion of institutions for delinquent youth. Although some attributed support of the project to the personal dynamism of Clifford Shaw, this ignores the basic material and ideological motivation behind it. It would be equally shortsighted to conclude that child saving would not have occurred without Charles Loring Brace or that the child guidance clinic movement resulted solely from the labors of William Healy. Certainly Shaw was an important advocate of the Chicago Area Project approach, and his books influenced professionals in the field, but the growth of the project was also a product of the times.

Because no detailed history exists of the founding and operation of the project, we can only speculate about the forces that shaped its development. We do know that Chicago at that time was caught in the most serious economic depression in the nation's history. Tens of thousands of people were unemployed, especially immigrants and blacks. During this period, a growing radicalization among impoverished groups resulted in urban riots (Cloward & Piven, 1971). The primary response by those in positions of power was to expand and centralize charity and welfare systems. In addition, there was considerable experimentation with new methods of delivering relief services to the needy. No doubt, Chicago's wealthy looked favorably upon programs such as the Area Project, which promised to alleviate some of the problems of the poor without requiring a redistribution of wealth or power. Both the prestige of the University of Chicago and the close supervision promised by Shaw and his associates helped assuage the wealthy and the powerful. Shaw and his associates did not advocate fundamental social change, and project personnel were advised to avoid leading communities toward changes perceived as too radical (Alinsky, 1946). Communities were encouraged to work within the system and to organize around issues at a neighborhood level. Project participants rarely questioned the relationship of urban conditions to the political and economic superstructure of the city.

Later interpreters of the Chicago Area Project did not seem to recognize the potentially radical strategy of community organization within poor neighborhoods. Its immediate legacy was twofold—the use of detached workers, who dealt with gangs outside the agency office, and the idea of using indigenous workers in social control efforts. Although detached workers became a significant part of the delinquency prevention strategy of the next three decades, the use of indigenous personnel received little more than lip service, because welfare and juvenile justice agencies hired few urban poor.

The success of the Chicago Area Project depended upon relatively stable and well-organized neighborhoods with committed local leaders. Changes in the urban structure that developed over the next two decades did not fit the Chicago Area Project model. The collapse of southern agriculture and mass migration by rural blacks into the cities of the North and West produced major social structural changes. This movement to the North and West began in the 1920s, decreased somewhat during the depression years, and later accelerated due to the attraction provided by the war industry jobs. During this same period, large numbers of Puerto Ricans settled in New York City and other eastern cities. Although economic opportunity attracted new migrants to the urban centers, there was little satisfaction for their collective dreams. Blacks who left the South to escape the Jim Crow laws soon were confronted by de facto segregation in schools, in the workplace, and in housing. Job prospects were slim for blacks and Puerto Ricans, and both groups were most vulnerable to being fired at the whims of employers. In many respects, racism in the North rivaled that of the South. The new migrants had the added difficulty of adapting their primarily rural experiences to life in large urban centers (Coles, 1967; Handlin, 1959).

Racial ghettos became places of poverty, disease, and crime. For the more privileged classes, the situation paralleled that of 16th-century European city dwellers who feared the displaced peasantry or that of Americans at the beginning of the 19th century who feared the Irish immigrants. During this period, riots erupted in East St. Louis, Detroit, Harlem, and Los Angeles. To upper-class observers, these new communities of poor black and brown peoples were disorganized collections of criminals and deviants. Racism prevented white observers from recognizing the vital community traditions or the family stability that persisted despite desperate economic conditions. Moreover, the label *disorganized communities* could be used ideologically to mask the involvement of wealthy whites in the creation of racial ghettos (Ryan, 1971). A liberal social theory was developing that, though benign on the surface, actually blamed the victims for the conditions in which they were caught. Attention was focused upon deviant aspects of community life, ascribing a culture of poverty and violence to inner-city residents and advocating remedial work with individuals and groups to solve so-called problems of adjustment. The following quote from the National Commission on the Causes and Prevention of Violence (1969) is illustrative of this posture:

> The cultural experience which Negroes brought with them from segregation and discrimination in the rural South was of less utility in the process of adaption to urban life than was the cultural experience of many European immigrants. The net effect of these differences is that urban slums have tended to become ghetto slums from which escape has been increasingly difficult. (p. 30)

Delinquency theorists suggested that lower-class communities were becoming more disorganized, because they were not characterized by the stronger ties of older ethnic communities:

> Slum neighborhoods appear to us to be undergoing progressive disintegration. The old structures, which provided social control and avenues of social ascent, are breaking down. Legitimate but functional substitutes for these traditional structures must be developed if we are to stem the trend towards violence and retreatism among adolescents in urban slums. (Cloward & Piven, 1971, p. 211)

Irving Spergel, leading authority on juvenile gangs, suggests that social work agencies made little use of indigenous workers after World War II because delinquency had become more aggressive and violent. Welfare and criminal justice officials argued that only agencies with sound funding and strong leadership could mobilize the necessary resources to deal with the increased incidence and severity of youth crime.

The movement toward more agency involvement brought with it a distinctly privileged-class orientation toward delinquency prevention. Social service agencies were preeminently the instruments of those with sufficient wealth and power to enforce their beliefs. The agencies were equipped to redirect, rehabilitate, and, in some cases, control those who seemed most threatening to the status quo. Workers for these agencies helped to perpetuate a conception of proper behavior for the poor consistent with their expected social role. For example, the poor were told to defer gratification and save for the future, but the rich often were conspicuous consumers. Whereas poor women were expected to stay at home and raise their families, the same conduct was not uniformly applied to wealthy women. The well-to-do provided substantial funding for private social service agencies and often became members of the boards that defined policies for agencies in inner-city neighborhoods. The criteria for staffing these agencies during the two decades following World War II included academic degrees and special training that were not made available to the poor or to people of color.

Social agencies, ideologically rooted and controlled outside poor urban neighborhoods, were often pressured to respond to "serious" delinquency problems. During this period, the fighting gang, which symbolized organized urban violence, received the major share of delinquency prevention efforts. Most agencies, emphasizing psychoanalytic or group dynamic approaches to delinquency, located the origin of social disruption in the psychopathology of individuals and small groups. The consequence of this orientation was that special youth workers were assigned to troublesome gangs in an attempt to redirect the members toward more conventional conduct. Little effort was made to develop local leadership or to confront the issues of racism and poverty.

Detached worker programs emphasized treatment by individual workers freed from the agency office base and operating in neighborhood settings. These programs, with several variations, followed a basic therapeutic model. Workers initially entered gang territories, taking pains to make their entrance as inconspicuous as possible. The first contacts were made at natural meeting places in the community such as pool rooms, candy stores, or street corners:

> Accordingly, the popular image of the detached worker is a young man in informal clothing, standing on a street corner near a food stand, chatting with a half dozen rough, ill-groomed, slouching teenagers. His posture is relaxed, his countenance earnest, and he is listening to the boys through a haze of cigarette smoke. (Klein, 1969, p. 143)

The worker gradually introduced himself to the gang members. He made attempts to get jobs for them or arranged recreational activities, while at the same time persuading the members to give up their illegal activities. Manuals for detached workers explained that the approach would work because gang members had never before encountered sympathetic, nonpunitive adults who were not trying to manipulate them for dishonest purposes. A typical report states, "Their world (as they saw it) did not contain any giving, accepting people—only authorities, suckers and hoodlums like themselves" (Crawford, Malamud, & Dumpson, 1970, p. 630). This particular account even suggests that some boys were willing to accept the worker as an "idealized father." The worker was expected to influence the overall direction of the gang, but if that effort failed, he was to foment trouble among members and incite disputes over leadership. Information that the workers gathered under promises of confidentiality was often shared with police gang-control officers. Thus, despite their surface benevolence, these workers were little more than undercover agents whose ultimate charge was to break up or disrupt groups that were feared by the establishment. These techniques, which focused on black and Latino youth gangs in the 1950s, were similar to those later used with civil rights groups and organizations protesting the Vietnam War.

There were many critics of the detached worker programs. Some argued that the workers actually lent status to fighting gangs and thus created more violence. Other critics claimed that the workers often developed emotional attachments to youthful gang members and were manipulated by them (Mattick & Caplan, 1967). Community residents often objected to the presence of detached workers, because it was feared they would provide information to downtown social welfare agencies. Although studies of the detached worker programs did not yield positive results, virtually all major delinquency programs from the late 1940s to the 1960s used detached workers in an attempt to reach the fighting gang.

The Mobilization for Youth

During the late 1950s, economic and social conditions were becoming more acute in the urban centers of the United States. The economy was becoming sluggish, and unemployment began to rise. Black teenagers experienced especially high unemployment rates, and the discrepancy between white and black income and material conditions grew each year. Technological changes in the economy continually drove more unskilled laborers out of the labor force. Social scientists such as Daniel Moynihan (1969) and Sidney Wilhelm (1970) view this period as the time in which a substantial number of blacks became permanently unemployed. Social control specialists for the privileged class surveyed the problem and sought ways to defuse the social danger of a surplus labor population.

The Ford Foundation was influential during this period in stimulating conservative local officials to adopt more enlightened strategies in dealing with the poor (Marris & Rein, 1967; Moynihan, 1969). Once again an ideological clash occurred between those favoring scientific and rational government programs and those who feared the growth of the state, demanded balanced government budgets, and opposed liberal programs to improve the quality of life of the poor. The Ford Foundation, through its Grey Area projects, spent large amounts of money in several U.S. cities to foster research and planning of new programs to deal with delinquency and poverty.

The most significant program to develop out of the Grey Area projects was the Mobilization for Youth (MFY), which began in New York City in 1962 after 5 years of planning. It aimed to service a population of 107,000 (approximately one-third black and Puerto Rican), living in 67 blocks of New York City's Lower East Side. The unemployment rate of the area was twice that of the city overall, and the delinquency rate was also high. The theoretical perspective of the project was drawn from the work of Richard Cloward and Lloyd Ohlin:

> "a unifying principle of expanding opportunities has worked out as the direct basis for action." This principle was drawn from the concepts outlined by the sociologists Richard Cloward and Lloyd Ohlin in their book *Delinquency and Opportunity*. Drs. Cloward and Ohlin regarded delinquency as the result of the disparity perceived by low-income youths between their legitimate aspirations and the opportunities—social, economic, political, education—made available to them by society. If the gap between opportunity and aspiration could be bridged, they believed delinquency could be reduced; that would be the agency's goal. (Weissman, 1969, p. 19)

The MFY project involved five areas—work training, education, group work and community organization, services to individuals and families, and training and personnel—but the core of the mobilization was to organize area residents to realize "the power resources of the community by creating channels through which consumers of social welfare services can define their problems and goals and negotiate on their own behalf" (Brager & Purcell, 1967, p. 247). Local public and private bureaucracies became the targets of mass protests by agency workers and residents. The strategy of MFY assumed that social conflict was necessary in the alleviation of the causes of delinquency. Shortly after MFY became directly involved with struggles over the redistribution of power and resources, New York City officials charged that the organization was "riot-producing, Communist-oriented, left-wing and corrupt" (Weissman, 1969, pp. 25–28).

In the ensuing months, the director resigned, funds were limited, and virtually all programs were stopped until after the 1964 presidential election. After January 1965, MFY moved away from issues and protests toward more traditional approaches to social programming, such as detached-gang work, job training, and counseling.

Another project, Harlem Youth Opportunities Unlimited (Haryou-Act), which developed in the black community of Harlem in New York City, experienced a similar pattern of development and struggle. The Harlem program was supported by the theory and prestige of psychologist Kenneth Clark, who suggested in *Dark Ghetto* (1965) that delinquency is rooted in feelings of alienation and powerlessness among ghetto residents. The solution, according to Clark, was to engage in community organizing to gain power for the poor. Haryou-Act met sharp resistance from city officials, who labeled the staff as corrupt and infiltrated by Communists.

Both MFY and Haryou-Act received massive operating funds. Mobilization for Youth received approximately $2 million a year, Haryou-Act received about $1 million a year, and 14 similar projects received more than $7 million from the federal Office of Juvenile Delinquency.[16] It was significant that, for the first time, the federal government was pumping large amounts of money into the delinquency prevention effort. Despite intense resistance to these efforts in most cities because local public officials felt threatened, the basic model of Mobilization for Youth was incorporated into the community-action component of the War on Poverty.

In 1967, when social scientists and practitioners developed theories of delinquency prevention for President Lyndon Johnson's Crime Commission, MFY was still basic to their thinking (President's Commission on Law Enforcement and the Administration of Justice, 1967). Their problem was to retain a focus upon delivery of remedial services in education, welfare, and job training to the urban poor without creating the intense political conflict engendered by the community action approach. The issue was complicated because leaders such as Malcolm X and Cesar Chavez and groups such as the Black Muslims and the Black Panther Party articulated positions of self-determination and community control. These proponents of ethnic pride and "power to the people" argued that welfare efforts controlled from outside were subtle forms of domestic colonialism. The riots of the mid-1960s dramatized the growing gap between people of color in the United States and their more affluent "benefactors."

It is against this backdrop of urban violence, a growing distrust of outsiders, and increased community-generated self-help efforts that delinquency prevention efforts of the late 1960s and early 1970s developed.

A number of projects during this period attempted to reach the urban poor who had been actively involved in ghetto riots during the 1960s. In Philadelphia, members of a teenage gang were given funds to make a film and start their own businesses. Chicago youth gangs such as Black P. Stone Nation and the Vice Lords were subsidized by federal funding, the YMCA, and the Sears Foundation. In New York City, a Puerto Rican youth group, the Young Lords, received funds to engage in self-help activities. In communities across the nation there was a rapid development of summer projects in recreation, employment, and sanitation to help carry an anxious white America through each potentially long, hot summer. Youth patrols were even organized by police departments to employ ghetto youths to "cool out" trouble that might lead to riots. Few of the programs produced the desired results and often resulted in accusations of improperly used funds by the communities. Often financial audits and investigations were conducted to discredit community organizers and accuse them of encouraging political conflicts with local officials.

One proposed solution that offered more possibility of controlled social action to benefit the young was the Youth Service Bureau (YSB; Norman, 1972). The first YSBs were composed of people from the communities and representatives of public agencies who would hire professionals to deliver a broad range of services to young people. The central idea was to promote cooperation between justice and welfare agencies and the local communities. Agency representatives were expected to contribute partial operating expenses for the programs and, together with neighborhood representatives, decide on program content. Proponents of the YSB approach stressed the need for diverting youthful offenders from the criminal justice system and for delivering necessary social services to deserving children and their families. Ideally YSBs were designed to increase public awareness of the need for more youth services.

The YSBs generally met with poor results. Intense conflict often arose between community residents and agency personnel over the nature of program goals, and YSBs were criticized for not being attuned to community needs (Duxbury, 1972; U.S. Department of Health, Education, and Welfare, 1973). Funds for these efforts were severely limited in relation to the social problems they sought to rectify. In some jurisdictions YSBs were controlled by police or probation departments, with no direct community input. These agency-run programs temporarily diverted youths from entering the criminal justice process by focusing on services such as counseling.

The most important aspect of the YSBs was their attempts to operationalize the diversion of youth from the juvenile justice process, although the effort's success seems highly questionable. Some argue that diversion programs violate the legal rights of youths, as they imply a guilty plea. Others warn that diversion programs expand the welfare bureaucracy, because youths who once would have simply been admonished and sent home by police are now channeled into therapeutic programs. Still others believe that diversion without social services does not prevent delinquency. In any case, a major shift has occurred from the community participation focus of the Mobilization for Youth to a system in which community inputs are limited and carefully controlled. This change in operational philosophy often is justified by the need to secure continued funding, as well as by claims of increasing violence by delinquents. It is important to remember, however, that these same rationales were used to justify a move away from the community organizing model of the Chicago Area Projects of the 1930s. Whenever residents become involved in decision making, there are inevitably increased demands for control of social institutions affecting the community. Such demands for local autonomy question the existing distributions of money and power and thus challenge the authority of social control agencies.

Institutional Change and Community-Based Corrections

Correctional institutions for juvenile delinquents were subject to many of the same social, structural pressures as community prevention efforts. For instance, there was a disproportionate increase in the number of youths in correctional facilities as blacks migrated to the North and the West. In addition, criticism of the use of juvenile inmate labor, especially by organized labor, disrupted institutional routines. But, throughout the late 1930s and the 1940s, increasing numbers of youths were committed to institutions. Later on, the emergence of ethnic pride and calls for black and brown power would cause dissension within the institutions.

The creation of the California Youth Authority just prior to World War II centralized the previously disjointed California correctional institutions.[17] During the 1940s and 1950s, California, Wisconsin, and Minnesota developed separate versions of the Youth Authority concept. Under the Youth Authority model, criminal courts committed youthful offenders from 16 to 21 years old to an administrative authority that determined the proper correctional disposition.[18] The CYA was responsible for all juvenile correctional facilities, including the determination of placements, and parole. Rather than reducing the powers of the juvenile court judge, the Youth Authority streamlined the dispositional process to add administrative flexibility. The Youth Authority was introduced into California at a time when detention facilities were overcrowded, institutional commitment rates were rising, and the correctional system was fragmented and compartmentalized.

The Youth Authority model was developed by the American Law Institute, which drew up model legislation and lobbied for its adoption in state legislatures. The American Law Institute is a nonprofit organization that seeks to influence the development of law and criminal justice. The institution is oriented toward efficiency, rationality, and effectiveness in legal administration.

The treatment philosophy of the first Youth Authorities was similar to the approach of William Healy and the child guidance clinic. John Ellingston, formerly chief legislative lobbyist for the American Law Institute in California, related a debate between Healy and Clifford Shaw over the theoretical direction the new Youth Authority should follow. The legislators, persuaded by Healy's focus on diagnosis of individual delinquents, ensured that the clinic model became the dominant approach in California institutions.

Sociologist Edwin Lemert attributed the emergence of the CYA to the growth of an "administrative state" in the United States. In support of this assertion, Lemert noted the trend toward more centralized delivery of welfare services and increased government regulation of the economy, together with the "militarization" of U.S. society produced by war. Lemert, however, did not discuss whether the purpose of this administrative state was to preserve the existing structure of privilege. The first stated purpose of the CYA was "to protect society by substituting training and treatment for retributive punishment of young persons found guilty of public offenses" (Lemert & Rosenberg, 1948, pp. 49–50).

The centralization of youth correction agencies enabled them to claim the scarce state delinquency prevention funds. In-house research units publicized the latest treatment approaches. In the 1950s and the 1960s, psychologically oriented treatment approaches, including guided-group interaction and group therapy, were introduced in juvenile institutions. During this period of optimism and discovery, many new diagnostic and treatment approaches were evaluated. Correctional administrators and social scientists hoped for a significant breakthrough in treatment, but it never came. Although some questionable evaluation studies claimed successes, there is no evidence that the new therapies had a major impact on recidivism. In fact, some people began to question the concept of enforced therapy and argued that treatment-oriented prisons might be more oppressive than more traditional institutional routines (Mathieson, 1965). Intense objections have been raised particularly against drug therapies and behavior modification programs. Takagi views this as the period when brainwashing techniques were first used on juvenile and adult offenders.[19]

Another major innovation of the 1960s was the introduction of community-based correctional facilities. The central idea was that rehabilitation could be accomplished more effectively outside conventional correctional facilities. This led to a series of treatment measures such as group homes, partial release programs, halfway houses, and attempts to decrease commitment rates to juvenile institutions. California was particularly active in developing community-based correctional programming. The Community Treatment Project, designed by Marguerite Warren in California, was an attempt to replace institutional treatment with intensive parole supervision and psychologically oriented therapy. Probation subsidy involved a bold campaign by CYA staff to convince the state legislature to give cash subsidies to local counties to encourage them to treat juvenile offenders in local programs. Probation subsidy programs were especially oriented toward strengthening the capacity of county probation departments to supervise youthful offenders.[20]

Proponents of the various community-based programs argued that correctional costs could be reduced and rehabilitation results improved in a community context. Reducing state expenditures became more attractive as state governments experienced the fiscal crunch of the late 1960s and the 1970s.[21] It also was thought that reducing institutional populations would alleviate tension and violence within the institutions, but it appears that these community alternatives have created a situation in which youngsters who are sent to institutions are perceived as more dangerous and, as a result, are kept in custody for longer periods of time.

The ultimate logic of the community-based corrections model was followed by the Department of Youth Services in Massachusetts, which closed all of its training schools for delinquents. Youngsters were transferred to group home facilities, and services were offered to individual children on a community basis (Bakal, 1973). The Massachusetts strategy met intense public criticism by juvenile court judges, correctional administrators, and police officials. Some recent attempts have been made to discredit this policy and to justify continued operation of correction facilities, but the Massachusetts strategy has influenced a move to deinstitutionalize children convicted of status offenses—offenses that are considered crimes only if committed by children, such as truancy, running away, or incorrigibility. In 1975, the federal government made $15 million available to local governments that developed plans to deinstitutionalize juvenile status offenders.

At the moment, the forces opposing institutionalized care are making ideological headway due to past failures of institutional methods in controlling delinquency. However, previous experience suggests that the pendulum is likely to swing back in favor of the institutional approaches. Already there is increased talk about the violent delinquent and the alleged increases in violent youth crime; these words have always signaled the beginning of an ideological campaign to promote more stringent control measures and extended incarceration or detention. It is also significant that most states are not firmly committed to community-based treatment. Most jurisdictions still rely on placement in institutions, with conditions reminiscent of the reform schools of 100 years ago. Children continue to be warehoused in large correctional facilities, receiving little care or attention. Eventually they are returned to substandard social conditions to survive as best they can.

Changes in Juvenile Court Law

In the late 1960s the growing awareness of the limitations of the juvenile justice system resulted in a series of court decisions that altered the character of the juvenile court. In *Kent v. United States* (1966) the Supreme Court warned juvenile courts against "procedural arbitrariness," and in *In re Gault* (1967) the Court recognized the rights of juveniles in such matters as notification of charges, protection against self-incrimination, the right to confront witnesses, and the right to have a written transcript of the proceedings. Justice Abe Fortas wrote, "Under our Constitution the condition of being a boy does not justify a kangaroo court" (*In re Gault*, 1967). The newly established rights of juveniles were not welcomed by most juvenile court personnel, who claimed that the informal humanitarian court process would be replaced by a junior criminal court. Communities struggled with methods of providing legal counsel to indigent youth and with restructuring court procedures to conform to constitutional requirements.

The principles set forth in Kent, and later in the Gault decision, offer only limited procedural safeguards to delinquent youth (Kittrie, 1971). Many judicial officers believe the remedy to juvenile court problems is not more formality in proceedings, but more treatment resources. In *McKiever v. Pennsylvania* (1971), the Supreme Court denied that jury trials were a constitutional requirement for the juvenile court. Many legal scholars believe the current Supreme Court has a solid majority opposing extension of procedural rights to alleged delinquents. The dominant view is close to the opinion expressed by Chief Justice Warren Burger in the Winship case:

> What the juvenile court systems need is less not more of the trappings of legal procedure and judicial formalism; the juvenile court system requires breathing room and flexibility in order to survive the repeated assaults on this court. The real problem was not the deprivation of constitutional rights but inadequate juvenile court staffs and facilities. (*In re Winship*, 1970)

The Supreme Court's decision in *Schall v. Martin* (1984) signaled a much more conservative judicial response to children's rights. Plaintiffs in *Schall v. Martin* challenged the constitutionality of New York's Family Court Act as it pertained to the preventive detention of juveniles. It was alleged that the law was too vague and that juveniles were denied due process. A federal district court struck down the statute and its decision was affirmed by the U.S. Court of Appeals. However, the U.S. Supreme Court reversed the lower courts, holding that the preventive detention of juveniles to protect against future crimes was a legitimate state action.

The Emergence of a Conservative Agenda for Juvenile Justice

From the late 1970s and into the 1980s, a conservative reform agenda dominated the national debates over juvenile justice. This new perspective emphasized deterrence and punishment as the major goals of the juvenile court. Conservatives called for the vigorous prosecution of serious and violent youthful offenders. They alleged that the juvenile court was overly lenient with dangerous juveniles.

Conservatives also questioned the wisdom of diverting status offenders from secure custody. The Reagan administration introduced new programs in the areas of missing children and child pornography, which were problems allegedly created by the liberal response to status offenders. Substantial amounts of federal funds were spent on police intelligence programs and enhanced prosecution of juvenile offenders.

Changes in federal policy were also reflected in the actions of many state legislatures. Beginning in 1976, more than half the states made it easier to transfer youths to adult courts. Other states stiffened penalties for juvenile offenders via mandatory minimum sentencing guidelines.

The most obvious impact of the conservative reform movement was a significant increase in the number of youths in juvenile correctional facilities. In addition, from 1979 to 1984, the number of juveniles sent to adult prisons rose by 48%. By 1985 the Bureau of Justice Statistics reported that two-thirds of the nation's training schools were chronically overcrowded.

Another ominous sign was the growing proportion of minority youth in public correctional facilities. In 1982 more than one half of those in public facilities were minority youths, whereas two thirds of those in private juvenile facilities were white. Between 1979 and 1982, when the number of incarcerated youth grew by 6,178, minority youth accounted for 93% of the increase. The sharp rise in incarceration occurred even though the number of arrests of minority youth declined.

Summary

We have traced the history of the juvenile justice system in the United States in relation to significant population migrations, rapid urbanization, race conflicts, and transformation in the economy. These factors continue to influence the treatment of children. The juvenile justice system traditionally has focused on the alleged pathological nature of delinquents, ignoring how the problems of youths relate to larger political and economic issues. Both institutional and community-based efforts to rehabilitate delinquents have been largely unsuccessful. Those with authority for reforming the juvenile justice system have traditionally supported and defended the values and interests of the well-to-do. Not surprisingly, juvenile justice reforms have inexorably increased state control over the lives of the poor and their children. The central implication of this historical analysis is that the future of delinquency prevention and control will be determined largely by ways in which the social structure evolves.[22] It is possible that this future belongs to those who wish to advance social justice on behalf of young people rather than to accommodate the class interests that have dominated this history (Krisberg, 1975; Liazos, 1974). However, one must be cautious about drawing direct inferences for specific social reforms from this historical summary. William Appleman Williams (1973) reminds us, "History offers no answers per se, it only offers a way of encouraging people to use their own minds to make their own history."

Review Questions

1. Describe the "moral panic" that led to the founding of the houses of refuge. Who were the leaders of this movement and what did they hope to accomplish?

2. What led to the creation of the first juvenile court in America in 1899?

3. How did legal decisions shape the contours of juvenile justice in the 1960s?

4. How did the philosophy of the Chicago Area Projects differ from that of the Child Guidance Clinic movement?

Notes

1. Thorsten Sellin, *Pioneering in Penology,* provides an excellent description of the Amsterdam House of Corrections.

2. This issue is well treated by Winthrop Jordan in *The White Man's Burden.*

3. Sources of primary material are N. R. Yetman, *Voices from Slavery,* and Gerda Lerner, *Black Women in White America.* Another fascinating source of data is Margaret Walker's historical novel, *Jubilee.*

4. Historical data on the 19th century rely on the scholarship of Robert Mennel, *Thorns and Thistles;* Anthony Platt, *The Child Savers: The Invention of Delinquency;* Joseph Hawes, *Children in Urban Society: Juvenile Delinquency in Nineteenth Century America;* and the document collection of Robert Bremner et al. in *Children and Youth in America: A Documentary History.*

5. *Delinquent children* are those in violation of criminal codes, statutes, and ordinances. *Dependent children* are those in need of proper and effective parental care or control but having no parent or guardian to provide such care. *Neglected children* are destitute, are unable to secure the basic necessities of life, or have unfit homes due to neglect or cruelty.

6. A good description of anti-Irish feeling during this time is provided by John Higham, *Strangers in the Land.*

7. The preoccupation with the sexuality of female delinquents continues today. See Meda Chesney-Lind, "Juvenile Delinquency: The Sexualization of Female Crime."

8. This routine is reminiscent of the style of 18th-century American Indian schools. It represents an attempt to re-create the ideal of colonial family life, which was being replaced by living patterns accommodated to industrial growth and development.

9. The term *dangerous classes* was coined by Charles Loring Brace in his widely read *The Dangerous Classes of New York and Twenty Years Among Them.*

10. The classic of these studies is that of E. C. Wines, *The State of Prisons and Child-Saving Institutions in the Civilized World,* first printed in 1880.

11. Platt, *The Child Savers: The Invention of Delinquency,* pp. 101–136, and Hawes, *Children in Urban Society: Juvenile Delinquency in Nineteenth Century America,* pp. 158–190, provide the most thorough discussions of the origins of the first juvenile court law.

12. Roy Lubove, *The Professional Altruist,* is a good discussion of the rise of social work as a career.

13. A few earlier clinics specialized in care of juveniles, but these mostly dealt with feeble-minded youngsters.

14. Anthropometric measurements assess human body measurements on a comparative basis. A popular theory of the day was that criminals have distinctive physical traits that can be scientifically measured.

15. Longitudinal studies analyze a group of subjects over time.

16. By comparison, the Chicago Area Project operated on about $283,000 a year.

17. John Ellingston, *Protecting Our Children from Criminal Careers*, provides an extensive discussion of the development of the California Youth Authority.

18. California originally set the maximum jurisdictional age at 23 years, but later reduced it to 21. Some states used an age limit of 18 years, so that they dealt strictly with juveniles. In California, both juveniles and adults were included in the Youth Authority model.

19. Paul Takagi, in "The Correctional System," cites Edgar Schein, "Man Against Man: Brainwashing," and James McConnell, "Criminals Can Be Brainwashed—Now," for candid discussions of this direction in correctional policy.

20. Paul Lerman, *Community Treatment and Social Control*, is a provocative evaluation of the Community Treatment Project and Probation Subsidy.

21. See James O'Connor, *The Fiscal Crisis of the State*, for a discussion of the causes of this fiscal crunch.

22. This perspective is similar to that of Rusche and Kirchheimer in their criminological classic, *Punishment and Social Structure*.

Four

The Current Juvenile Justice System

The goal of this chapter is to describe how the historical legacy of juvenile justice has been translated into the modern justice system practices that one encounters today. The approach will be to describe the processing of cases through the modern juvenile court system, comparing and contrasting these practices with the adult criminal justice system. Keep in mind that there remains significant variation among states and localities. What is presented below is an attempt to capture the present reality in the largest number of juvenile court jurisdictions. The National Center for Juvenile Justice is the preeminent source of more current information on how legislative changes impact the structure and process of the juvenile justice system.

The original scope or jurisdiction of the juvenile justice system is defined in each state by specific statutes. The first level of this definition process involves the age of the youth at the time of arrest or referral to the juvenile justice system. Most states set the upper age of juvenile court jurisdiction at age 18. Connecticut, New York, and North Carolina have established a much lower upper limit, at 16 years of age. Eleven other states employ age 17 as the upper limit of original juvenile court jurisdiction. However, several states permit the juvenile court to retain its jurisdiction of cases already in the system until age 21. Several states actually allow this continuing jurisdiction for some youths as old as 25 who are under the control of the state youth corrections authority (Snyder & Sickmund, 1999).

There is also variability in the lower boundary of the juvenile court's authority—the age below which the child is deemed too young to be subject to court laws. Eleven states set this lower age boundary at 10 years old, whereas another five states use boundaries of age 6 (North Carolina), age 7 (Maryland, Massachusetts, and New York), and age 8 (Arizona). Other jurisdictions have no statutorily mandated lower age threshold, although the usual practice is to recognize the tradition of the English Common Law standard of age 7 for the lowest age of criminal court jurisdiction (Snyder & Sickmund, 1999).

These general age limits have been further refined by state laws specifying circumstances and legal mechanisms through which the original jurisdiction of the juvenile court may revert to the criminal court or be shared with the criminal court system. The overall trend in juvenile law in the past decade has been to extend these exceptions and to extend the range of transfer procedures. Some would say that the most important development in contemporary juvenile court law has been the "blurring of the line" between the juvenile court and the criminal law system.

A further complication in understanding the juvenile justice system is the overlap, in many locales, between the criminal law system as applied to minors and the laws governing the protection of dependent, neglected, and abused children. It is common that children appearing before the juvenile court are still under the auspices of child welfare and protection laws. Judges sometimes use either legal structure or a combination of the two systems to fashion remedies in individual cases. Often, it is the same judge who hears cases in both systems. Moreover, many states have established hybrid categories, such as Children in Need of Supervision (CHINS), Persons in Need of Supervision (PINS), or Minors in Need of Supervision (MINS), that overlap the traditional categories of dependent children with behavior that might be considered criminal law violations in other states. Most often these hybrid categories are meant to be used in cases involving behaviors such as truancy, running away, curfew violations, underage drinking or smoking, or incorrigibility. Traditionally, state laws prohibit the secure confinement of these non-offenders or forbid their confinement with youngsters charged with criminal law violations. However, these finite legal categories often merge together in cases in which the youth is already under juvenile court control (e.g., under probation supervision or in some sort of diversion program). In the world of contemporary juvenile justice nothing is simple and consistent.

Before discussing the various components of the juvenile justice process, it is worth considering how the modern juvenile and criminal justice systems differ and converge. Table 4.1, prepared by the federal Office of Juvenile Justice and Delinquency Protection, provides a convenient summary of these common and differing aspects of the two justice systems (Snyder & Sickmund, 1999).

Table 4.1   Comparison of Juvenile and Criminal Justice Systems

Although the juvenile and criminal justice systems are more alike in some jurisdictions than in others, generalizations can be made about the distinctions between the two systems and about their common ground.

Juvenile Justice System	Common Ground	Criminal Justice System
Operating Assumptions		
• Youth behavior is malleable. • Rehabilitation is usually a viable goal. • Youths are in families and not independent.	• Community protection is a primary goal. Law violators must be held accountable. • Constitutional rights apply.	• Sanctions should be proportional to the offense. • General deterrence works. Rehabilitation is not a primary goal.
Prevention		
• Many specific delinquency prevention activities (e.g., school, church, recreation) are used. • Prevention is intended to change individual behavior and is often focused on reducing risk factors and increasing protective factors in the individual, family, and community.	• Educational approaches are taken to specific behaviors (drunk driving, drug use).	• Prevention activities are generalized and are aimed at deterrence (e.g., Crime Watch).
Law Enforcement		
• Specialized "juvenile" units are used. • Some additional behaviors are prohibited (truancy, running away, curfew violations). • Some limitations are placed on public access to information. • A significant number of youth are diverted away from the juvenile justice system, often into alternative programs.	• Jurisdiction involves the full range of criminal behavior. • Constitutional and procedural safeguards exist. • Both reactive and proactive approaches (targeted at offense types, neighborhoods, etc.) are used. • Community policing strategies are employed.	• Open public access to all information is required. • Law enforcement exercises discretion to divert offenders out of the criminal justice system.

(Continued)

Table 4.1 (Continued)

Juvenile Justice System	Common Ground	Criminal Justice System
Intake—Prosecution		
• In many instances, juvenile court intake, not the prosecutor, decides what cases to file. • The decision to file a petition for court action is based on both social and legal factors. • A significant portion of cases are diverted from formal case processing. • Intake or the prosecutor diverts cases from formal processing to services operated by the juvenile court, prosecutor's office, or outside agencies.	• Probable cause must be established. • The prosecutor acts on behalf of the state.	• Plea bargaining is common. • The prosecution decision is based largely on legal facts. • Prosecution is valuable in building history for subsequent offenses. • Prosecution exercises discretion to withhold charges or divert offenders out of the criminal justice system.
Detention—Jail/Lockup		
• Juveniles may be detained for their own protection or the community's protection. • Juveniles may not be confined with adults unless there is sight-and-sound separation.	• Accused offenders may be held in custody to ensure their appearance in court. • Detention alternatives of home or electronic detention are used.	• Accused individuals have the right to apply for bond/bail release.
Adjudication—Conviction		
• Juvenile court proceedings are quasi-civil (not criminal) and may be confidential. • If guilt is established, the youth is adjudicated delinquent regardless of offense. • Right to jury trial is not afforded in all states.	• Standard of proof beyond a reasonable doubt is required. • Rights to be represented by an attorney, to confront witnesses, and to remain silent are afforded. • Appeals to a higher court are allowed. • Experimentation with specialized court (i.e., drug courts, gun courts) is underway.	• Defendants have a constitutional right to a jury trial. • Guilt must be established on individual offenses charged for conviction. • All proceedings are open.

Juvenile Justice System	Common Ground	Criminal Justice System
Disposition—Sentencing		
• Disposition decisions are based on individual and social factors, offense severity, and youth's offense history. • Dispositional philosophy includes a significant rehabilitation component. • Many dispositional alternatives are operated by the juvenile court. • Dispositions cover a wide range of community-based and residential services. • Disposition orders may be directed to people other than the offender (e.g., parents). • Disposition may be indeterminate, based on progress demonstrated by the youth.	• Decisions are influenced by current offense, offending history, and social factors. • Decisions hold offenders accountable. Decisions may give consideration to victims (e.g., restitution and no-contact orders). • Decisions may not be cruel or unusual.	• Sentencing decisions are bound primarily by the severity of the current offense and by the offender's criminal history. • Sentencing philosophy is based largely on proportionality and punishment. • Sentence is often determinate, based on offense.
Aftercare—Parole		
• Function combines surveillance and reintegration activities (e.g., family, school, work).	• The behavior of individuals released from correctional settings is monitored. • Violation of conditions can result in reincarceration.	• Function is primarily surveillance and reporting to monitor illicit behavior.

SOURCE: Snyder and Sickmund (1999, p. 94).

At the most basic level, the two systems differ in their core assumptions. For example, the juvenile justice system assumes that young people are capable of positive change. Rehabilitation is considered a possible and desirable goal. Juvenile justice interventions assume that youths are part of families, and attempts are made to involve parents in the various programs of the system. By contrast, the current criminal justice system does not place much emphasis on rehabilitation as a goal, although many criminal law systems did value rehabilitation in the past. The contemporary criminal justice system assumes that general deterrence is an effective crime control strategy (Zimring & Hawkins, 1973). This means that the criminal law assumes that others will be discouraged from law breaking by knowledge of the severity and certainty of punishments meted out to apprehended offenders. Inherent in the concept of deterrence is the assumption that humans operate principally through a process of rational calculations of the benefits of committing crimes compared to the costs of apprehension and punishment (Wilson, 1983). The juvenile justice system assumes that in addition to cost–benefit calculations, young offenders are motivated by a range of rational and irrational forces. The reader will recall that this latter assumption is directly related to the early scientific work supporting the creation of the juvenile court (Healy, 1915).

Both the juvenile and the criminal justice systems recognize protection of the public as a major goal. In each system there is value placed on holding offenders accountable for their specific actions. Most important, since the late 1960s, the juvenile justice system has mirrored the adult court system in its attention to the protection of the constitutional rights of the accused. Both systems are increasingly interested in advancing the rights of victims in various aspects of its legal processes. Legislation establishing the rights of victims in the juvenile court has trailed behind the criminal court system, but the 1990s was a period in which many lawmakers sought to extend rights to victims within the juvenile justice system.

The two systems also differ markedly in their approaches to crime prevention. As noted earlier, the criminal justice system depends on general and specific deterrence to prevent future crimes. Prevention strategies often entail increasing the capacity and willingness of citizens to report crimes to the police. This type of public participation is reflected in programs such as Crime Watch or Crime Stoppers. Crime Watch programs often involve organizing neighborhood residents to conduct informal patrols, pass along information about recent local crimes, or hold meetings with police to learn how to better protect one's person or property. Crime Stoppers is a national program that pays cash rewards for information leading to the arrest of criminals. Juvenile crime prevention programs tend to rely more on educational efforts (an example is the D.A.R.E. program, in which police officers enter schools and teach children about the dangers of drug use) and the delivery of services including recreational, vocational, and counseling efforts. OJJDP funds prevention programs through a number of grants to states and localities. Units of state and local governments typically devote some funding each year to service-oriented prevention efforts. These services are designed to reduce certain risk factors that researchers have linked to the onset of delinquent behavior in individuals, families, schools, and communities (Hawkins & Catalano, 1992). Prevention programs also seek to increase protective or buffering factors that insulate youngsters from risk factors. We will discuss these approaches to delinquency prevention in Chapter 7. There are some more limited educational prevention efforts in the criminal justice system such as classes for drunk drivers, educational programs for domestic violence offenders, or courses on traffic safety. Participation in these adult prevention programs is often a condition of diverting the case from formal court processing or of reducing penalties.

Law enforcement policies and practices differ between the two justice systems. Police agencies often assign special units to handle juvenile offenders, and there is an expectation that public access to information about juvenile offenders will be more limited than for adults. The overall philosophy of enforcing laws with minors is to divert a significant number of these cases away from the justice system. In policy, and often in practice, the ideal is to handle cases informally, allowing parents or other community agencies to take the lead. The ethos of juvenile justice is to exercise extreme constraint when intervening in the lives of children. Chapter 3 explained why and how these ideas became part of the modern juvenile justice, and it is true that this noninterventionist paradigm is regularly questioned and reexamined.

It is also worth noting that police respond to behaviors by juveniles that would not engage their attention if committed by adults. For example, police enforce truancy laws but do not arrest adults who fail to attend their classes. Except in times of emergency, adults do not have to adhere to curfews, whereas minors cannot be out in public places during certain hours. Adults are free to purchase highly toxic and addictive substances such as tobacco and alcohol, but these commodities are forbidden for juveniles. Minors can be confined for running away from their homes, whereas adults are free to change their living situation without criminal penalty.

Police divert adult offenders from further criminal justice processing, although the rationale is rarely that there are better places from which to get services. Diversion of adult offenders is often based on police obtaining information from them that can be used to arrest others. The exercise of police discretion in adult cases has led to serious criticism of law enforcement agencies who are alleged to employ racial, gender, or social class factors in making their decisions. For example, police handling of domestic violence incidents has moved toward mandatory arrest policies, in lieu of allowing the street officers to decide the appropriate resolution of individual cases. While these mandatory arrest policies have been promoted based on research findings (Sherman et al., 1997), the evidence supporting the efficacy of these approaches is less than totally convincing.

More recently, police practices for adults and juveniles have converged in the theory of problem-solving law enforcement in which informal dispute resolution and mediation strategies are encouraged in lieu of making arrests. For both juveniles and adults, police are governed by common constitutional requirements pertaining to the limitations on powers to stop individuals, rules pertaining to search and seizure, and safeguards against self-incrimination.

As one moves further along in the process, the juvenile and adult systems begin to diverge. In the adult system, it is the prosecutor who decides if a person who is arrested by the police is brought into the criminal justice system. Typically, there is a preliminary hearing in which the prosecutor presents the charges to a judge, the defendant enters a plea of guilty or not guilty, and either bail is set or the defendant is remanded to jail. Later in the process, usually after a variety of evidentiary motions are considered (such as the inclusion of evidence, the face validity of the charges, or other procedural matters), the prosecutor decides either to bring the case forward or to drop it. In many jurisdictions a panel of citizens known as a grand jury will hear the prosecutor's preliminary evidence and will decide if the criminal case should be brought forward. Prosecutors have the discretion to either drop the case or defer prosecution, usually in situations in which the defendant agrees to enter some treatment or counseling program. Failure to complete this agreement often results in the original charges being filed.

The juvenile justice system usually employs an intake unit to evaluate whether a case should be brought forward. Although it is increasingly common for prosecutors to participate in the intake process, it is most often accomplished by staff of the juvenile probation department. The sufficiency of legal evidence is a strong consideration, but the primary emphasis of the juvenile intake process is problem solving—how best to rectify the youth's misconduct with a minimum of court intervention. The juvenile court almost always is governed by the principle of utilizing the least restrictive alternative consistent with protecting public safety. The intake process is also guided by a search for ways to protect the child from adverse community, family, or peer influences. It is sometimes the case that the child welfare or mental health systems may provide more appropriate responses to the child's behavior than the juvenile justice system.

In the juvenile court the decision is made whether to file a petition to declare the child a ward of the court. This decision is guided by both legal and social service considerations. The child and his or her attorney may contest the petition, but they do not typically enter a plea of guilt or innocence. In most locales a juvenile court judge will decide whether it is in society's or the child's best interests to proceed with a formal hearing on the petition. In smaller jurisdictions this hearing is conducted by a lower court judge or magistrate. Unlike the criminal justice system, there is no automatic right to bail. Youths who are not released to their guardians are confined in juvenile detention facilities. The juvenile court is permitted broad latitude to detain youngsters for society's protection (similar to the adult system) or for the protection of the child. Whereas there are very strict constitutional limitations on preventive pretrial detention for adults, the U.S. Supreme Court has approved a much wider set of detention criteria for minors (*Schall v. Martin,* 1984).

It is at the adjudication stage that the two justice systems are most different. Juvenile court hearings are not viewed as criminal law proceedings; they are quasi-civil hearings. If the facts of an alleged petition are sustained by the court, the petition is sustained and the youth is declared to be a ward of the juvenile court. In the criminal law system the offender is found guilty of a very specific set of criminal offenses; in the juvenile court the petition relates to a general pattern of behavior or family circumstances. Criminal court hearings must be open to the public, whereas juvenile courts operate primarily on a confidential basis. Adults charged with criminal offenses are entitled to a jury of their peers, but there is no legally recognized right to jury trials in the juvenile court system.

Both the criminal and juvenile justice systems require a standard of proof of beyond a reasonable doubt, and persons in each court have rights to be represented by attorneys, to confront their accusers, and to not testify against themselves. The right to appeal is available in both systems. Both court systems are beginning to introduce specialized sections of their courts that focus on particular offenses such as drug courts, gun courts, and reentry courts.

During the dispositional phase of juvenile court hearings there is great weight placed on in-depth social, psychological, and individual factors. Dispositions are, by design, to be *individualized.* Juvenile courts may even direct their dispositional orders to other individuals such as the youth's guardians. Juvenile courts employ a broad range of dispositional options— orders to make restitution or to perform community service, as well as a wide range of residential placements. Juvenile courts often impose curfews or require regular attendance in school. Parents and youths may be ordered to attend counseling sessions. These more creative dispositions are sometimes utilized in criminal courts, but on a far more limited basis.

Criminal courts generally rely more on a limited set of legal factors such as the gravity of the current offense and the prior record of the offender. Criminal court sentences are very often rigidly determined by state laws, whereas juvenile court dispositions are far more open-ended— the youth is declared under the juvenile court's supervision based on regular reviews of his or her progress up to the statutory age maximum jurisdiction of the court. Neither the criminal nor juvenile court system may impose sanctions that are deemed cruel or unusual.

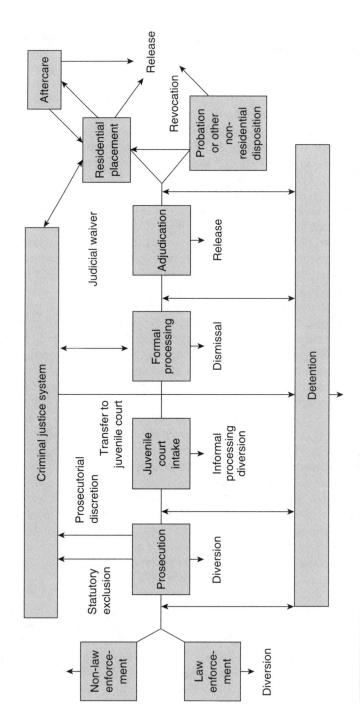

Figure 4.1   The Stages of Delinquency Case Processing in the Juvenile Justice System

SOURCE: Snyder and Sickmund (1999, p. 98).

The Flow of Cases Through the Juvenile Justice System

Figure 4.1 (Snyder & Sickmund, 1999) shows a typical flow of cases through the juvenile justice system. It cannot be repeated often enough that there are many state variations that alter how this process operates across the nation. Let's examine this case flow using data from the National Center for Juvenile Justice (Snyder & Sickmund, 1999).

Law enforcement agencies are the primary source of referrals into the juvenile justice system. Approximately 86% of cases come from police agencies. The remaining 14% are referred by schools, social service agencies, or parents. In the case of minor assaults, there are a larger number of referrals coming from schools, probably a reflection of campus fights among students.

Police agencies have a range of policies on handling juvenile arrests. Some departments operate their own special programs that are designed to divert youngsters from further court processing. There are police agencies that work diligently to return back to their parents those juveniles that are stopped for minor offenses. Other law enforcement agencies take virtually every youth into custody, relying on the probation department to sort out the next steps. A recent development in police handling of juveniles is community/juvenile assessment centers—places at which the police drop off youngsters in instances in which an arrest is not mandatory. An assessment center consists of staff who are multidisciplinary and knowledgeable about community-based treatment options. The primary goal of an assessment center is to perform a treatment assessment for the youth and to quickly move that youngster into more appropriate community services. Police appreciate the assessment center concept because they can drop off the youngsters with responsible adults, it saves them paperwork, and the patrol officers can more quickly return to service.

Because police decisions to arrest or release juveniles are subject to a great deal of external scrutiny, it is difficult to accurately describe how these decisions are actually made. There is much speculation that race and social class factors unfairly bias law enforcement decisions. Statistics are very hard to collect on such low-visibility decision making. Anecdotal evidence suggests that police are more likely to return youths to their homes if their parents are at home (or reachable by telephone) and if the parents are regarded as reputable by the officers. It is easy to see how class and racial considerations might impact the judgment of a law enforcement officer, particularly one who does not know much about the youngster or his or her community. One of the goals of community policing is to better connect police officers with the residents of the areas that they patrol, setting up the possibility of better decision making as to whether a young person should be arrested.

Researchers have suggested that the demeanor of the youth may play a large factor in whether a formal arrest will be made (Piliavin & Briar, 1964). A belligerent and verbally abusive youth is far more likely to be taken into custody. Moreover, some have observed that teenagers who simply assert their constitutional rights are more likely to be treated in a more formal and harsh manner. The factor of demeanor is sometimes used as a rationale for why it appears that minority youths seem to be arrested in higher proportions than their white counterparts (Piliavin & Briar, 1964). But, it should be considered that race differences are pivotal in the way in which different people interpret the behavior of others. A youth who averts his or her eyes from the arresting officer may be showing deferential behavior, although this might be interpreted as a sign of disrespect. Because demeanor is so subjective and situational in its interpretation, it is difficult to comprehend how ethnic, racial, gender, or class differences could not influence this communication process.

Of those youths who are brought by the police to the juvenile court intake process, slightly more than half of these cases result in the filing of delinquency petition. About one fifth of the cases that are referred to intake are dismissed outright, and another one quarter receive some informal sanction that might include dismissal, restitution, community service, or a minimal level of probation supervision. For the cases that the intake unit sends forward to the court, about two thirds of these result in formal adjudications. The juvenile court relies on a range of informal sanctions to handle the rest of the cases. Only about 6 in 1,000 referrals to the juvenile court result in the transfer of the case to the criminal court. However, we noted earlier that in some jurisdictions there are statutory provisions permitting the waiver of a juvenile to criminal court without the agreement of the juvenile court (Snyder & Sickmund, 1999).

Most youths who are adjudicated by the juvenile court and who have their petitions sustained by the court are placed on probation or receive lesser penalties. Of all youths that are referred to the juvenile court, about 9% of these cases result in some form of out-of-home placement (Snyder & Sickmund, 1999). These data illustrate how the philosophy of utilizing the least restrictive alternative remains a core principle of the juvenile court.

Because the decision to remove a child from his or her home is such a dramatic (and costly) step, it is worth examining the process by which such determinations are made. The very first placement decision made by the juvenile justice system involves whether a youth should be held in a juvenile detention facility. Approximately 600,000 juveniles are admitted to juvenile detention centers each year. Although many of these youths spend less than 24 hours in detention centers, the average length of stay for all detained youngsters is about 15 days (Krisberg et al., 2001). Federal law requires that the holding of juveniles in police lockups be of very short duration and that youth be moved to an appropriate juvenile facility. Further, this law requires strict "sight and sound" separation of juveniles from adult offenders.

Initial detention decisions are typically made by intake workers. While there are some states that define general criteria for detention, there is often very wide latitude given to the juvenile justice system. Unlike the adult court system, juveniles may be detained "for their own protection," as well as to maintain public safety. Juveniles do not have the right to post bail in most jurisdictions. Many states bar the confinement of status offenders in secure detention facilities, although there are often statutory loopholes that allow for the incarceration of youngsters who have committed status offenses. These exceptions to the ban against confining status offenders can include youths who have violated a valid court order or a youngster who is already on probation.

In recent years several juvenile justice systems have employed structured risk assessment instruments (RAIs) to assist in making detention intake decisions. These RAIs employ a limited set of variables that have been demonstrated via research to determine the risk of committing another crime before the case is adjudicated or the risk of the youth failing to make scheduled court hearings. Similar instruments have been utilized in making pretrial confinement decisions in the criminal court system since the 1950s. The primary focus of the RAI is the protection of public safety. The intake worker scores a specific case and generally follows the presumptive custody or release decision that is suggested by the RAI. Intake workers can override the presumptive decision of the instrument, but many departments require that a supervisor review and approve this override.

The use of more structured and objective detention intake instruments has led to significant declines in admissions in a number of locations (Krisberg et al., 2001; Schwartz & Barton, 1994). Reducing detention admissions through the use of well-designed RAIs does not appear to endanger public safety, nor does it lead to increased failure-to-appear rates (Krisberg et al., 2001; Steinhart, 1994). Moreover, it appears that the use of RAIs can reduce the amount of racial, gender, and class bias that often enters into more subjective detention intake systems (Wiebush, Baird, Krisberg, & Onek, 1995).

In most locales the alternatives to secure detention are fairly limited. Intake workers either decide to hold the youth pending a court review, or they generally release the child to a legal guardian. More recently, a range of additional alternatives to detention have been attempted. For example, some jurisdictions have employed electronic monitoring devices that allow the probation department to determine if the minor is at home during specified hours. Other locales have funded day reporting programs, in which the youth lives at home but is expected to show up daily at a program, usually after school. Detention alternatives may also involve intensive home-based visits by probation staff or by a designated community-based agency. For youths who do not pose a threat to public safety but need a safe place to live temporarily, some juvenile courts have established nonsecure shelters where the youngster can stay until the court proceedings are completed. Research has demonstrated that properly implemented alternatives to detention are considerably less costly than secure confinement, and youths placed in alternatives make their court hearings and do not commit many new offenses while they are living at home (or in the community) awaiting the final disposition of their cases. In fact, well-designed alternatives can actually reduce failures to appear and pretrial crimes, because youths in these programs are in greater contact with court personnel in the preadjudication period. Youths who are initially detained are often released before their court hearings are completed and may reoffend even though they have been initially incarcerated (Krisberg et al., 2001; Schwartz & Barton, 1994).

Reducing the number of youngsters who are inappropriately incarcerated during the preadjudication period is desirable for a number of reasons. As noted earlier, the decision to detain is expensive and often creates crises within families trying to reconcile differences and reunite. Minors who are detained pretrial are more likely to be placed out of their homes after their cases are disposed (Schwartz & Barton, 1994). While this correlation may be a function of the severity of the offense or the past delinquent history of the child, there is some evidence that the initial decision to detain is a "self-fulfilling prophesy" in that court officials assume that detained youths must be more serious threats to public safety.

Too often, detention centers do not have effective custody classification systems, so that minor offenders may share the same living unit with more aggressive and criminally sophisticated youths. Many detention centers are dominated by gang conflicts and violence. Little in the way of treatment or education takes place in most secure detention centers. Youngsters in detention do "dead time." There are few medical, behavioral, or mental health services available to children in detention. Youths with serious health issues often deteriorate in these stark settings (Hartney, Wordes, & Krisberg, 2002). Most progressive thinkers in the juvenile justice system view detention as a necessary evil to be limited as much as possible.

As problematic as the conditions in juvenile detention centers are, the practice of some jurisdictions of putting minors in adult jails is even more dangerous. Historically, minors placed in adult jails have experienced much higher rates of violence and sexual exploitation than youths placed in specialized youth facilities. The suicide rate for juveniles in jails is much higher than youths in juvenile detention centers.

The passage of the federal Juvenile Justice and Delinquency Prevention Act of 1974 (JJDPA) was, in part, motivated by an effort to end the abuses suffered by children who were held in adult jails and police lockups. At the time of the enactment of the JJDPA, it was estimated that nearly 500,000 minors entered adult jails each year. There were 100,000 minors admitted to jails in California alone in the early 1980s. Initially, the JJDPA sought to impose strict separation between adult and juvenile inmates. Later amendments to the law called for the complete removal of children from adult facilities. Congress allowed each state to apply its own legal definition of a juvenile. A more conservative Congress voided the jail removal standard and returned to the goal of separating adult and juvenile jail inmates, but the overall trend has been to provide more loopholes for jurisdictions that wish to continue this practice.

The national reform to reduce the jailing of children met with substantial success. By the late 1980s juvenile admissions to jails had declined to roughly 65,000 per year (Austin, Krisberg, & DeComo, 1995). The more conservative juvenile justice policies of the 1990s led to a 35% increase in children in jails between 1994 and 1997 (Snyder & Sickmund, 1999). In 1997, of the approximately 9,100 youth under age 18 who were jail inmates, three quarters were awaiting trials or were convicted in criminal courts (Snyder & Sickmund, 1999).

The jailing of children has historically been a problem for rural jurisdictions and those locales where large distances prevent law enforcement officials from quickly transporting youngsters to juvenile facilities. However, very punitive attitudes among some judges also contributed to the dangerous practice of holding minors in adult facilities. Reformers employed a range of tactics to reduce the jailing of children. Some jurisdictions built new juvenile facilities, while others provided funding for community-based shelter facilities. A major bipartisan legislative campaign in California made it illegal to jail minors for more than 6 hours and then only for the purpose of moving them to a more appropriate setting (Steinhart, 1988). The practice of jailing children in California virtually disappeared after the enactment of this law.

Sending minors to adult prisons was not part of the national jail reform campaign. There are no federal laws prohibiting states from placing very young adolescents in state prisons if they have been convicted in criminal courts. Indeed, this practice has become much more common over the past 10 years (Torbet et al., 1996).

No one knows for sure how many juveniles are transferred to adult courts. Hamparian and her colleagues estimated that in 1978 there were more than 9,000 youths transferred to criminal courts by juvenile courts, another 2,000 cases moved to adult courts by prosecutors, and more than 1,300 minors prosecuted as adults due to statutes that excluded certain offenses from juvenile court jurisdiction (Hamparian, 1982). Later estimates from a variety of sources suggest that as many as 200,000 youths under age 18 are tried in adult courts (Krisberg, 1997).

The National Correctional Reporting Program (NCRP) found that there were nearly 7,400 persons under age 18 who entered prisons in 1992 from the 37 states participating in that national data system (Strom, 2000). These minors represented about 1% of all prison admissions from these states. These youngsters were predominantly African American males (58%) and were typically 17 years old at the time of their prison admission. About 47% of these youths were convicted of violent crimes, and 53% were charged with drug offenses or property crimes (Krisberg, 1997). Youths under age 18 who enter prison receive longer sentences and actually serve three times as long in prison compared to adults convicted of similar offenses. Howell (1997) notes that juveniles in prisons are more likely to get involved in disciplinary problems that extend their prison stays, and they serve a very large proportion of their sentences in prison administrative segregation units.

Although there are many studies of the process through which juvenile courts select cases to transfer to criminal courts, virtually nothing is known about how prosecutors choose cases to file directly in criminal courts or how laws restricting the jurisdiction of the juvenile court are actually enforced. Howell (2003) found 38 studies of judicial waiver that sought to account for the decision-making process. He found that legal factors such as severity of the crime and prior record influenced the waiver decision. Howell also found that race, the age of the offender, victim–offender relationships, and local juvenile court practices exerted strong effects on the decision to transfer youngsters to adult courts. For example, compared to white minors who were charged with the same offenses, African American youths had significantly higher rates of transfer for drug crimes and violent offenses (Snyder & Sickmund, 1999). Frazier (1991) found clear evidence of racial differences in the use of prosecutorial discretion to file juvenile cases in adult courts in Florida. Eigen (1972) reports that African American teenagers who murdered white victims were much more likely to be tried as adults than as juveniles in Philadelphia. Singer and McDowall (1988) showed how New York State's tough laws on trying juveniles as adults were selectively enforced in a number of different New York counties. Krisberg (2003) illustrated how racial bias and inadequate legal representation can propel minority youngsters into the adult criminal court system.

The decision to remove juvenile offenders from the juvenile justice system constitutes a very dramatic change in a young person's legal status. We noted earlier that juveniles in prisons are less likely to receive treatment services, they are more likely to be victimized by older inmates, and they spend large parts of their incarceration time in solitary confinement units (Forst, Fagan, & Vivona, 1989; Howell, 2003). Transfer decisions, however, have even more stark consequences for young offenders. For example, no juvenile court permits the imposition of capital punishment, but youths who are 16 and older and are tried in criminal courts may be put to death. In 1998 there were 76 death-row inmates who committed their crimes before the age of 18. Forty percent of these cases were in just two states—Texas and Florida. The United States is virtually alone among countries in the developed world in permitting juveniles to be put to death (Streib, 1987).

In the last few years we have witnessed ever younger adolescents being tried as adults and sent to state prisons. The tender age of these prison-bound youths has shocked the conscience of some but has not yet fueled a national reform movement to stop this policy (Amnesty International, 1998). In fact, federal and state laws continue to encourage the wider use of transfer procedures.

Summary

There is major variation among the states and even within states with regard to the structure and operation of the juvenile justice system. Previously, my colleagues and I referred to this situation as "Justice by Geography." Most states set the upper age boundary of original jurisdiction of the juvenile court at 18, but this age limit can be as low as 16 years old in some states and as high as 25 years old in others. Juvenile justice systems have become more like criminal justice systems over the past 30 years, but there remain major differences between the two. Unlike the adult system, the juvenile justice system is guided by a philosophy of rehabilitation and child protection. Juvenile justice systems are more focused on preventive practices and actively try to divert young people from the formal court process. The criminal justice system has a lesser emphasis on diversion and principally pursues prevention through the notion that its penalties serve as a deterrent to potential offenders.

Most cases enter the juvenile justice system through police referrals, but schools, social agencies, and parents also bring cases to juvenile court.

Most communities operate juvenile intake units that evaluate individual cases and attempt to find alternative methods of resolving the immediate issue. Of youths brought to intake units, slightly more than one half go on to formal court hearings. Discretionary decision making is a core part of how the juvenile justice system operates. Much of the research on juvenile justice has focused on the determinants of these decisions.

Increasingly, states have enacted more ways to transfer young people to the criminal courts. This is a very controversial trend, and there is a great deal of research suggesting that trying very young people in criminal courts is bad public policy. For example, no juvenile court can impose the death penalty, but juveniles transferred to adult courts can receive capital punishment.

Review Questions

1. Compare and contrast ways in which the criminal justice and juvenile justice systems work.

2. What are the main findings of research on how decisions are made in various stages of the juvenile justice process?

3. What are the presumed benefits and problems of transferring youths from the juvenile justice system to the adult system?

Five

Juvenile Justice and the American Dilemma

A t the dawn of the 20th century the great American sociologist and social activist W. E. B. DuBois proclaimed that the "problem of the color line" would be the central issue of that century (DuBois, 1903). As we enter the 21st century, his prophetic words still ring true. The juvenile justice system is plagued by racial disparities and inequities that challenge its legitimacy. Despite a dominant philosophy that seeks to be "race neutral," the decision-making processes of the juvenile justice system are anything but neutral for children of color. In this chapter the extent of this grave problem will be examined, explanations for its existence will be explored, and potential remedies will be considered.

In 1992 the federal Juvenile Justice Act was amended by Congress to require that all participating states wishing to receive funding from OJJDP be required to examine the extent of disproportionate minority confinement (DMC) in their juvenile justice systems. Besides conducting in-depth studies of the problem, participating states were required to make "good faith efforts" to reduce DMC where appropriate. Since the late 1990s there have been annual attempts from some members of Congress, most notably Senator Orrin Hatch of Utah, to remove the DMC mandate from the federal justice program. Although these efforts have weakened the mandate and given states great flexibility, Congress has not yet eliminated the requirement for states to examine racial disparities in their juvenile justice systems.

In 1987, Krisberg and his colleagues utilized data from the national Children in Custody survey to document the disproportionate presence of African American, Native American, and Latino youths in juvenile correctional facilities. Further, they found that minority youths were more likely to be housed in more secure facilities and to be held in places that were chronically overcrowded. Moreover, Krisberg and his associates noted that reform efforts in the 1970s that were intended to deinstitutionalize youths, removing them from secure facilities to community settings, had primarily resulted in white youth incarceration rates going down and far less of a decline in the confinement of minority youngsters. As the public policy agenda embraced tougher penalties and longer stays in custody in the 1980s, minority youths bore the overwhelming brunt of these "get tough" policies. Throughout the last two decades of the 20th century, racial disparities continued to worsen.

Before examining some of the key data on DMC, it is important to clarify some basic terminology. Although it is common to use the word *race* to describe certain groups, it must be noted that mainstream scientists regard race as a meaningless biological category. Research on human genetics has consistently shown that human genetic diversity is very limited in comparison to other living organisms. Increasingly, scientists believe that observable human differences are attributable more to geographic communities (i.e., people who have lived in close proximity for generations) than to genetic differences. It is highly questionable science to use race as an explanatory variable, in and of itself, although several conservative, media-promoted criminologists such as Charles Murray and James Q. Wilson have consistently produced flawed research using scientifically questionable data in this area (Herrnstein & Murray, 1994; Wilson & Herrnstein, 1985). Further, the extensive sexual contacts among racial groups, which is often publicly denied, makes pure racial distinctions moot. Most Americans have interracial heritages and there are no scientifically valid rules by which an individual should be assigned to one group or another. Race is, first and foremost, a social construct and a powerful life-defining category. Race-conscious societies often have intricate rules, because assignment to one or another racial group *does* have profound social and even legal consequences. For years, many southern states such as Louisiana made very fine distinctions based on the presumed percentage of one's blood that came from different racial groups. For some, even "one drop of blood" defined a person as belonging to a particular racial category. There is a rich literary and folk tradition about people who attempted to "pass" as members of another group (for example, the classic American musical *Showboat* or the classic movie starring Lana Turner, *Imitation of Life*). Racial categories are fluid and change as society changes. At the turn of the century, Jewish and Italian immigrants were regarded as nonwhite. During certain historical periods, being part Native American was a badge of honor, but at other times this racial background was a stigma.

Related to the concept of race is that of *ethnicity*. *Ethnicity* refers to a group of people who generally share a common culture. The commonality of an ethnic group might include history, values, aesthetics, family and community traditions, and language. Most of the groups who are referred to as ethnic groups may share some of these common social and cultural elements, but more often than not, there is notable diversity within these groups. For example, the category *Latino* may refer to people with a heritage from North American, South American, Central American, or Caribbean nations. They practice several different religions and speak English, Spanish, or Portuguese, among other languages. Similarly, there is enormous cultural diversity in the African American community, whose antecedents may have originated in Africa but who lived in virtually every nation on earth. Even for those born in one nation, regional differences or rural-versus-urban experiences profoundly affect a person's ethnic identity. There is a serious question as to whether a person can self-select an ethnic identity such as the white teenager who totally embraces the culture of urban African Americans or the Eastern European immigrant who attempts to embrace the culture of white Anglo-Saxon Protestants. As with race, the concept of ethnicity is a social construct and is most meaningful in terms of how others react and respond to an individual, as well as the ethnic identity that one projects to the outside world.

Both race and ethnicity are further complicated by differences in gender and social class. Often in discussions about DMC, people will ask whether the observed differences are really a function of economics or other indicators of social prestige. As some would observe in the trial of famous football star O. J. Simpson, the true color of justice may be green. There is no easy answer to this question. While justice agencies routinely collect data on the presumed race or ethnicity of defendants, they rarely compile data on socioeconomic status. Only more detailed data collection sometimes teases out these relationships. Further, there is almost as much ambiguity about the social meaning of class as there is about race and ethnicity. How gender differences further complicate matters will be discussed in the next chapter.

If you are feeling confused and getting a mild headache after considering these complexities, you are probably getting the right messages. Terms such as *race*, *ethnicity*, and *social class* are used imprecisely and sometimes interchangeably. This is a big problem that is embedded in the existing data and research. There is no simple solution to this conceptual quagmire except to recognize that it exists and frustrates both good research and sound public policy discussions on this topic. One thing is clear—all of these categories are socially constructed, and therefore they can be made and unmade by people.

Disproportionate Minority Representation and the Juvenile Justice Process

The federal DMC mandate has produced a rich mix of data and analytic insights on the problems of race and juvenile justice across many states. OJJDP called for analyses of the entire juvenile justice process—the ways in which decisions at each level of the process might culminate in DMC. A national summary report of dozens of these state-specific studies that was authored by Hamparian and Leiber (1997) found that overrepresentation of minority youths increased at every stage of the juvenile justice process. Although the research indicates that the largest gap between white youths and children of color occurred at the front end of juvenile justice— at the point of arrest, court intake, and detention—the data also revealed that the initial disparities got worse at later stages in the juvenile justice process. This finding has led some observers to talk about a "cumulative disadvantage" for minority youths in the justice system (Leonard, Pope, & Feyerherm, 1995; Males & Macallair, 2000).

The most comprehensive description of this cumulative disadvantage was produced by Poe-Yamagata and Jones (2000) in their path-breaking report titled *And Justice for Some.* In this study the authors incorporate data on DMC from a very wide range of federal data sources on juvenile justice as well as on youths in the adult corrections system. The report traces the disproportionate representation of minority children from arrest through the dispositional or sentencing process.

The vast majority of youths first encounter the juvenile justice system through contacts with the police. Law enforcement responses to alleged instances of juvenile misconduct can cover a broad range of actions, including verbal reprimands and informal case handling to arrest and detention. The first decision that is made is whether to make an arrest, and police are given fairly wide latitude in making this decision. Typically, police divert or dismiss about 25% of the youths that they arrest; about two thirds of these cases are referred to the juvenile court, and about 10% are sent to the criminal court system or are referred to other community agencies. Studies of police practices by Wilson (1968),

Cicourel (1968), and Emerson (1969) have shown that there are very wide differences among police agencies in the ways in which these discretionary decisions are made at the front end of the juvenile justice system.

There were roughly 2.6 million persons under the age of 18 who were arrested in 1998, with 71% of these arrests involving white youngsters. However, African American youths are disproportionately represented, composing 26% of those arrested compared with being 15% of the total population of youths under age 18 (Poe-Yamagata & Jones, 2000). Table 5.1 breaks down these data for several ethnic groups and offense categories. The reader should note the inability of current federal statistics to provide information on Hispanic or Latino youths. For most data sources, Hispanic youths are combined with whites. Also, we will later discuss how the aggregate crime statistics mask the very high rates of juvenile justice involvement of youths from certain Pacific Islands and first and second generation migrants from Southeast Asian countries.

Table 5.1   Racial Proportions of Youth Under Age 18, 1998

Most Serious Offense Charged	Estimated No. of Juvenile Arrests	Percent of Total Arrests			
		White	African American	Native American	Asian
Total	2,603,300	71	26	1	2
Violent Crime Index	112,200	55	42	1	1
Murder	2,100	47	49	3	2
Rape	5,300	59	39	1	1
Robbery	32,500	43	54	1	2
Aggravated assault	72,300	61	37	1	2
Property Crime Index	596,100	70	27	1	2
Burglary	116,000	73	24	1	2
Larceny-theft	417,100	70	26	1	2
Motor vehicle theft	54,100	61	36	1	2
Arson	9,000	80	18	1	1
Nonindex	1,895,000	73	25	1	1
Other assaults	237,700	64	33	1	1
Forgery and counterfeiting	7,100	77	21	1	2

(Continued)

Table 5.1 (Continued)

Most Serious Offense Charged	Estimated No. of Juvenile Arrests	Percent of Total Arrests			
		White	African American	Native American	Asian
Nonindex (Continued)					
Fraud	11,300	64	34	<1	2
Embezzlement	1,600	61	37	1	1
Stolen property— buying, receiving, possessing	33,800	60	38	1	2
Vandalism	126,800	80	17	1	1
Weapons carrying, possessing, etc.	45,200	66	32	1	1
Prostitution	1,400	56	43	1	1
Sex offenses (except forcible rape and prostitution)	15,900	70	28	1	1
Drug abuse violations	205,800	66	32	1	1
Gambling	1,600	15	84	—	1
Offenses against the family and child	10,200	79	19	1	2
Driving under the influence	21,000	91	6	2	1
Liquor laws	157,300	92	5	3	1
Drunkenness	24,600	89	7	3	1
Disorderly conduct	183,700	67	32	1	1
Vagrancy	2,900	71	27	1	<1
All other offenses (except traffic)	453,000	73	25	1	2
Suspicion	1,300	79	20	1	1
Curfew and loitering law violations	187,800	71	27	1	1
Runaways	165,100	78	18	1	3

Note: Detail may not add to total due to rounding.

The data do not disaggregate Latino youth from race. In 1998, 91% of Latino youth were identified as white.

SOURCE: Adapted from Poe-Yamagata and Jones (2000).

African American youths made up 42% of those under 18 who were arrested for violent offenses (Poe-Yamagata & Jones, 2000) and 2% of minors arrested for offenses such as weapon possession, drugs, and disorderly conduct. The only offense categories in which white youth are disproportionately arrested are liquor-law violations, driving under the influence, and public drunkenness. Because these latter offenses usually occur in conjunction with traffic violations, the greater likelihood of white youths having access to cars may explain these findings.

Research by David Huizinga and Delbert Elliott (1987) suggests that the overrepresentation of minority youths, and especially African American youngsters, cannot be explained by a higher level of offending by those groups. Using self-report questionnaires as part of the National Youth Survey, Elliott and others were able to construct national estimates of the age, race, gender, and social class distribution of offending by juveniles. There has been some concern expressed that African American youths underestimate the extent of their criminal behavior. However, Elliott, Huizinga, and Ageton conclude that this alleged underreporting is not statistically significant (Elliott, Huizinga, & Ageton, 1985). In general, African American youths report a slightly higher level of delinquency, but these differences were not statistically significant. Further, African American youths did report somewhat higher proportions involved in the more serious offenses, and their frequency of offending was greater than for white youths, but these modest differences could not explain the wide discrepancies among the groups in terms of arrests or other indices of system processing. Huizinga and Elliott also report that the delinquent acts that African American youths admit to are far more likely to result in arrests than if those same offenses are claimed by white youths (Huizinga & Elliott, 1987). Their conclusion may reflect, among other factors, the density of deployment of police in minority communities compared to white areas. Police rarely go into middle- and upper-class neighborhoods looking for teen crime violations. Most police contact with juveniles takes place in public settings, including schools, playgrounds, and city streets. Also, it appears that police use informal adjustments and voluntary referrals to a greater extent for white youths. Police may perceive (sometimes correctly) that white communities possess more prevention and treatment resources to deal with offending youths.

There is some reason to believe that the legacy of police violence against persons of color and the history of excessive use of force against minority citizens exert a profound influence on the ways in which minority youths and adults interact with the police. Some observers have tried to explain the more formal and restrictive response of predominantly white law enforcement officers to minority youths in terms of the concept of demeanor. Minority youths are allegedly more hostile, more confrontational, and more verbally challenging to white authority figures than their white counterparts. There is scant empirical evidence to back these claims, but it is not hard to understand how historical racial patterns influence the perceptions of demeanor in tense situations (Piliavin & Briar, 1964).

The disparity among ethnic groups seen at the arrest stage is reflected in the composition of the juveniles that come to court. African American youths comprise 31% of those sent to the juvenile court—more than twice their proportion in the general youth population. This suggests that court intake workers may further exacerbate the racial differentials seen at the arrest level. At the point of the decision to detain, things get even worse for minority youths. For example, white youngsters comprised 66% of those referred to the juvenile court but 53% of those detained. African Americans make up 31% of the referrals, but 43% of those detained (Poe-Yamagata & Jones, 2000). The higher likelihood that African American youths will be detained is true for both violent offenses and property crime. However, the greatest differential among the groups occurs with drug offenses. Black youths make up about one third of those referred to the juvenile court for drug offenses, but they constitute 55% of those who are detained for drug crimes. Put differently, an African American youth who is brought to court for a drug offense is twice as likely to be locked up pretrial than is his or her white counterpart. Minority youngsters also spend more time in detention than white youths. These disparities hold even when one controls for whether the youth had prior referrals to the juvenile court before the current charge (National Council on Crime and Delinquency, 2001).

Detention is a dramatic loss of liberty and may begin a further downward spiral toward deeper penetration in the justice system. Being more likely to be detained also means that the youth is more likely to be placed out of home or incarcerated upon adjudication (Poe-Yamagata & Jones, 2000). African American youths are more likely held in overcrowded and substandard urban detention centers in which treatment and educational resources are virtually nonexistent.

Current statistical data on the juvenile court suggest that there is a smaller disadvantage for minority youths as they move through the adjudication stage compared to earlier steps in the juvenile justice process. Still, African American teens are more likely to receive a formal adjudication for delinquency for virtually every offense category. This disparity is the most pronounced for drug offenses. In 1997, roughly 78% of drug cases involving African American youths resulted in a formal petition of delinquency, compared to 56% of cases involving white youths (Snyder,

Finnegan, Stahl, & Poole, 1999; Snyder, 1999). Here again, we see that the War on Drugs has had an extremely adverse impact on young people of color.

As noted earlier, there is an increasing tendency in law and practice to transfer cases from the juvenile court to the adult criminal courts. This decision can be made mandatory based on state statutes or may result from prosecutors having the discretion to send juvenile defendants directly to the adult courts. Roughly 8,400 cases per year that are referred to juvenile courts are transferred to the criminal courts by virtue of a hearing in the juvenile court. As with other juvenile justice decision points, white youths are underrepresented in the population of those sent to the criminal courts, whereas African American young people are overrepresented in the referred population. For example, African American teens comprise about 34% of those referred to the juvenile court, but they are 46% of those referred, or waived, to the criminal court. The racial disparity is especially evident in the way in which the juvenile court handles crimes against persons and drug crimes (Poe-Yamagata & Jones, 2000).

A study by the Pretrial Services Resource Center based on 18 urban jurisdictions showed that minority youths sent to the criminal courts suffered a similar cumulative disadvantage to those retained in the juvenile court. During the first 6 months of 1998, a stunning 82% of all minors sent to adult courts in these 18 jurisdictions were youths of color (Juszkiewicz, 2000). In six of the studied jurisdictions, minority youths comprised more than 90% of those children tried in criminal courts. For example, in Jefferson County, Alabama, African American youths comprised roughly 30% of those arrested for felonies, but they made up nearly 80% of those tried in criminal courts.

The most glaring race disparities found in the Pretrial Services Resource Center study were for drug crimes and for public order offenses. Adult felony drug charges were filed against African American youths at a rate five times that of white youths and three times that of Latino youths (Juszkiewicz, 2000).

In most instances the adult court charges resulted from the actions of prosecutors, as opposed to waiver decisions made in the juvenile court. Depending on the locale, youths tried in the criminal courts were confined pretrial in either jails or juvenile facilities. Large numbers of these youths who were tried in criminal courts were not convicted. For example, less than half (43%) of the African American youths who were charged with felonies were actually convicted, compared with 28% of Latino youths and 24% of whites. About 20% of the African American youths were transferred back to the juvenile court. These data are somewhat ambiguous in their interpretation. One might conclude that criminal courts are more lenient toward minority youngsters (a highly unlikely hypothesis); alternatively, it might be argued that prosecutors overcharge these cases and bring weaker cases to court when these involve African American teenagers. For those convicted in criminal courts, African American youths were more likely to receive a sentence of imprisonment for virtually every offense category. Of those sentenced to incarceration, African American youths received longer sentences than other youths (Juszkiewicz, 2000).

If cases remain in the juvenile court system through adjudication, the familiar pattern of racial disparity continues. African American youths are more likely than white youths to be placed out of their homes for every major offense category. White youths are more likely to be placed on probation. As observed above, drug offenses seem to produce the largest differences in outcomes among the racial groups. For white youths adjudicated as delinquents for drug crime, 61% receive probation; for African American youths, 49% receive probation.

Youths of Color in Confinement: The National Picture and State Differences

The national-level data on juvenile justice processing shed considerable light on the tragic overrepresentation of minority children in confinement. However, it is important to remember that the localized variations in juvenile justice laws and practices leading to this problem are even more severe in certain jurisdictions. OJJDP has promulgated a very simple measure of disproportionate minority confinement. The calculation compares the proportion of a given ethnic group in the confined population to that same population in the general youth population. A ratio of 1.0 would suggest that minority youths are represented in the confinement population at roughly the same level as that of the general youth population. If this same ratio is less than 1.0, this would signify underrepresentation. The more the ratio exceeds 1.0, the larger the extent of overrepresentation of minorities in custody. Let us examine the problem of DMC in a range of custody settings.

An obvious place to start is juvenile detention facilities. Detention is the entry point for the confinement system, and these lock-ups are the most frequent form of secure custody experienced by young people. A summary study of DMC reports submitted to OJJDP found that all but one state reported disproportionate minority confinement in juvenile detention centers (Hamparian & Leiber, 1997). This report found an average index of minority overrepresentation of 2.8—meaning that minority

Table 5.2   Indices of Overrepresentation for African American Youth in Detention

Alabama	1.3	Delaware	2.3	Massachusetts	5.9	Oregon	4.2
Alaska	1.6	District of Columbia	1.1	Minnesota	10.7	South Carolina	1.7
Arizona[a]	4.0	Florida	1.7	Missouri	3.3	Tennessee	3.7
Arizona[b]	3.2	Illinois	3.1	Nevada[c]	3.3	Texas	2.6
Arkansas	1.3	Indiana	4.1	New Jersey	3.8	Vermont	0.7
California	3.0	Kansas	4.5	New Mexico	1.5	Virginia	1.8
Colorado	4.4	Louisiana	1.6	New York	3.2	Washington	4.0
Connecticut	4.8	Maryland	2.8	North Carolina	1.7	Wisconsin	6.6

Note: The indices of minority overrepresentation were calculated by dividing the African American proportion of detained youth by the proportion of African Americans in the juvenile population.

a. Maricopa County only

b. Pima County only

c. Washoe County only

SOURCE: Community Research Associates (1997).

youths were confined in detention centers at a rate that was 280% higher than their proportion of the general youth population. Only Vermont reported an underrepresentation of minority youth in detention, or a ratio of 0.7. By contrast, Iowa reported the highest overall DMC ratio of 7.9.

Table 5.2 presents data on the overrepresentation in detention of African American youngsters across a number of states. Topping this list is Minnesota with a DMC ratio of 10.7 and Wisconsin at 6.6. Table 5.3 shows the same DMC ratio for Latino youths in detention. Here we can see that there are more states in which Latino youths are underrepresented in detention (Illinois and Florida, for example), and there are states in which Latino youths are confined roughly proportionally to the general youth population (California, Texas, and Arizona). However, Latino youths are confined in Colorado at a rate that is 190% of their presence in that state's youth population. The states of Connecticut and Massachusetts report even higher ratios of DMC of Latino youths (4.8 and 2.1, respectively). But, these state data on Latino youths in custody must

Table 5.3   Indices of Overrepresentation for Latino Youth in Detention

Arizona[a]	1.5	Connecticut	4.8	Nevada[c]	1.4	Oregon	1.3
Arizona[b]	1.0	Florida	0.7	New Jersey	1.5	Texas	1.0
California	0.9	Illinois	0.1	New Mexico	1.2	Washington	1.1
Colorado	1.9	Massachusetts	2.1	New York	1.6		

Note: The indices of minority overrepresentation were calculated by dividing the Latino proportion of detained youth by the proportion of Latinos in the juvenile population.

a. Maricopa County only

b. Pima County only

c. Washoe County only

SOURCE: Community Research Associates (1997).

be reviewed with some skepticism because jurisdictions utilize very different criteria in labeling youngsters as Latino and there is far less care taken in data collection with respect to Latino youngsters (Villarruel & Walker, 2002).

Looking at the broader youth corrections data, the status of minority youth in confinement is grim. As of 1997 there were 105,790 youths residing in youth corrections facilities. Of these, almost two thirds (63%) were children of color. The residential custody rate per 100,000 youths was 1,018 for African American youngsters, 515 for Latino youths, 525 for Native Americans and 204 for whites (Snyder & Sickmund, 1999). The incarceration rate for Asian youths appears comparable to that of whites, but we will see later that this aggregate rate is misleading.

Minority youths were overrepresented in confinement for virtually every offense group. They were more than twice as likely as white youths to be confined for crimes against persons and twice as likely to be confined for public order crimes. They were more than three times more likely to be in custody for drug crimes. Minority youngsters are more likely than white youths to be locked up for technical violations of probation (59% versus 40%, respectively). There are other data suggesting that minority youths are primarily confined in public correctional programs and white youths are sent in greater numbers to private facilities (Poe-Yamagata & Jones, 2000). Private facilities are smaller, are not likely to be locked facilities, have a greater investment in treatment and educational programs, and are rarely overcrowded. Public juvenile corrections facilities are chronically understaffed and underbudgeted and often have very poor conditions of confinement.

An analysis of data on admissions to state juvenile correctional facilities showed that African American and Latino youngsters had much higher admissions rates—and this held true both for youths with no previous experiences in state custody and for chronic offenders. See Figures 5.1 and 5.2 (Austin, Krisberg, & DeComo, 1995). These same data revealed that both Latino and African American youths had longer stays in custody facilities compared to whites, even when one controlled for the severity of their commitment offenses.

Postadjudication incarceration rates differ for white and minority youths across the various states. For these commitment facilities, Iowa and West Virginia had DMC ratios higher than 5.0. Connecticut, Kansas, Kentucky, Minnesota, New Hampshire, Pennsylvania, Rhode Island, and Wisconsin had DMC ratios such that minority youths were confined at levels over 300% of their representation in the general population of those states (Poe-Yamagata & Jones, 2000). When commitment facilities are examined, Latino youths are disproportionately confined in Arizona, California, New Mexico, and Texas.

Youths in Prison

There were approximately 7,400 persons under the age of 18 who were admitted to state prisons in 1997 (Poe-Yamagata & Jones, 2000). Sentenced by criminal courts and regarded as adults for the purposes of their punishment, these young people are not protected by the provisions of the federal Juvenile Justice and Delinquency Prevention Act, which mandates sight and sound separation between juveniles and adult inmates. Three quarters of these adolescents in prison were minority youths. African American young people alone account for more than one half of these prisoners younger than age 18; Latino youth make up 15% of this group. The African American teenage population in prisons grew from 53% of the total to 61% from 1985 to 1990. During this same period, the proportion of the population of white prisoners younger than age 18 declined from 32% to 21%. Drug crimes have played a major role in the increasing presence of African American teenagers in prison. In 1985 the proportion of teenagers in prison for drug crimes was roughly 2% for both African Americans and whites. By 1997 this proportion of drug offenders had grown to 5% for whites but was 15% for African Americans (Poe-Yamagata & Jones, 2000).

In Alabama, Georgia, Mississippi, Virginia, South Carolina, and North Carolina, African Americans were more than three quarters of those

Youth With No Prior Admissions**

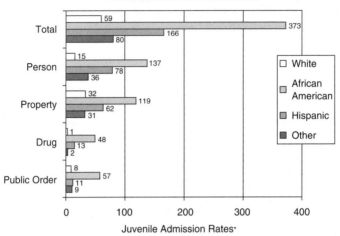

Juvenile Admission Rates*

Youth With One to Two Prior Admissions**

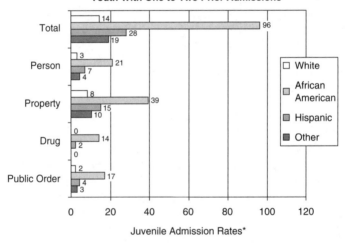

Juvenile Admission Rates*

Figure 5.1   1993 Admission Rates* of Juveniles to State Public Facilities

* Rates are calculated per 100,000 youth age 10 to the upper age of juvenile court jurisdiction in each state.

** States include AK, AZ, AR, CA, DE, GA, ID, IL, IN, IA, KY, LA, ME, MD, MA, MN, MS, MO, NE, NH, NJ, NY, ND, OH, OK, OR, SC, SD, TN, TX, UT, VT, VA, WV, and WI.

Note: Persons of Hispanic origin may be of any race. White and African American categories do not include youth of Hispanic origin.

Totals contain offenses not shown.

SOURCE: Poe-Yamagata and Jones (2000).

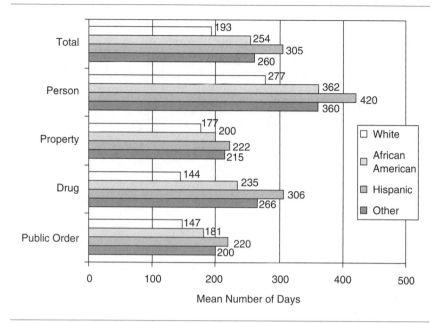

Figure 5.2   1993 Youth Mean Lengths of Stay in State* Public Facilities

* States include AK, AZ, AR, CA, DE, GA, ID, IL, IN, IA, KY, LA, ME, MD, MA, MN, MS, MO, NE, NH, NJ, NY, ND, OH, OK, OR, SC, SD, TN, TX, UT, VT, VA, WV, and WI.

Note: Persons of Hispanic origin may be of any race. White and African American categories do not include youth of Hispanic origin.

Totals contain offenses not shown.

SOURCE: Poe-Yamagata and Jones (2000).

under age 18 that were sent to prisons. In Utah and Colorado, Latino youths made up almost one half of prison admissions of minors. In South Dakota and North Dakota, Native American youngsters constitute 45% and 40%, respectively, of new underage prisoners (Perkins, 1994). There is little question that as states continue to send more juveniles to adult prisons, the burden of this ill-conceived penal policy will be most heavily borne by young people of color.

Beyond Black and White

The issue of racial disparity in the juvenile justice system is not limited to the experience of African American youths. Although the data presented in this chapter clearly demonstrate the harsh treatment received by African

American youngsters in the juvenile justice system, it is worth examining how youths from other minority communities are treated by the system. More research is needed on the plight of African American youngsters, but there is a virtual absence of data on youths who are Latinos, Asian and Pacific Islanders (API), and Native Americans. A recent literature review conducted by OJJDP found fewer than 15 articles over the last decade that cover the experiences of these significant ethnic communities and the justice system (Pope, Lovell, & Hsia, 2002). Statistical data that would help clarify key issues are almost nonexistent or are confusing at best.

One major problem is that the way in which the federal government collects and reports statistical data on a range of ethnic communities. For example, the U.S. Bureau of the Census has only recently permitted people of mixed racial heritage to acknowledge that reality in the 10-year population counts. Further, the federal government imposes the arbitrary rule that Latinos (or Hispanics in their terminology) constitute an "ethnic category" whose members might be of any racial group. Why this distinction is reserved only for Hispanics and not other groups is not well explained. Moreover, federal data are extremely uneven with respect to more detailed breakdowns of subpopulations within the racial categories. This is becoming an increasing problem as the United States welcomes immigrants from a long list of other countries and these newer immigrants are lumped into statistical categories with long-standing immigrant populations. Most federal reports mix together groups that have little or nothing in common based on culture, citizenship status, life experiences, or language. For example, more than 50 nations have contributed to the U.S. population of Asian Americans, including ethnic groups that speak more than 100 distinct languages. The U.S. government adds to this broad category current and former residents of the Pacific Islands and Native Hawaiians. Despite the more accepted term of Native Americans, the U.S. Census continues to refer to "American Indians," although the many ethnic groups within this category contain virtually no persons with historic connection to the Indian subcontinent. It has been more than five centuries since those hopelessly lost European explorers thought that they had sailed to India rather than the New World, yet our government continues to institutionalize their mistake. To make matters worse, the various Native American peoples are merged with a variety of indigenous groups who primarily come from Alaska and parts of Canada. These arbitrary and apparently meaningless statistical categories render virtually useless most of the data on these groups.

This data situation gets worse at the state and local levels. Every state has its own policies with respect to the racial and ethnic identifications used to compile statistics on crime and justice. There is virtually no training for law enforcement and other justice personnel on how to correctly identify an individual's racial or ethnic affiliation. Some agencies ask the defendant to self-identify, but others rely on guesses. Because the justice system employs far too few people of color, one cannot be too sanguine about the accuracy of these racial and ethnic identifications. Moreover, as indicated at the beginning of this chapter, the categories traditionally used in analyses of race and ethnicity are highly interconnected and subjective in their interpretations and practical impacts. Despite these enormous problems, it is worth examining some of the unique juvenile justice issues faced by Latino, Asian American, Pacific Island, and Native American youths.

¿Dónde Está la Justicia?

Despite the great difficulties in obtaining accurate data on Latino youths and the juvenile justice system, the Institute for Children, Families, and Youth at Michigan State University produced an extremely valuable summary of the issues (Villarruel & Walker, 2002). Similar to the findings for African American youngsters, Latino youth are overrepresented at virtually every stage of the justice system. They appear to receive harsher treatment than white youths, even if the alleged offenses are the same. As noted earlier, an NCCD study reported that Latino youths were more likely than their white counterparts to be sent to state juvenile correctional facilities, even when one controlled for the severity of the commitment offense and prior record (Poe-Yamagata & Jones, 2000). These disparities also existed for the lengths of stay that individuals from each ethnic group spent in state facilities. Data from Villaruel and Walker (2002) reveal that Latino youths are incarcerated in adult prisons and jails at 3–6 times the rate of whites in nine states, and 7–17 times the white rate in four states. An in-depth study in Los Angeles County, California, covering the period 1996–1998, showed that Latino youths were more than twice as likely to be arrested compared to white youths; they were more than twice as likely to be prosecuted as adults, and more than seven times more likely to be sent to state prisons.

Solid information on Latino youths in the justice system requires a significant investment in both staff time and resources to improve the glaring gaps in data. There are also very important definitional and conceptual problems that must be solved. The federal government and many states do not have a uniform definition of who is Latino or Hispanic. Different agencies utilize different categories. Further, these categories are treated as overlapping with existing racial statistical designations—meaning that a Hispanic person may be of any race. Due to the fact that most Latinos are designated as white, the net result is an overestimation of the number of whites and an undercounting of minorities in confinement.

Currently, states and counties may or may not participate fully in federal data collection efforts, so that the effort aimed at achieving accurate categorization is extremely varied. Moreover, there are little or no funds made available either to train justice system personnel in collecting data on Latinos or to support supplementary data gathering on Latino populations. The absence of bilingual staff in the justice system poses another challenge to achieving accurate data collection. Traditionally, states with large Latino populations such as Arizona, California, Colorado, and Texas have made a greater attempt to assemble data on Latinos. But, as this fastest growing segment of the U.S. population continues to expand in many other states, especially in the Southeast and the Midwest, data collection has not kept pace. The consequence of these discrepancies in data collection is that comparisons among states on Latino youths are virtually meaningless.

Beyond the problems of data collection, the absence of bilingual staff in the justice system has profound and negative consequences for Latino youths and their families. It is estimated that as many as half of Latino youths possess limited proficiency in the English language and that this issue may even be greater for their parents (Villarruel & Walker, 2002). For many of these youths and their families, the failure to have adequate bilingual services means that legal documents go untranslated and unread. Youth and their families may not be fully aware of how to exercise their legal rights or to adequately participate in their own defense. Difficulties in communication among families and justice system personnel tend to exacerbate an already critical situation. Further, the failure to offer meaningful bilingual services may mean that various social and psychological assessment tools that are used by the court may be grossly inaccurate; identifying and diagnosing mental health issues is especially problematic. The limits on communication can also hamper the effectiveness of counseling, aftercare, and other treatment services and fuel the perception that Latino youths are less amenable to home-based services, thus propelling them to out-of-home settings.

Language barriers are just the tip of the iceberg. Lack of understanding of cultural nuances within diverse Latino cultures may lead to harsher treatment of these youngsters. Villarruel and his associates point out that a downcast gaze in the presence of an authority figure is a sign of embarrassment in many Latino cultures, but may be interpreted by the non-Latino juvenile justice person as a sign of disrespect or a lack of remorse.

Moreover, given that the Latino community consists of a broad array of cultures, including Mexican, Puerto Rican, Cuban, Guatemalan, Salvadoran, Nicaraguan, to name a few, there exists a wide range of more specific cultural values, family structures, socioeconomic statuses, and immigration histories. The ability or inability of the juvenile justice system to provide services that are "culturally competent" can help or hinder the system's ability to provide meaningful interventions and services. For example, those who have recently immigrated from countries with totalitarian regimes may feel an understandably strong hostility toward or fear of law enforcement officials. The ability to trust that one's family will be treated fairly by authority figures is key to the successful functioning of the juvenile justice system. When juvenile justice personnel appear to have no understanding or appreciation of various Latino cultures, it is difficult to build a foundation of trust.

Latino youths are also detained for both short and long periods by the Immigration and Naturalization Service (INS). Each year almost 5,000 immigrant youths are confined in more than 90 INS facilities across the nation (Villarruel & Walker, 2002). While not all of these youngsters are Latino, the vast majority are from Mexico and other Central and South American nations. These youths have committed no crimes other than being in the United States without proper documentation. Many of these youngsters migrated with their families, but they are often separated from family members and held in different facilities. Detention may take a few days or many months. Parents may be reluctant to visit their detained children for fear that they themselves will be deported. These youths are given virtually no legal representation, nor are they told what is likely to happen to them. The INS often has few bilingual staff. Culturally competent programming is virtually nonexistent. Some INS facilities do not meet even minimum standards for housing children. Even worse, the INS record-keeping and computer systems are so inadequate that it is difficult to determine how long these youths remain in custody or what happens to them upon release.

Latino youths suffer disadvantages in the juvenile justice system due to questions about their immigration status. Youths who are citizens or who are in the United States via legal immigration are often presumed by law enforcement officials to be illegals. Latino youths are often stopped and searched by police using the sole rationale that they are potentially illegal immigrants. The assumption that a youth is breaking U.S. immigration laws can result in incarceration until parents or guardians are located. Also, a youth who is wanted by the INS may be housed in a juvenile detention facility until INS officials decide how they wish to handle that particular case. Such youngsters are not eligible for release to their parents or to any other alternatives to detention. These youths are in limbo—they are charged with no offense, but the legal process sits in suspension, sometimes for extended periods of time.

In the aftermath of the attack on the World Trade Center in New York City, the U.S. Justice Department encouraged local law enforcement agencies to assist in the work of identifying persons with questionable immigration statuses. This policy, if fully implemented, will result in even higher numbers of Latino youngsters being arrested and incarcerated.

Another serious burden faced by Latino youths is the popular stereotype that most are gang members. Even though there is scant evidence that Latino youths are more involved in gang activities than youths from other ethnic groups, media portrayals of the "Mexican bandit" have shaped public perceptions and law enforcement responses to Latino young people. Being labeled as a gang member increases one's likelihood of arrest and detention. Under certain state laws (such as California's Proposition 21), even the allegation that one is a gang member can result in a wide range of adverse consequences. Proposition 21 permits a youth as young as 14 to be tried as an adult at the discretion of prosecutors. Offenses allegedly tied to gang activities permit automatic filing of juvenile cases in criminal courts. Many law enforcement agencies have implemented computerized gang intelligence systems. Every time a youth comes in contact with the police, officers may access this gang intelligence file. The problem with these systems is that there is no real legal standard for defining a person as a gang member. Having a relative or friend who is alleged to be part of a gang is enough to get a youth labeled. School officials have identified youths as gang members based on the clothes they wear, including the logos of most professional and college sports teams. Likewise, driving certain types of cars may lead school personnel or police to conclude that an individual is a gang member.

Even worse, once one is labeled as a gang member, it is nearly impossible to be deleted from these automated files. Youths and their parents are not informed that they are included in these files and have no means to expunge their names once in the database. Being labeled a gang member, for all too many Latino youths, is a lifetime disadvantage.

In juvenile correctional facilities it is not uncommon for virtually all incarcerated youths to be treated as if they are active gang members. If a fight between two suspected Latino gang members breaks out, correctional officials may lock down all Latino youths in the facilities, whether they were part of the altercation or not. Housing assignments in prisons and juvenile facilities are sometimes dictated by staff perceptions of gang membership. A youth who is unaffiliated is faced with the difficult choice of joining a gang or being victimized by other gang members.

Hysteria about gangs has led to intensified police patrol in Latino neighborhoods and targeted police sweeps in these areas. Some cities, such as Los Angeles, have also enacted laws that prohibit presumed gang members from associating with one another—this can include family members. Latino youths are frequently harassed by police as probable gang members. The image of the Latino gang member is often merged with sinister racial stereotypes of the "illegal alien." In the aftermath of the September 11 tragedies, there have been several instances in which Latino youths were treated as if they were terrorists. There was a somewhat ambiguous case of a young Puerto Rican man in Chicago who had taken on an Islamic name and was allegedly found with some nuclear waste material. Although it now seems highly unlikely that this case was in any way related to Al Qaeda, there was enhanced surveillance on Latino gangs in many cities. This is yet another example of how Latino youngsters are marginalized and feared by white Americans.

Asian Americans and Pacific Islanders: The Burden of Invisibility

Between 1977 and 1997, arrests of Asian Americans and Pacific Islanders (API) increased by 726% (Federal Bureau of Investigation, 1997). During this same time period, arrests of African Americans declined by 30%. The increase in API arrests far outstripped API increase in the general population (which virtually tripled from the 1980 Census to the 2000 Census). Although the FBI data do not break down the API arrests by specific ethnic groups within this population category, data presented below demonstrate that refugee populations from Southeast Asia were very involved with the justice system. Migrants from Southeast Asia contained high concentrations of war victims, refugees, and other dispossessed populations. Youths who are Samoan have very high rates of arrest and confinement in California (Asian/Pacific Islander Youth Violence Prevention Center, 2001). For example, Samoan young people had a higher arrest rate than African American youths in San Francisco. Southeast Asian youngsters and Samoan youths are much more likely to be placed in out-of-home settings than white youths. In the state of Hawai'i, Native Hawaiian youngsters are disproportionately detained and imprisoned.

Vietnamese youths make up a highly disproportionate number of juvenile arrestees in both Alameda and San Francisco counties in California (Le, Arifuku, Louie, & Krisberg, 2001; Le, Arifuku, Louie, Krisberg, & Tang, 2001). Statewide, the number of Asian youths committed for the first time to the CYA rose from 4% to 7.4% of the total new commitments during the 1990s (State of California, Department of the Youth Authority, n.d.). A survey of the February 2002 residents of CYA found that 25% of the API youths in custody were committed for homicide, compared to 6% for whites, approximately 9% for Hispanics, 12% for Native Americans, and 8% for African Americans. Thai, Laotian, and Cambodian youths from California's Central Valley are overrepresented in the CYA population (National Council on Crime and Delinquency, in press). Although API groups have been left out of many studies of self-reported delinquency, the limited available data suggest that Southeast Asian youths self-report higher rates of antisocial behavior than non-API youths (Asian/Pacific Islander Youth Violence Prevention Center, 2001). A recent report suggested that young women from Southeast Asian communities have the highest rates of teenage pregnancy compared to girls from other ethnic groups (Asian/Pacific Islander Youth Violence Prevention Center, in press).

These facts are striking in contrast to the dominant perception of API youths as members of the "model minority." A very pervasive view of the API population is that they are a racial minority group that has overcome its disadvantaged status and achieved a very high degree of educational success, financial independence, and social acceptance. The myth of the "model minority" is that APIs prove that strong family values, a strong work ethic, and a commitment to educational attainment can overcome generations of racism and legal discrimination against Asian Americans (Lee & Croninger, 1996; Sue & Kitano, 1973). The presumed success of the API population is offered as evidence of the powerful existence of the American meritocracy that transcends racial or class differences. Other ethnic groups are advised, by implication, to follow the lead of the API population to find the keys to advancement in American society. API achievement has been used to attack affirmative action programs, social welfare policies, and the decline in family values among other ethnic groups. It is certainly true that some segments of the API population are doing better after years of suffering under racial discrimination and legally imposed barriers; however, there are many segments of the API community that are not succeeding at all (Takagi, 1989). For example, the 1990 Census reported that Laotian and Hmong Americans had rates of poverty that were more than six times those of the general U.S. population. Cambodian Americans had a poverty rate of 47%, and Vietnamese Americans had a poverty rate of 34% (President's Advisory Commission on Asian Americans and Pacific Islanders, 2001). Whereas 38% of all Asian Americans held college degrees in 1990, this was true for only 6% of Cambodian Americans, 7% for Laotian Americans, 3% of Hmongs, and 17% of Vietnamese Americans (Sok, 2001).

The myth of the model minority means that very needy segments of the API community are ignored by government agencies and social services agencies (Lee & Zahn, 1998). Moreover, the API population exhibits very low rates of voting and consequently has very few elected representatives at any level of government (Espiritu, 1992). With few exceptions, API populations live in ethnically segregated communities along with other disenfranchised ethnic groups (Ong & Miller, 2002). This further contributes to the political invisibility of the API population.

API youths are confronted with many of the problems discussed above in connection with Latinos. Despite the growing numbers of API youths entering the justice system, there have been few, if any, accommodations to the special needs of the API population. There are very few police, judges, prosecutors, defense lawyers, or correctional officials from the API community and even fewer justice officials. Language barriers are enormous for groups that together speak over 100 different languages and dialects. Interpreters are virtually nonexistent. Even in jurisdictions such as San Francisco, in which APIs constitute almost a majority of the youth population, there has been little attention paid to developing culturally competent programming.

API youths also suffer from a range of racist stereotypes in their encounters with justice system officials. Contemporary law enforcement officials are fond of promulgating the images of the evil Chinese gangs that originate in Hong Kong, Taiwan, or China and victimize American citizens. These images are as old as those presented to the gullible public in the late 19th and early 20th centuries by the Hearst and McClatchy newspaper chains that showed cartoons of sinister Asian men luring attractive white women into opium dens, forcing them into lives of degenerate white slavery. These racist images set the stage for a wide range of anti-Asian legislation and exclusionary immigration policies. The mass media has trumped-up the Asian American criminal as one of its most frightening images.

Immigration issues also plague youths from API communities. They face many of the same kinds of injustice and insensitivity encountered by Latino youngsters. The image of the Asian youth gang leads police to arbitrarily stop many API youths. Laws designed to crack down on gangs are disproportionately applied in API communities.

Native American Youths: Outsiders in Their Own Land

Ironically there are less data available on the involvement of Native American youths in the juvenile justice system than for any other major ethnic group. Although the FBI reports that there were 20,295 "American Indian or Alaskan Native" juveniles who were arrested in 1999, it is impossible to determine the accuracy of this number. Native Americans reside both inside and outside tribal territories. Some of the tribal areas are regarded as sovereign nations; others are not. The bulk of the juvenile arrests reported by the FBI are from urban areas, suggesting an under-reporting of arrests occurring in tribal areas (Maguire & Pastore, 2000).

Melton (1998) points out that reliable statistics on Native American crime are missing for several reasons. First, data collection methods differ from tribe to tribe, and there are no uniform methods governing these data. Second, many crimes that occur in tribal territories are not even reported to the FBI. Other federal data on Native American crime are collected by the Bureau of Indian Affairs (BIA) or U.S. Attorneys on cases under investigation, but these data are very incomplete. Law enforcement in tribal areas is provided by a mixture of local, state, and federal agencies. According to Melton (1998), about 60% of 304 Native American reservations operate their own tribal police with financial support from the federal government. The BIA of the U.S. Department of the Interior has only about 400 sworn law enforcement officers that are assigned to about 40 locales, primarily in the western states. The BIA also has criminal investigators that support the work of these police officers. As mentioned earlier, there are circumstances in which U.S. Attorneys, the FBI, and other federal law enforcement agencies are involved in policing Native American territories. Observers have raised concerns about the poor level of coordination among these multiple law enforcement agencies, which contributes to the absence of reliable data about crime and the operation of the justice system in tribal areas. There are also concerns that services to Native American victims are inadequate, prosecutions are often hindered by confusing jurisdictions, and law enforcement training is uneven (Melton, 1998).

Adult and juvenile correctional facilities on tribal territories are operated by the BIA. In 1995, there were a total of four juvenile facilities operated by the BIA. There are also nearly 40 adult facilities that have some capacity to hold juveniles. In all, there many be as many as 339 beds to hold Native American juvenile offenders (Melton, 1998). Besides the correctional beds operated by the BIA, there are a number of contracted facilities used to house minors. There are very little reliable data on the programs and conditions of confinement in these contracted facilities. Some Native American youths who are convicted of federal offenses are transferred to the custody of the Federal Bureau of Prisons, which in turn contracts with state and private agencies to hold these youngsters. One consequence of this arrangement is that Native American youngsters are often confined in facilities that are hundreds of miles from their home communities. For example, Navaho youths from Arizona are often sent to the facilities of the California Youth Authority. It is rare that these contracted programs have either staff or programs that are culturally appropriate for Native American youngsters.

Native American families and youths confront many serious problems related to youth crime. Substance abuse, especially alcoholism, is a major problem. Child maltreatment is a major problem in tribal areas (Hammond & Yung, 1993). There are increasing reports of the growth of gang membership among Native American youths (Coalition for Juvenile Justice, 2000; Melton, 1998). Community resources that are available to respond to these challenges are extremely underfunded and in some instances nonexistent. Community-based options, home-based services (in lieu of confinement), or out-of-home placements are badly needed. Not surprisingly, this situation leads to disproportionate incarceration among Native Americans, both in tribal areas and in the outside community. Because many Native Americans live in rural communities, the excessive confinement of these youngsters is further propelled by the general lack of alternatives to incarceration in rural areas, as well as the punitive philosophies that tend to dominate rural justice systems (Parry, 1996).

The task of bringing justice to Native American youths is enormous. There is a paucity of solid research to guide program development. There are few well-tested models of working effectively with Native American youngsters and their families. We need to travel the long journey to educate justice system officials about culturally appropriate interventions. The severe balkanization of law enforcement services and correctional programs must be reduced.

As with API and Latino youths, we must focus positive public attention on these children and families. The American legacy of violence against and exploitation of its native peoples is an issue of enduring national shame. The continuing plight of Native American youths should not be allowed to perpetuate that tragic history.

In Search of Answers

In our society, race and ethnic differences affect virtually all aspects of life. One's racial or ethnic identity exerts a major influence on where one lives, the quality of health care one receives, where one's family attends religious services, the friends that one associates with, the neighborhoods that one is likely to live in, the range of educational and vocational opportunities available, and the quality of justice one can expect. Indeed, race and ethnicity affect a person's life expectancy and where bodily remains will be placed after death. It would be odd if the juvenile justice system were *not* profoundly impacted by race and ethnicity.

Though there is little doubt that American society has made significant strides to eliminate legally sanctioned segregation and discrimination, the remaining disparities are nevertheless extremely important. America's long and tragic history of racism is still with us. Like a virus, we are all infected by racist concepts and fears. The virus may lie dormant for a time, but it is nearly impossible to escape its pernicious influence. The benefits that accrue without effort to all white Americans (sometimes referred to as "white privilege") is a seductive reason to deny that racism still exists or that one has any specific responsibility in the nation's legacy of racial oppression. Some of the racial disparities discussed in this chapter are the result of prejudiced individuals who consciously set out to harm people of color. If these individuals were the major source of the problem, the remedies would be rather straightforward—screen out biased criminal justice personnel and punish those who use race or ethnicity as inappropriate criteria in the exercise of their legal responsibilities. Unfortunately, the issue is far more complex, and the unconscious influence of racism is far more pervasive and difficult to purge from the operations of the justice system. One example of the effects of unconscious race bias is offered by the research of Bridges and Steen (1998). They systematically reviewed the court reports produced by probation officers in a Northwestern urban juvenile court. The findings were startling. The probation officers were much more likely to attribute the delinquency of white youths to environmental factors, of which the youths were victims. For black youths, the probation officers concluded that the misconduct was due to fundamental character flaws. It was typical to read that black youths "showed no remorse" or were "cold-blooded" offenders. The white youths were often portrayed as tragic figures of family maltreatment, mental health problems, or bad companions. Bridges and Steen found that these probation officer analyses differed even when the circumstances of the offenses were almost identical. Similarly, the probation officers were more likely to recommend incarceration as the appropriate punishment for African American youngsters. They were more willing to consider home-based treatment approaches for white youths.

The contrasting stories of two youths from Southern California further illuminate the forces that influence disparate treatment of minority youths by the justice system. In 1995 the California legislature enacted a new law that permitted youths as young as 14 to be tried in adult courts for murder. It should be noted that since that time California voters have voted for even more expansive procedures to prosecute very young children in criminal courts.

The first two youths who were tried under the 1995 statute were both from Orange County, California. While the names of the youths have been changed to protect their confidentiality, the facts of the case illustrate how racial and ethnic bias can corrupt the justice process (Krisberg, 2003). The first youngster, whom we will call Sean, is a white youth. Sean took his father's gun and killed his mother in a dispute over cookies that Sean wanted to eat. The second youth, whom we will refer to as Hector, was Latino. Hector was an accomplice to an armed robbery in which his co-defendant murdered a convenience store clerk. Hector had no gun and fired no shots. He was simply at the wrong place at the wrong time. Both youngsters were 14 years old at the time of these events.

Under the 1995 law, both youths were eligible to be tried as adults, but the outcomes of these cases were quite different. Hector was tried in a criminal court and is serving a prison sentence of 25 years to life. Sean was kept in the juvenile court, was sent to the California Youth Authority, and was eligible for parole in a few years. Both Hector and Sean were initially sent to a Youth Authority Reception Center for a diagnostic assessment. Sean had no prior criminal record, whereas Hector had a few prior arrests for minor property crimes. Neither youth had an official history of past violent behavior. Correctional professionals from the Youth Authority concluded that both young people were amenable to the treatment programs of the juvenile justice system.

Sean became the focus of national media coverage. His father appeared on the *ABC Nightline* show pleading for leniency for his 14-year-old son. Hector's case achieved minimal media attention, with only a very brief report in the Orange County version of the *Los Angeles Times*.

During his hearing, Sean was portrayed by his counsel as a tragic and sympathetic figure in need of mental health treatment services. In court, Sean, a tall and muscular high school football player, acted contrite and despondent. Hector, who was very slight of build, swaggered and grinned, showing the adolescent bravado that he had learned on the streets of Long Beach, California. The judge in Hector's case referred to him as "a cancerous growth on society." Neither boy said he could remember the details of his crime. Hector's lack of memory was interpreted by the prosecution as "a lack of remorse." Sean's claim of not recalling the murder was explained by a court-appointed psychiatrist as "post traumatic amnesia" (Krisberg, 2003).

Neither family had much money, and both boys were represented by public counsel. In Sean's case, he was defended by a very able public defender that put on a "virtual capital defense" to allow the court to see him as a sympathetic figure. Sean's public defender asked the court to pay for a psychiatrist who examined the troubled 14-year-old and made a convincing case for leniency. The court heard from a broad range of adults who knew Sean his whole life. By contrast, Hector was given an assigned counsel, a private lawyer who periodically takes on cases of indigent clients. In general, the assigned counsels are somewhat less familiar with the local juvenile court culture. Unlike Sean's adroit public defender, Hector's lawyer did not request a court-appointed psychiatric exam and did not put on a lengthy case. In fact, there was no formal court hearing for Hector; his plea for leniency amounted to the filing of papers.

Sean clearly benefited from skillful legal representation as well as community sentiments favoring compassion and understanding. Hector was not as fortunate. As one observer reported, "There is a sea of Hectors in Southern California, and we can hardly even distinguish them as individuals" (Krisberg, 2003).

Blatant racism would be an easy explanation for the disparate outcomes between Hector and Sean. After all, the white youth got the benefit of the doubt and the Latino youth was harshly punished—even though the offense committed by Sean seems much more frightening than that of the unarmed codefendant, Hector. The racially charged atmosphere in Southern California, especially the bias against Latino citizens, surely contributed to the end result. Clearly, there were two standards of justice that were applied in these two cases. Yet it is unlikely that the criminal justice officials set out to conspire against Hector. More realistically, unconscious race and class prejudices came into play. No less pernicious, racism that exists below the cognitive level can exert a very powerful influence on human decision making (Lawrence, 1987). One might raise the broader issue that unarticulated racial biases were crucial to convincing legislators that children as young as 14 should be tried in adult courts (Krisberg, 2003).

The cases of Hector and Sean provide humanistic texture to the social science research of Bridges and Steen (1998). These data also point us in the direction of possible remedies to the unfair treatment of minority youths at every level of the juvenile justice process (Krisberg et al., 1987; Poe-Yamagata & Jones, 2000). One such solution, which seeks to make decision makers more aware of their unconscious biases, involves training in racial and ethnic sensitivity. Diversity training has become increasingly important in criminal justice training curricula. Though we have little completed empirical research on the effectiveness of these training investments, there is scant evidence that actual decision-making practices have changed in very many locales. Typically, justice system workers deny that they are using inappropriate decision-making criteria; they put forth a range of explanations and justifications for unfair outcomes. Most prominent is the erroneous assertion that solving racial bias in the justice system will require the imposition of a quota system for who gets arrested and detained. Diversity trainers confront predominantly white justice system employees who feel defensive about claims that the system is racially slanted. Moreover, diversity training is often subtly presented as something to be done for public relations reasons. Front-line workers often do not get a clear message that top management is totally committed to changing policies and practices.

More promising results have been reported in jurisdictions that have an explicit goal to reduce minority penetration into the juvenile justice system, especially in those places that have moved to more objective decision-making tools. For example, two sites supported by the Annie E. Casey Foundation, Santa Cruz, California, and Multnomah, Oregon, have achieved impressive results in lessening racial and ethnic disparities in their detention centers (Hoytt, Schiraldi, Smith, & Ziedenberg, 2001). The Building Blocks for Youth project is now working actively with a number of jurisdictions that are willing to make a commitment to reducing racial disparity and that are willing to examine every level of decision making throughout their systems. NCCD's research has consistently demonstrated that research-guided decision systems can reduce the racial disparities that seem endemic to clinical or subjective systems in both juvenile justice and child welfare (Baird, Ereth, & Wagner, 1999).

Another reform direction suggested by the research and case examples is to increase the quality and extent of legal representation that is available to all youths. Often this is an issue of money—who can pay for adequate legal representation or which jurisdictions provide the best quality of legal defense of indigent clients. Research and demonstration projects need to be launched to test whether improved legal services can help reduce the racial biases of the juvenile justice process.

Because the decision to transfer youths to the criminal court seems to have an especially significant impact on minority youths in the justice system, it makes sense to oppose the expansion of transfer practices and even attempt to reverse some of the very bad laws that have been enacted during the past decade. Franklin Zimring (in press) has argued that focusing on reducing the growing trend to try juveniles as if they were adults is a "harm reduction" strategy that will positively impact minority youngsters without explicitly challenging the racial biases in decision making.

Finally, it appears that early interactions between minority youngsters and the police or detention intake workers are crucial to the ultimate disparate outcomes. It is very important to create a range of new community-based options that will be available in the communities in which most children of color reside. Diversionary programs have too often been instituted only in predominantly white communities. Specific attention should be paid to developing inner-city program options to keep nonviolent offenders out of the justice process whenever possible.

Research pointing to proven alternatives is woefully inadequate. We need to know more, but we also need to *do* more. Large-scale demonstrations of how to reduce racial disparity in the juvenile justice system have not been undertaken. Simple justice demands a course of action different from the current one. Indeed, if the reality of the justice system for children of color is that "justice means just us," the very legitimacy of the legal process is compromised. There are few issues more central to the reform of juvenile justice than rectifying the racial biases that seem to infect every aspect of the process.

Summary

In 1992 the federal JJDPA was amended to require all states wishing to receive funds from OJJDP to examine the extent of DMC in their juvenile justice systems. In addition to conducting the studies, states were required to make "good faith efforts" to reduce DMC. Many of these studies have documented the disproportionate presence of children of color at every stage in the juvenile justice process. In particular, African American, Latino, and Native American youngsters are much more likely than white youths to be detained, to be placed out of the home, and to be sent to prisons.

Research that explains why these disparities occur is less well defined. The available data on race and ethnicity and juvenile justice are very uneven. It appears that many factors contribute to an "accumulated disadvantage" that pulls children of color into the deep end of the juvenile justice system. There are previously ignored issues that adversely affect the handling of Latino, Native American, Asian American, and Pacific Islander youngsters. These include inadequate language and cultural resources in the juvenile justice system, excessive focus on gangs, racial biases that are embedded in juvenile justice decision making, and detrimental policies of the Immigration and Naturalization Service and the Bureau of Indian Affairs. There are several promising approaches to reduce DMC, and some jurisdictions have made significant progress in this area.

Review Questions

1. What is the best way to measure the extent of DMC, and what stages of the juvenile justice process are most important in generating disproportionate treatment of children of color?

2. What is "cumulative disadvantage," and how does it increase DMC?

3. What are some of the key conceptual and data problems that limit our ability to really understand the causes of DMC?

4. What approaches have proven successful in reducing the extent of DMC?

Six

Young Women and the Juvenile Justice System

Of the approximately 2.8 million arrests of persons younger than age 18 in 1997, about one quarter involved young women. Whereas young women were 16% of those arrested for violent crimes and 28% of serious property crimes, they were 56% of juveniles arrested for prostitution and commercialized vice and 58% of those arrested as runaways. Girls accounted for less than 10% of juveniles who were arrested for drug or weapons offenses (Snyder & Sickmund, 1999). Data from self-report surveys suggest that young men and women are about equally likely to engage in sexual behavior, underage drinking, and the use of illicit drugs (Snyder & Sickmund, 1999).

Since the 1980s, the arrest rate of young women has been increasing at a rapid rate compared to that of their male counterparts, and they are being drawn into the juvenile justice system at younger ages (Community Research Associates, 1997; Puzzanchera et al., 2000; Snyder, 1999). The number of cases of delinquency involving a female increased 83% between 1988 and 1997 (Scahill, 2000). This significant increase in the number of young women being arrested and brought into the juvenile justice system has fueled considerable interest in the underlying forces behind this trend.

At least one controversial book has attributed this rise in crime among young (and older women) as a by-product of the Women's Liberation Movement (Adler, 1975). However, a number of studies designed to test this thesis have not provided much empirical support. Other popular and media explanations of the increase in crime among young women include the effects of the War on Drugs or the trend toward the earlier physical maturation of young women. Some have asserted that the trends in official data are reflective of law enforcement practices in which behaviors that were traditionally labeled as juvenile status offenses are now treated as criminal offenses—a practice known as "bootstrapping" (Chesney-Lind, 1997). It is not uncommon for girls who are placed on probation as status offenders to be subsequently detained for the offense of "violating a valid court order." Thus, a young woman who initially enters the juvenile justice system for truancy may have her legal problems exacerbated if she violates a judge's order to attend school. Youth advocates claim that bootstrapping is a way in which juvenile courts can get around the legislative barriers to incarcerating status offenders. The severity of delinquent acts by girls is also exaggerated by relabeling family disputes as criminal events. For example, a study of girls who were referred to the Maryland juvenile justice system found that almost all of the young women referred for "assaults" involved family-centered arguments (Mayer, 1994). Young women have been inadequately represented in most large-scale and well-designed studies of delinquency. Consequently, there is very little evidence that could be utilized to adequately describe or analyze changing patterns of female delinquency (Hoyt & Scherer, 1998).

As noted earlier, girls are underrepresented in arrests of juveniles for violent offenses, but they are overrepresented in arrests for juvenile status crimes such as running away, incorrigibility, and curfew violations (Snyder & Sickmund, 1999). Several commentators have suggested that juvenile crime enforcement patterns appear to be protecting society from the criminal behavior of young males, but the same juvenile justice system seems focused on protecting young women from themselves (Bishop & Frazier, 1992; Chesney-Lind & Shelden, 1992; Mann, 1984; Weiss, Nicholson, & Cretella, 1996). Female delinquency has been traditionally interpreted by justice system agencies as wrapped up with concerns about sexuality and moral depravity (Hoyt & Scherer, 1998).

Data on the processing of girls by the juvenile justice system reveal a pattern and practice of handling delinquency cases via informal and diversionary programs (Poe-Yamagata & Butts, 1996). However, there has been speculation that some of these diversionary options may involve equally restrictive sanctions, albeit occurring in the welfare, mental health, or special education systems. Girls are far more likely than boys to be placed in privately operated group homes, shelters, and other residential programs. On the other hand, it is clear that girls are often detained and placed out of home for minor offenses that would not result in the same disposition for boys (American Bar Association & National Bar Association, 2001; Weiss et al., 1996).

Partly because boys are more numerous in the juvenile justice system, especially in locked correctional programs, there are few, if any, specialized programs for young women. A popular comment is that current girls' programs involve little more than taking a boys' program and "painting it pink." Such programs are often guided by gross stereotypes about the adolescent development of young women (e.g., girls like tea parties, young women are inherently deceitful, the principal focus of girls' programs should be helping them find an acceptable mate, and girls need to learn to control their sexual urges). Moreover, girls' programs are often given less budgetary resources, and young women are given second-class access to educational, vocational, and recreational resources in juvenile corrections system. For example, a recent investigation of a co-correctional facility in the CYA revealed that the young women had to wait for males to complete their recreational activities before they were allowed access to any of these facilities. This practice often resulted in the young women getting less physical exercise time than required by CYA policies. Other studies have pointed to gross deficiencies in the allocation of medical and other treatment resources to incarcerated young women. Programming for young women, especially in detention centers and other confinement settings is severely underdeveloped. These same studies have uncovered patterns of verbal, physical, and sexual abuse of young women in the juvenile corrections system (Acoca, 1998; Acoca & Dedel, 1998). It has also been noted that specifically designed prevention programs for young women are sorely lacking (Weiss et al., 1996). The low numbers of young women relative to young men who enter the juvenile justice system have been used to excuse the lack of services.

Gender-Specific Juvenile Justice Services

Despite this bleak picture of services for at-risk young women, there is growing awareness and concern about the need to do better. For example, a number of states have convened task forces on gender equity in the court system, and these groups have focused more attention on the disparate treatment of women, both juveniles and adults, in the judicial system. Professional groups such as the American Bar Association and the National Bar Association (2001) have stressed equity issues and attempted to rally advocacy resources for young women who are caught up in the juvenile justice system. Others such as the NCCD, the American Correctional Association, and Girls Incorporated have issued detailed reports of the plight of incarcerated young women, and they have offered specific recommendations for action (Weiss et al., 1996).

The growing professional consensus is that a priority must be placed on (1) ensuring equitable treatment of young women in the juvenile justice system and (2) establishing high-quality gender-specific services. The goal of equity requires that juvenile justice officials and legal advocates for young women purge sexual and gender stereotypes from the operation of the justice system. This includes ending the dubious practice of incarcerating young women for their "self-protection." Jurisdictions must carefully examine the disproportionate use of status offender laws to pull girls into detention and out-of-home placements. The practice of using court orders or bench warrants to bootstrap status offenders into allegedly more serious incidents of misconduct must be eliminated.

Using more objective detention and placement screening tools should reduce the numbers of inappropriately confined young women. These instruments highlight the fact that most girls who are detained represent a very low risk to public safety in terms of violence or further reoffending. The available research indicates that many young women in the justice system possess very high profiles for treatment needs. While the juvenile court should attempt to provide the necessary treatment interventions, there must be a higher priority placed on home-based or community-located services. Most important, the services that are provided must be developmentally appropriate for young women—no more boys' programs that are "painted pink."

Several exploratory studies have pointed to crucial service needs for young women. For example, Acoca and her associates have documented that court-involved young women have been exposed to tremendous amounts of violence in their home environments and at very young ages (Acoca, 2000; Acoca & Dedel, 1998). A profile of young women in a gender-specific probation program in Alameda County, California, produced parallel results. Boys who engage in violent behavior also have been subjected to high levels of violence in the home, either as victims of abuse or as witnesses to it (Widom, 1989). For young men, it appears that the "cycle of violence" leads them into more aggressive behavior with peers as well as violence against intimate partners. For girls, heavy exposure to violence seems to lead to self-abusive behavior, maltreatment of their children, depression, mental illness, drug use, and suicide (Baerger et al., 2001; Freitag & Wordes, 2001; Hoyt & Scherer, 1998; Obeidallah & Earls, 1999).

Studies are also beginning to document very high rates of sexual violence and abuse among girls in the juvenile justice system (Acoca, 1998; National Council on Crime and Delinquency, 2001).

Researchers have pointed to etiological factors such as early educational failure, family disruption, drug abuse, and gang involvement as decisive to propelling young women toward chronic and serious law-breaking. Although these factors have also been identified as causal factors in male delinquency, there are crucial differences in the way in which these forces differentially impact males and females (Acoca, 1999; Brown & Gilligan, 1992; Dryfoos, 1990; Hoyt & Scherer, 1998; Moore & Hagedorn, 2001). These findings are interesting; however, it is vital to point out that the scientific literature on delinquency among young women is woefully incomplete. For instance, although there may well be risk factors that are common in delinquent pathways to both girls and boys, we have few clues to more subtle ways in which these factors interact over the course of adolescent development.

Another major knowledge gap involves protective factors that might insulate young women from adverse social and environment forces or those steps that we could take to build resiliency for young women who have already been victimized and harmed (Greene, Peters, & Associates, 1998; Poe-Yamagata, Wordes, & Krisberg, 2002). There is some speculation that there are many areas in which protective factors could be found. For example, it has been assumed that positive female role models would be especially useful to young women who are struggling with losses of self-esteem, those who lack caring and concerned adults in their lives, and those who are looking for affirmative examples of successful transitions from adolescence to adulthood. Another area that has been identified involves teaching appropriate and effective relationship skills (Loeber & Hay, 1997). Related to relationship-building skills is knowledge about how to identify destructive and potentially dangerous personal relationships.

Other national organizations have pointed to the loss of self-esteem experienced by young women during the teen years (American Association of University Women, 1991). It is argued that boosting self-esteem and counteracting negative self-images can insulate girls from some risk factors. Related to this are efforts to promote individualism and a sense of personal boundaries among at-risk young women. Also important is the development of a sense of hope for a positive future (Weiss et al., 1996). There has been increased emphasis on the productive role of sports and other physical challenges in helping at-risk teens through difficult life transitions.

While many of these ideas appear to make sense on the surface, there is virtually no research supporting the value of these efforts as protective factors. It is easy to see that some adolescent boys could benefit from the same sorts of preventive services. There are virtually no proven program models that could demonstrate how best to deliver these protective factors. Further, researchers have not been given adequate support to determine if these positive protective factors should be delivered in culturally relevant ways. This latter point is especially important given that the vast majority of girls entering juvenile correctional programs are young women of color (Morris, 2002).

What Works for At-Risk Young Women

Reviews of tested juvenile justice programs have rarely, if ever, covered programs for young women (Krisberg, Currie, Onek, & Weibush, 1995; Lipsey & Wilson, 1998). Similar to the literature on prevention, some writers have speculated about what sorts of services and interventions might help at-risk young women make the transition to law abiding conduct. These programs include pregnancy and parenting classes, mentoring and tutoring, opportunities for self-expression involving music and the arts, and wilderness challenges. There is virtually no research that backs up these ideas. At this writing, I know of only one program evaluation that incorporated an experimental design for a gender-specific program in Alameda County, California (National Council on Crime and Delinquency, 2001). It is worth reviewing the results of that research.

With funding made available from the state legislature, the Alameda County Probation Department launched a multiyear effort to develop a model approach to gender-specific services for girls on probation. The RYSE program (Reaffirming Young Sisters' Excellence) was named after a contest among its early participants. The central idea behind RYSE was to offer a complete array of gender-specific services to girls on probation. It was designed as a model of home-based services, not as a residential program. It was hoped that RYSE would become a meaningful sanctioning option for the juvenile court and might avoid out-of-home placements for some young women. All girls placed on probation were eligible for RYSE. A random selection process monitored by NCCD then determined if the girls were assigned to RYSE or regular probation caseloads. Two thirds of the eligible girls went into RYSE and the remaining were assigned in the usual manner. Probation caseloads in Alameda County generally exceeded 75 clients per officer. Because males predominated in the probation population, there were rarely more than a few girls in any one officer's ongoing cases. It was planned that girls would stay in RYSE for 12 months and then be transitioned back to conventional probation supervision. With the leadership of the Presiding Juvenile Court Judge and the Chief Probation Officer, it was decided that RYSE should be subject to a rigorous scientific testing. Generous funding from the state and county made the labor-intensive research possible over a 4-year period.

Like most juvenile justice programs, RYSE had multiple components, making it quite difficult to pinpoint the exact mix of services that were the most effective. RYSE clients were assigned to very small caseloads (usually less than 25 per officer) of specially trained probation staff. The girls saw their probation officers on a weekly basis. In addition, the RYSE clients attended a 12-week educational course called "Sister Friends" that was taught by community volunteers and the probation officers. The curriculum included a broad range of subjects including self-esteem, women's health issues, social skills, educational and vocational topics, reproductive health issues, managing family conflicts, leadership roles for young women, and the arts. Sister Friends included field trips so that the young women could test out their new skills in positive settings that emphasized the achievement of women from their communities.

Each probation officer had access to funds to purchase appropriate treatment services, especially drug and alcohol treatment, and mental health services for their clients. There were also dollars available for "concrete services." The probation staff could access these funds for direct emergency financial assistance for their clients (e.g., paying a month's rent, covering overdue utility or phone bills, or purchasing needed school supplies or clothing). The idea of concrete services had been used by the Probation Department in its Family Preservation Unit, which was working to keep young people out of costly foster care placements. Utilizing the vouchers for services or the concrete service dollars required that the probation officer develop an overall case management plan that explained how these funds would support the youth's successful adjustment. In addition, the Probation Department contracted with local mental health professionals to assist the officers in dealing with especially difficult client and family situations. County health officials provided medical exams for those girls who had not received adequate medical care during the previous year.

RYSE served more than 450 young women over 3 years. As could be expected, the clients of RYSE exhibited many serious needs for treatment services. An intensive diagnostic screening tool was administered to all RYSE clients and to the control group. This assessment showed the family pattern of young women who had experienced extensive exposure to violence in the formative years. Many of the girls had family members who were in prisons and jails. A very large proportion of the young women had been victimized sexually, often by relatives and family friends. There were serious indications of mental health problems and substance abuse.

Although the girls expressed interest in school, they were not enrolled in many school-based programs such as sports, music and arts, leadership clubs, or other extracurricular activities. Despite often tragic histories of family maltreatment, these young women sought to reconnect to family members and to create positive and loving family environments. They wanted to learn and find gainful employment, but they lacked the personal resources to achieve their goals.

As with many innovative juvenile justice programs, RYSE experienced a number of fits and starts on its way to full implementation. In the main, however, the program met many of the hopes of its designers. One of the most interesting developments was the concern expressed by the RYSE probation staff that they were overwhelmed by their caseloads. This seemed a bit hard to understand given that their workloads were less than one third of those of their fellow officers. It was learned that the girls-only caseloads confronted the probation officers with a number of clients with enormous needs, who could be simply ignored within a larger caseload of boys and girls. The probation officers had multiple interactions with their troubled clients each week and could not avoid knowing about a range of very serious problems, including potential suicide attempts. Not much older than their clients, the probation officers called for more clinical resources for advice in dealing with individual cases. Once this issue was properly understood by probation leadership, the clinical resources were identified and made available.

The immediate outcome results of RYSE were encouraging. During the time that the young women were receiving intensive services and attention, the RYSE clients had a lower recidivism rate than the control group. Further, even when violations of the conditions of probation occurred, the court was more inclined to keep girls in RYSE, whereas it was more likely to escalate the sanctions for girls on regular probation. Thus, there was some evidence that RYSE did divert girls from detention or out-of-home placements.

Longer term outcome results were less positive. In the 12-month period in which the RYSE clients were transitioned back to conventional probation supervision or to no supervision, the failure rates of the RYSE clients were quite similar to those of the control group. This suggests that RYSE was not able to inoculate the girls from the adverse risk factors in their young lives, nor was RYSE able to substantially change those risk factors. This finding is virtually identical to research on a number of innovative juvenile sanction programs. Benefits are clearly observable when services are being delivered in an intensive manner, but the effects decline as these services are withdrawn. One lesson may be that services to at-risk adolescents must be sustained for a much longer time than has been previously assumed. Overcoming years of maltreatment and neglect cannot be accomplished in a narrow time frame.

After the state funding for RYSE was reduced, Alameda County decided to continue a less intensive version of the program for all girls assigned to probation. The Sister Friends curriculum has been shortened and perfected. Caseloads are larger than under the original RYSE program, but county officials continue to believe that gender-specific services should be a key component of juvenile probation services. Following the launching of RYSE, several other counties have attempted to replicate the program or develop their own versions of gender-specific probation services. The results of research on some of these programs are still pending.

Other Promising Gender-Specific Approaches

To date, most of the innovative gender-specific programs have focused on prevention and early intervention services. The best known national program is operated by Girls Incorporated (formerly Girls Clubs of America), which annually serves more than 350,000 in 900-plus program locations (Weiss et al., 1996). Serving young women aged 7–18 years, Girls Inc., through its affiliates, offers a broad range of educational programs and peer group support. The Girls Inc. program in Alameda County has paid special attention to conflict resolution and violence prevention curricula. In Harrisburg, Pennsylvania, Girls Inc. has pioneered an innovative approach aimed at assisting at-risk girls to learn business entrepreneurship skills and to improve their job skills. The employment and business curriculum is connected to other Girls Inc. areas including reproductive health, sports, and peer education.

The Girl Scouts Behind Bars program serves adult women in custody and their daughters, ages 5–18 years. Children whose parents are incarcerated are at very high risk of delinquent behavior, and there are very few services or programs for these children (Acoca & Austin, 1996; Mann, 1984). Volunteers from the Girl Scouts of America help the young girls to visit their incarcerated parents and maintain positive relationships. The children are also introduced to the beneficial aspects of traditional Girl Scouts programming. Incarcerated mothers and their daughters participate together in scouts activities.

Very promising community-based programs for young women involved in the justice system include the Female Intervention Team (FIT) in Baltimore, Maryland, which provided a catalyst for starting the RYSE program. The

FIT program attempts to work with young women in ways that emphasize personal strength and building resiliency. There is a Rites of Passage curriculum and girls celebrate their accomplishments at a graduation ceremony. The Kalamazoo County, Michigan, juvenile court operates a female offender program that offers wilderness and other physical challenge experiences to court-involved girls. The program uses many community-based groups and volunteers to deliver its services.

Perhaps the best known agency for gender-specific services is the PACE Center for Girls, Inc., which offers a range of educationally focused, community-based services throughout Florida. PACE operates alternative schools and supports local juvenile courts with high-quality counseling and educational services.

Increasingly, there are high-quality gender-specific residential programs such as the Harriet Tubman Residential Center in New York, the Marycrest Euphrasia Center in Ohio, the Touchstone Program in Connecticut, and First Avenue West in Iowa. Each of these programs is attempting to evolve an effective treatment response for very troubled young women that is developmentally appropriate and draws from the best professional wisdom on gender-specific services (Weiss et al., 1996).

None of the programs listed in this section have been subject to adequate research. Although promising, we simply cannot say for sure that their programs are truly effective. Further, the state-of-the-art research on girls' programming is so lacking that we cannot be certain that the intervention models that are employed by these programs are at all useful.

Conclusions

The sorry state of knowledge and innovative programming for at-risk girls cannot be allowed to continue. Although young women may continue to represent a smaller percentage than boys in the juvenile justice system, we ignore their plight at our own risk. These troubled young women are being drawn into the justice system in larger numbers. Moreover, often young parents themselves, some are locked into recreating the cycle of violence and abuse that affects the entire society.

Simple fairness demands that young women not be subjected to excessive social control merely to protect them from themselves, even as we ignore similar behavior for young males. We cannot tolerate an inferior justice system response for girls, even as we acknowledge that the system for boys is grossly inadequate as well. There needs to be an adequate supply of gender-specific services and programs so that girls are not routed into detention and other out-of-home placements when home-based services would be more cost-effective. Finally, we need to build effective community continua of responses that reduce violence and sexual abuse against young women in their homes, in their schools and neighborhoods, and in the justice system.

Summary

Young women make up approximately 25% of all of the arrests of persons under age 18, but they account for a much larger share of arrests for running away and prostitution. Since the 1980s, the arrest rate for young women has been increasing. Research on young women who enter the juvenile justice system suggests that they often have histories of physical and sexual abuse. Girls in the juvenile justice system have severe problems with substance abuse and mental health issues.

There are very few juvenile justice programs that are specifically designed for young women. Gender-responsive programs and policies are urgently needed. Further, there is concern that young women are not getting equitable treatment by the juvenile justice system. Girls are often detained or placed in residential programs "for their own protection." The juvenile justice system is likely to incarcerate some young women for minor law-breaking behavior, such as juvenile status offenses, that would not result in the confinement of young men. Once in the juvenile justice system, girls experience substandard health care, poor education programs, and few staff that are trained in female adolescent development. Even worse, there are well-documented instances in which young women have been sexually abused by juvenile justice personnel.

A few promising gender-responsive programs have been attempted, although not many of them have been rigorously evaluated. The RYSE program in Alameda County, California, is one example of a gender-specific program that was tested and showed some success compared to conventional methods. OJJDP has paid little attention to the unique needs of girls in the justice system.

Review Questions

1. What are the crimes for which young women are arrested? What are recent trends in terms of young women and juvenile delinquency?

2. What is bootstrapping and how has this played a role in the growing numbers of young women entering the juvenile justice system?

3. What are the core principles that should guide the design of more gender-responsive juvenile justice programs?

Seven

Is There a Science of Prevention?

The Politics of Prevention

During the highly partisan debate in 1993 on the federal Crime Bill, congressional Republicans seized on the theme that delinquency prevention was little more than political pork and that this funding was little more than a payoff to selected jurisdictions in exchange for votes to support the Crime Bill package. An Oakland, California, program that was designed to divert high-risk youths from the streets in the evening, Midnight Basketball, was especially singled out as a worthless expenditure of taxpayer dollars. President Bill Clinton had proposed that there be a large expenditure of funding for youth development programs. Further, Vice President Al Gore championed a federal Ounce of Prevention Council that would distribute these funds and conduct additional research to discover new prevention strategies. The political battle was quite heated.

There was an important sense in which political considerations did loom very large in the debate over crime-prevention funding. Traditional Democrats, especially the Black Congressional Caucus, were opposed to the provisions of the Crime Bill that expanded the federal death penalty and toughened such sentencing provisions as the Three Strikes and You're Out policy that vastly lengthened sentences for repeat offenders. Liberals were told to take the funding for prevention to placate their constituents so that the president could convince more conservative members of Congress

125

to support his bill. Ultimately, funding for the prevention programs was diminished. The ambitious Ounce of Prevention Council was given less than $1 million, while billions were allocated for more police, additional prison construction, and correctional boot camps.

This was not the first time that funding for prevention had become a political battleground. As early as the 1950s, Congress held hearings on the rising tide of juvenile crime and considered serious proposals to fund prevention programs on a national scale. President Eisenhower vetoed one proposal, arguing that crime control was a local responsibility. This changed rapidly during the John F. Kennedy administration. Attorney General Robert F. Kennedy set up the federal Office of Juvenile Delinquency that began testing community-wide prevention efforts. These early efforts were enlarged as a core component of President Lyndon B. Johnson's War on Poverty. Throughout the Richard Nixon administration, significant federal funding for positive youth development was earmarked to fight youth crime. It was in 1974, during Gerald Ford's brief presidency, that Congress created OJJDP to establish a concerted federal effort to encourage prevention of youth crime and establish community-based responses. In the wake of the Watergate scandals, President Ford, a nonelected chief executive, signed OJJDP into law despite his reservations about the value of prevention, but proposed minimal funding for the new agency. President Jimmy Carter later increased support for prevention programs through substantially expanded funding of OJJDP—the budget grew 20-fold in the first years of the Carter administration. Neither Presidents Ronald Reagan nor George Bush supported prevention funding. On the contrary, they both tried to eliminate OJJDP throughout their administrations.

Building a Foundation for Prevention Programming

Throughout those years, many academic critics bemoaned the poor scientific foundations of most prevention efforts. Many others echoed the tough judgment of distinguished criminologist Peter Lejins:

> The field of prevention is by far the least developed area in criminology. Current popular views are naive, vague, most erroneous, and mostly devoid of any research findings; there is a demand for action based on bygone days and other equally invalid reasons. In scientific and professional circles the subject of prevention has received remarkably little attention. Even the basic concepts in the field of prevention lack precision. There has been very little theory-building, and attempted research under these circumstances has failed to produce any significant results. (Lejins, 1967)

As OJJDP started national research and demonstration efforts on youth development programs, the claims that these efforts would impact serious youth crime were questioned. Through the National Assessment of Prevention, Walker, Albert, Cardarelli, and Billingsley (1976) conducted a literature search on existing programs, finding that few programs possessed a coherent theoretical foundation. Even worse, most prevention programs were so badly designed that there were significant logical inconsistencies in their program elements—client selection criteria, services, and disconnected stated outcome measures. Another national survey of delinquency prevention programs, funded by the National Science Foundation, reached a similarly dismal conclusion about the state of the art based on a review of evaluation studies (Wright & Dixon, 1977).

The first major national OJJDP initiative attempted to demonstrate that positive youth development activities offered to low income youths by established "character-building agencies" such as the Boys and Girls Clubs of America, the YMCA, the Salvation Army, and the United Neighborhood Centers of America would divert youngsters from careers in youth crime. Many of the grantees, especially the national organizations, had been very active in lobbying Congress for the establishment of OJJDP. Some viewed this program somewhat cynically, as a payback to loyal supporters.

More than $20 million was distributed to a total of 168 agencies across the nation. The national evaluation of the initiative estimated that nearly 20,000 youngsters received some services as part of this effort. The evaluator faced innumerable obstacles. Few of these agencies could differentiate between their ordinary services and those activities that were targeted to prevent delinquency. Data collection on clients was not part of regular agency operations. There were very few chances to implement even minimally rigorous research designs. Further, many program staff resented the very concept of accountability. One often heard the opinion that "saving one youth is worth a million dollars," so more quantitative assessments of impact were viewed as inappropriate.

The first OJJDP national prevention program produced few measurable results. The vast majority of clients were no different from previous recipients of agency services. These clients typically had very little contact with the juvenile justice system; they were the "good kids." Services were not well documented. It was hard to determine how many youths received which services or the intensity and duration of these services. These agencies often met with other character-building agencies in their communities but had few ongoing relationships with schools, law enforcement, or social service agencies. There was little doubt that many of the grantees preferred to work with the most amenable youngsters, often subtly excluding those at highest risk of delinquency. In sum, the

OJJDP grantees mirrored the full range of problems that had been identified by previous critics of delinquency prevention programs. Although it is hard to argue with the goal of providing healthy development experiences for all children, it is extremely questionable whether these efforts can seriously impact rates of youth crime (Krisberg, 1981).

In the aftermath of the disappointing results of the first OJJDP foray into the area of delinquency prevention, there was some effort to launch a more rigorous theory-based prevention program, the Seattle Social Development Project (Hawkins & Weis, 1985). The recommendation for the Seattle experiment emerged from a year-long literature search conducted by the OJJDP Assessment Center on Delinquent Behavior and Prevention.

The ambitious Social Development Project attempted to operationalize the precepts of delinquency theory, implement an experimental design, and follow youngsters over a 10-year period. However, the general lack of interest at the federal level in crime prevention during the 1980s doomed the Seattle project in its formative years.

Others argued for a different approach to prevention that emphasized comprehensive planning (National Advisory Committee on Criminal Justice Standards and Goals, 1976). Although this approach recognized the critical role of the systematic analysis of youth development programs and the identification of service gaps, there were few resources to help communities build or fund their plans.

Beginning in the early 1990s some of the OJJDP leadership embraced a very different approach to delinquency prevention. A series of large-scale longitudinal studies began in Pittsburgh, Pennsylvania; Denver, Colorado; and Rochester, New York as part of the comprehensive Program of Research on the Causes and Correlates of Delinquency (Thornberry, Huizinga, & Loeber, 1995). The goal of this research program was to discover empirical regularities in the initiation, persistence, and desistence of delinquent behavior. Further, the parallel studies would test common hypotheses, use similar measurements, and permit replication across sites. The OJJDP research staff expected that this major investment in basic research would yield substantial insight to guide effective prevention and intervention programs.

The Program of Research on the Causes and Correlates of Delinquency assumed that sound data could generate useful ideas for policy makers and practitioners. The program established the concept that there are "developmental pathways to delinquency" that could be discerned among preadolescents and that these might change as the youth matured (Kelley, Thornberry, & Smith, 1997). The researchers argued for a comprehensive community-wide approach that might involve multiple aspects of a child's life; they said different services would be more or less important at different ages. This was a significant departure from the single factor (and single agency) approach that had held sway in the past among youth development practitioners. OJJDP sponsored a number of subsequent study groups to produce ongoing assessments of research findings that could be used to guide national programming (Loeber & Farrington, 1998, 2001).

Implementing Effective Community Prevention Models

In 1992 Congress enacted Title V as an amendment to the federal Juvenile Justice Act. Title V, also known as the Community Prevention Grants Program was championed by local elected officials and youth advocates as a mechanism to direct limited federal funds to effective prevention programs. In fiscal year 1994 the Title V program allocated $13 million to local communities that participated in successful comprehensive planning efforts. The Community Prevention Grants Program was then funded at $20 million annually in FY 1995 through 1998, $45 million in 1999, and $42.5 million in both 2000 and 2001. To assist localities, OJJDP launched a training and technical assistance program to help communities meet the mandates of Title V. This provided both a challenge and a strategic opportunity for federal officials to translate the findings of the Causes and Correlates program, as well as other federally sponsored research projects, into practical guidance for youth workers and local elected officials.

The work of David Hawkins and Richard Catalano (1992) was well suited to bridge the worlds of research and prevention practice. Drawing heavily on concepts that were gaining currency in the health field, Hawkins and Catalano incorporated the foundations of health promotion into their model. They pointed out that most adults know about the primary risk factors for cardiac disease such as genetic predisposition, obesity, smoking, and lack of exercise. They also know about protective factors—steps to take to lower the probability of heart trouble even given several risk factors. Many Americans began taking greater note of their own risk profiles for heart disease and took action to increase their protective factors. This greater awareness of risk and protective factors, according to Hawkins and Catalano, resulted in a major decline in deaths from cardiac disease.

By analogy, delinquency prevention could be conceptualized as a process of ameliorating risk factors and increasing protective factors that are directly related to adolescent misconduct. Hawkins and Catalano developed a very sophisticated community planning model to accomplish these objectives. The model, based on the social development strategy, and titled Communities That Care, was utilized by OJJDP in its Title V training efforts.

Communities That Care derived its insights on risk factors from a range of longitudinal studies of adolescent development. It offered trainees an easy-to-comprehend framework through which a large body of research could be summarized, and communities could organize their prevention efforts. Table 7.1 shows the risk factors incorporated into the Communities That Care model. They are organized along the four domains of community, family, school, and individual and peers.

Table 7.1 covers five troublesome adolescent behaviors: substance abuse, delinquency, teenage pregnancy, dropping out of school, and violence. For a risk factor to get a check mark or be connected to a particular problem behavior, there had to be at least two rigorous studies linking that risk factor with the problem behavior. The absence of a check does not mean that there is no relationship but simply that the research is not conclusive.

Hawkins and Catalano chose not to assign statistical weights to the various risk factors to make it easier for nonresearchers to utilize this information. They did show that as more risks were present in a youth's life, the odds of engaging in the problem behavior increased geometrically (Hawkins & Catalano, 1992). The fact that some risk factors appear across multiple types of problem behavior illustrates how these behaviors are interrelated. For example, extreme economic deprivation, family management problems, family conflict, early and persistent antisocial behavior, and early academic failure are powerful risk factors for virtually all types of adolescent problem behavior. Moreover, reductions in some risk factors can have a multiplier effect across many areas of undesirable youth behavior.

It is worth noting that these risk factors operate at both the individual and community levels. In particular, the community risk factors are primarily attributes of neighborhoods in which at-risk families and youths live. The linkage between these risk factors and individuals is often mediated by protective factors, which will be discussed shortly. By contrast, the school risk factors are descriptive of negative individual youth experiences, although different school environments may produce more of these risk factors.

Protective factors are derived from the social development strategy and a theory of delinquent behavior that enjoys substantial empirical support (Howell, 1995). The ssocial development strategy suggests that young people can be insulated from risk factors by holding healthy beliefs and engaging in pro-social behaviors. Youngsters acquire these positive beliefs and clear standards by becoming bonded with individuals, community institutions, and peer groups that hold these views. The more that young people interact with and are surrounded by pro-social people,

Table 7.1   Adolescent Problem Behaviors

Risk Factor	Substance Abuse	Delinquency	Teenage Pregnancy	School Dropout	Violence
Community					
Availability of drugs	✓				
Availability of firearms		✓			✓
Community laws and norms favorable toward drug use, firearms, and crime	✓	✓			✓
Media portrayals of violence					✓
Transitions and mobility	✓	✓		✓	
Low neighborhood attachment and community organization	✓	✓			✓
Extreme economic deprivation	✓	✓	✓	✓	✓
Family					
Family history of the problem behavior	✓	✓	✓	✓	
Family management problems	✓	✓	✓	✓	✓
Family conflict	✓	✓	✓	✓	✓
Favorable parental attitudes and involvement in the problem behavior	✓	✓			✓
School					
Early and persistent antisocial behavior	✓	✓	✓	✓	✓
Academic failure beginning in elementary school	✓	✓	✓	✓	✓
Lack of commitment to school	✓	✓	✓	✓	
Individual/Peer					
Rebelliousness	✓	✓		✓	
Friends who engage in the problem behavior	✓	✓	✓	✓	✓
Favorable attitudes toward the problem behavior	✓	✓	✓	✓	
Early initiation of the problem	✓	✓	✓	✓	✓
Constitutional factors	✓	✓			✓

the less chance that they will be attracted by negative and antisocial groups such as youth gangs.

The bonding process occurs when young people can actively partici-pate in pro-social groups. It is here that young people acquire knowl-edge and skills, are given opportunities to demonstrate these new skills, and receive strong positive recognition, a sense of belonging, and public rewards for their behavior. Hawkins often illustrates the power of the bonding process by making an analogy to delinquent gangs. These neg-ative peer groups permit young people to acquire a wide range of crimi-nal knowledge and skills—how to buy and sell drugs, how to use guns, or how to avoid apprehension by law enforcement. Gangs offer emo-tionally powerful recognition, which is especially meaningful for vul-nerable and isolated young people. New gang members can demonstrate their new skills by acquiring drugs for the gang, attacking gang rivals, or being a lookout during robberies and burglaries. Gangs offer a sense of belonging that is vital to alienated young people who often refer to their gang as a family. Delinquent peer groups offer praise and tangible rewards (money and illegal goods and services). Seen from this vantage, a gang can make very effective use of the tenets of the social development strategy. The problem, however, is that young people are being bonded to individuals who hold unhealthy and pro-criminal beliefs and attitudes.

The social development strategy is suggestive of a broad range of positive learning experiences including music, the visual and theater arts, sports, and other areas that are very attractive to young people. These opportunities for acquiring knowledge and skills, participating, and being rewarded can be provided by families, faith-based groups, schools, and any number of community-based youth groups. Connecting young people to these positive development experiences is the primary means of protecting against risk factors. Hawkins and his colleagues have reported on research demonstrating that increasing the number and improving the quality of protective factors can substantially reduce the adverse effects of multiple risk factors. However, this research shows that sustained exposure to a large number of risk factors can overwhelm the long-term value of increasing protective factors. Thus, Hawkins and Catalano urge communities to work simultaneously on reducing the range of risk factors as they increase the number and extent of protective factors. A one-sided approach to prevention will not succeed (Hawkins & Catalano, 1992).

Communities That Care helps communities conduct self-inventories and assessments of the broad range of risk and protective factors present in their environments. Local key leaders are coached to measure their communities against others, using archival data or youth surveys. Based on these data, the leaders are asked to prioritize a limited set of prevention priorities that will receive primary attention. Once these areas are identified, training is given on research-based programs that can reduce the selected risk factors and increase protective factors. Communities are encouraged to establish multiyear plans to implement their localized prevention strategies. The Communities That Care model is a major departure from the traditional approach to prevention that emphasized initiating more programs without regard to whether these programs were effective or genuinely responded to local needs. The traditional failed method of prevention programming is to (1) latch onto media-created panaceas (the Scared Straight or Tough Love programs are two such examples), (2) dispense funding to programs that have no proven impact but have powerful backers (D.A.R.E. is an example of a politically favorable program with no or positive impact on participants), or (3) distribute public dollars to community groups that are adept at garnering political support through their well-connected board members or alumni (for example, Boys and Girls Clubs of America).

Research on the usefulness of the Communities That Care model through the Title V program was very encouraging in that it allowed both researchers and the communities themselves to understand which methods worked and why. This also benefited OJJDP by identifying which strategies were most efficient in preventing juvenile delinquency (Hsia, 2001; Chibnall, 2001). A subsequent OJJDP program that melded the risk-focused prevention approach of Communities That Care with research-based reforms of the juvenile sanctioning system produced similar and very positive results (Krisberg, Barry, & Sharrock, 2004).

A different perspective on prevention has been advanced by the advocates of an *assets* or *strength-based* approach to youth development (Benson, 1997). Proponents of this view assert that too much attention has been paid to weaknesses and problems, some of which cannot be easily changed. The goal of this approach is to recognize strengths and assets that exist in otherwise impoverished families and communities. One goal is to build on existing community resources in lieu of saturating communities with outside professional treatment professionals. Another key objective is to develop the resiliency of young people facing difficult life situations (Leffert et al., 1998). Whereas the research foundation for Communities That Care is largely dependent on large-scale empirical studies that incorporate longitudinal designs, the research support for the assets or strengths model is derived from the clinical insights of psychologists or social workers. These latter studies are usually based on a small number of case studies and qualitative research. The Communities That

Care approach draws more heavily on sociological theory and statistical analyses.

In several communities these two approaches to community-wide prevention efforts compete for public attention. There are for-profit organizations that are marketing training packages in these different approaches, as well as a range of products for parents, schools, and communities. Not infrequently, different governmental agencies will select one or the other approach, leading to heated battles over which perspective will predominate. The diffuse nature of government responsibility for funding and providing youth development services across multiple county and municipal departments makes turf competition endemic to the prevention field. In fact, the two broad approaches to delinquency prevention can be used to complement each other.

Further complicating the local discussion on juvenile crime prevention is the seemingly endless array of individual programs or curricula that claim to prevent troublesome adolescent behavior. Few of these prevention solutions have any empirical evidence to support their claims. A literal cottage industry exists, producing booklets, video and audio tapes, board games, and computer exercises that purport to prevent school violence, teenage pregnancy, drug abuse, tobacco use, and bullying. Often, the same materials or programs are modestly changed to focus on the adolescent social problem that gains current media attention and attracts public funding. For example, after the tragic shootings at a number of suburban and rural high schools, there was a sudden upsurge in the availability of allegedly effective school programs and curricula to prevent school killings. As the media began painting a picture of the offenders as victims of bullies, the prevention field sprang into action to market antibullying programs. Another media-driven area of prevention programs is the growth of private boot camps that promise worried parents that the in-your-face approach can head off a complex of risky adolescent behaviors, including substance abuse, promiscuity, rebelliousness, and poor school grades. There is not a shred of rigorous evidence supporting their claims. In fact, the research on the presumed effectiveness of government financed juvenile boot camps has been largely negative (MacKenzie, Grover, Armstrong, & Mitchell, 2001).

A particularly noteworthy prevention program is operated by a small police department in northern California. Called Elvis and the Lawmen, the program consists of a small number of law enforcement officers who visit local elementary and middle schools dressed up like Elvis Presley and perform some of the King's greatest hits. After the performance, Elvis and his friends speak about the consequences of drugs, violence, and smoking or try to promote traffic safety—depending on the latest funding stream. The group has its own newsletter that is distributed statewide and attracts significant funding from public sources and private contributions. The effectiveness of the Elvis and the Lawmen program has never been evaluated. Running a close second to the Elvis program was a well-funded program jointly sponsored by Hand Guns Incorporated and the National Basketball Association. In this program the staff, sometimes accompanied by professional basketball players, work with children in kindergarten and preschool. The program culminated when the 5- and 6-year-old children signed a pledge that they would not engage in violence or play with guns. This is hardly an effective long-term method for deterring delinquency. Another school antiviolence program funded by the U.S. Department of Education employed jugglers dressed as clowns to assist with school conflicts. The list of superfluous prevention programs is quite long, lending credibility to the claims of critics that prevention is pork.

An encouraging development in recent years has been the dissemination of a series of publications that report on prevention programs that have been vetted by solid research. For example, Lawrence Sherman and his colleagues at the University of Maryland produced a comprehensive evaluation for the National Institute of Justice of the research support for particular prevention programs that were sponsored by the federal government (Sherman et al., 1997). A series of more targeted research reviews was funded by OJJDP and formed the basis of a number of community training efforts across the nation (Howell, Krisberg, Hawkins, & Wilson, 1995; Lipsey & Wilson, 1998). The work of Delbert Elliott, through the Blueprints for Violence Prevention project, is especially noteworthy. A research team at the University of Colorado identified a limited number of prevention programs that had been carefully and rigorously evaluated. But beyond the usual brief description of successful programs, Elliott and his associates provided in-depth information on how they were structured, initiated, and maintained. A series of publications from the Blueprints project is an important resource for those communities genuinely interested in implementing proven approaches.

Interrupting the Cycle of Violence

Rigorous research on the lives of chronic and serious juvenile offenders and a number of highly encouraging program evaluations direct our attention to prevention efforts that focus on children caught up in the tragic world of family violence. Several cross-sectional studies have examined the prevalence of abuse and neglect among offender populations. For example, Pasawerat (1991) found that 66% of male offenders and 39% of female offenders in Wisconsin were victims of substantiated reports of abuse and neglect. Another study in three states of high-risk juveniles on parole who had allegedly been victims of abuse and neglect ranged from 29% in Virginia to 45% in Colorado and to 53% in Nevada (Osofsky, 2001). Moreover, several longitudinal studies have demonstrated the powerful developmental effects of child abuse and neglect (Kelley et al., 1997; Widom, 1992, 1995; Wordes & Nuñez, 2002).

Figure 7.1 from the work of Kelley and her associates illustrates that maltreatment in childhood is associated with much higher rates of violence, pregnancy, drug abuse, poor school grades, and mental health problems. For instance, 70% of child victims of abuse reported engaging in violent behavior as teenagers compared to 56% of nonabused children. Childhood abuse victims were more likely to have an official record of delinquency (45% versus 32%) and were twice as likely to have multiple problems during adolescence (Kelley et al., 1997).

Widom and her colleagues (1992) followed a cohort of 1,575 children through their adolescent years and into adulthood. Maltreated children were more likely to be arrested as juveniles (27% compared to 17% for nonmaltreated children). The two groups also differed in terms of

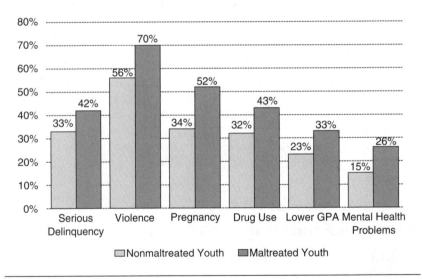

Figure 7.1   Relationship Between Prevalence of Child Maltreatment and Various Outcomes During Adolescence

SOURCE: Kelley et al. (1997, p. 8).

probability of adult arrests (42% versus 33%). Moreover, the maltreated children had a higher average number of adult arrests (5.7 compared to 4.2). Child victims of abuse and neglect also were likely to commit violent crimes as teenagers and adults.

America suffers from a serious epidemic of abuse and neglect of its children. While no one knows for sure how many children are maltreated, the nation's child protective service (CPS) agencies received official reports on approximately 3 million allegedly maltreated children in 1999. Of these reported cases, 28% were substantiated after investigations that led to some formal state intervention with these families (U.S. Department of Health and Human Services, 1999). Analyzing only the substantiated cases of maltreatment, children age 3 or younger had the highest rate of neglect, and boys ages 4–11 had the highest rates of physical abuse. Girls were most likely to be sexually abused, with 12- to 15-year-olds at the highest risk for sexual abuse. Children younger than 6 accounted for 86% of all fatalities due to child abuse and neglect, with half of this group being infants less than 1 year (Osofsky, 2001).

In addition to being the direct victims of violence, children also witness violence in their homes. Compared to other children, youth who witness domestic violence (whether or not they are victims themselves) are more likely to exhibit a wide variety of behavioral problems, more symptoms of anxiety and depression, and more aggressive conduct (Kolbo, Blakely, & Engleman, 1996). Further, several studies suggest that there is a significant overlap between cases involving violence against women and violence against children in these same families. For example, English (1997) found that 55% of referrals to child protective services for physical and emotional abuse involved children who were present during episodes of domestic violence. A study that examined hospital medical records of 116 children who were suspected of being abused or neglected found that 45% of the mothers had histories of partner abuse. When a similar analysis was conducted one year later, the researchers found that 59% of the mothers of abused children had medical records suggesting that they had been battered by their partners (U.S. Department of Health and Human Services, 1999). It is very clear from these studies that America's hidden victims of domestic terrorism, those who live in daily fear of domestic violence, comprise a very substantial segment of serious and chronic juvenile offenders. Further, there are several studies suggesting that poor parenting techniques involving inconsistent or overly harsh discipline or excessively frequent family conflicts (those that might stop short of battering) are causal factors for delinquency (Thornberry, 1994).

These research studies of child abuse and domestic violence suggest that targeted prevention programs aimed at these vulnerable children should produce substantial youth crime control impacts. There are several tested programmatic approaches that appear to be helpful in reducing the risks of family violence (Developmental Research and Programs, 2000). These prevention efforts can range from marital therapy to improved methods of responding to reports of child maltreatment.

Studies by Hahlweg and colleagues (1998) report that communication difficulties among couples before marriage and before conflicts arise are strong predictors of escalation in distress among couples. Marital counseling programs that teach effective communication skills and problem solving and conflict resolution techniques can be meaningful prevention programs. The best programs allow couples to learn and practice these skills with the assistance of a therapist or counselor. One such tested program is the Prevention and Relationship Enrichment Program (PREP), which involves approximately 15 hours of lectures, videotapes, and role-playing exercises. PREP couples report a range of positive outcomes, including fewer instances of physical violence with their spouses compared to couples in control groups (Markman, Renick, Floyd, Stanley, & Clements, 1993).

Prenatal programs and programs for infants have also proven their capacity to recognize the early predictors of maltreatment and offer meaningful prevention services (Barnard, Booth, Mitchell, & Telzrow, 1988; Horachek, Ramey, Campbell, Hoffman, & Fletcher, 1987; Olds & Kitzman, 1993). Often these programs are delivered by medical professionals as part of regular prenatal medical care that covers education for the mother on physiological and emotional stresses of pregnancy, preparing for child birth, and guidance on promoting the mental and physical well-being of newborns. The conversations and coaching in the doctor's office are supplemented by periodic home visits by nurses or other health professionals. For example, the Prenatal/Early Pregnancy Program developed by David Olds and his colleagues has proven that it can reduce tobacco, alcohol, and narcotics use among expectant mothers, thus significantly reducing perinatal childhood health problems. Participants in this program evidenced a 4% abuse and neglect rate compared with 19% for a control group in the two years after program involvement (Olds, Henderson, Chamberlin, & Tatelbaum, 1986; Olds & Kitzman, 1993). A subsequent follow-up study that tracked program participants for the next 15 years showed fewer signs of adolescent misconduct such as running away, substance abuse, and delinquency (Olds, Hill, & Rumsey, 1998).

There are several other tested programs that can avert or lessen the impact of family violence, for example, functional family therapy (FFT) (Alexander, Pugh, & Parsons, 1998). In this model, a well-trained therapist conducts home visits with a family for 12–36 hours over a 90-day period.

During these visits, generally one hour in duration, the therapist takes the family through a series of key developmental steps. First, the therapist engages the family and builds motivation for change. This process often involves breaking down ingrained negativity, increasing respect among family members for differing values and beliefs, and rebuilding trusting relationships. The FFT worker conducts a careful family assessment in which characteristics of family members are identified. This assessment should result in referrals to intensive services to respond to issues such as addiction, anger management, health, and mental health concerns that are underlying family problems. The therapist works to improve parental skills through teaching, specific family assignments, and other training techniques. The FFT worker deals with a broad range of internal and external family needs including interactions with schools, welfare agencies, the extended family, and employers. Through the Blueprints project Elliott and his colleagues located 13 articles in high-quality scientific journals that document the effectiveness of functional family therapy. Some of these studies followed families for up to 5 years and have reported reductions of offending by the children of at least 25% or as much as 60% compared with control group children (Alexander et al., 1998).

Other early interventions with maltreated children, or those who have witnessed domestic violence, include the Child Development-Community Policing (CD-CP) Program that was jointly conducted by the New Haven Police Department and the Yale University Child Study Center (Marans et al., 1995). This program forms teams of police and child development specialists who work together on behalf of physically or emotionally traumatized children. Besides joint training that equips the police with a greater ability to recognize the impacts of trauma on children, the CD-CP program provides on-call clinicians who immediately minister to children that are part of crime scenes involving violence. To date, there are several clinical observations that support the value of this effort (Marans et al., 1995). (There is ongoing research and evaluation on the project through the Child Study Center, the Northeast Program Evaluation Center at the Yale School of Medicine Department of Psychiatry, and the Department of Psychiatry Center for Health Care Services Research at the University of Connecticut Health Center, but no published results.)

Besides implementing a comprehensive continuum of *programs* responding to child treatment, effective prevention requires a *research-based decision-making system* that ensures that high-risk children and families get appropriate attention. This latter goal poses a major problem for many communities. CPS agencies are often inundated with reports of child abuse that are well beyond their ability to respond to due to limited staff resources. It is not uncommon for CPS agencies to investigate only 60% of the reports that they receive. Some urbanized jurisdictions do not even meet this frequency of investigations. In Michigan, for example, approximately 11% of reports of child abuse and neglect were fully investigated (Baird, Wagner, Healy, & Johnson, 1999). Further, the rate of worker turnover is quite high at these agencies, leaving the burden of often life or death decisions to inexperienced and untrained staff (Freitag & Wordes, 2001). Moreover, many CPS agencies depend on fairly unstructured methods requiring extensive individual worker judgments that may be affected by racial, ethnic, or social class biases. These *clinical decision-making systems* have been successfully challenged in federal courts as arbitrary and capricious (Baird et al., 1999).

Several locales are implementing structured decision-making (SDM) systems that are more effective in identifying high-risk cases and directing priority legal and social service attention to these cases. SDM systems, now in place in cities in Michigan, California, Wisconsin, Minnesota, and New Hampshire, among other states, utilize research-based risk and needs assessment tools to determine how cases should be handled. SDM agencies initiate staff training that outlines the presumptive actions that the worker should take based on the results of the research-based assessment tools. Workers need to consult with their immediate supervisors if they want to override these presumptive actions. Research completed in Michigan, and now under way in California, confirms the assumptions of the developers of SDM that rates of reabuse would be lower, that fewer serious and fatal injuries would occur in SDM locales, and that treatment resources would be targeted more effectively (Baird, Wagner, Caskey, & Neuenfeldt, 1995). As noted earlier, communities must have a full array of services to prevent chronic child maltreatment and effective methods for identifying families that would benefit from these early interventions.

The Cost-Effectiveness of Prevention

Several researchers have tried to quantify the relative costs and benefits associated with prevention programs compared to other crime-control policies. For instance, Yoshikawa examined the costs and benefits associated with nearly 40 parent-training programs. He identified four programs that appeared to reduce long-term effects of serious and chronic delinquency (Yoshikawa, 1994, 1995). A highly influential study by the RAND Corporation identified another set of prevention efforts that appeared to produce substantial crime reduction impacts for relatively modest amounts of program investments (Greenwood et al., 1996). RAND researchers focused on home visits to at-risk families by childcare professionals, training for parents with very young children who were acting out in school, cash and other incentives to encourage low-income high school students to graduate, and close monitoring of high school–age youths who were showing early signs of problem behavior. The RAND report cautions the reader that the cost and benefit estimates are based on the results of pilot studies and that results seen after taking these programs to scale may be somewhat different. Greenwood and his associates found that the graduation incentives save enough in averted crime costs to pay for the entire program. Parent training and intensive supervision of minor delinquents would save between 20% and 40% of program costs. The study concluded that home visits would be an effective but costly program. As noted earlier in this chapter, the use of research-based assessment tools to target the highest risk families could increase the cost-effectiveness of family visitation programs.

The RAND analysis also compared the effectiveness of prevention programs to a California law that significantly increased penalties for offenders with three felony convictions (the Three Strikes and You're Out provision). Greenwood and his colleagues had previously estimated that full implementation of Three Strikes could reduce crime in California by 21% (Greenwood et al., 1994). However, the same Peter Greenwood later concludes that prevention programs could reduce state crime rates by up to 15% at radically lower costs to the taxpayer. Figure 7.2 suggests that Three Strikes would cost California $5.5 billion to implement, but that a statewide investment of about $1 billion in early prevention programs would equal the crime reduction benefits of the Three Strikes policy (Greenwood et al., 1996). Greenwood and his associates called for more demonstration projects involving prevention programs to develop better estimates of the true potential of early intervention and prevention efforts.

Researchers from the state of Washington have also tried to identify cost-effective prevention programs through a sophisticated economic model (Aos, Phipps, & Korinek, 1999). These researchers caution us that not all prevention programs are effective in averting future offenses. Although a range of prevention programs were found to be effective, the Washington group emphasized that success rates were modest—even the most success-ful program lowered rates of adult offending by only 10%–15% (Aos et al., 1999). The research review suggested that some prevention programs do work for certain youths in certain contextual settings.

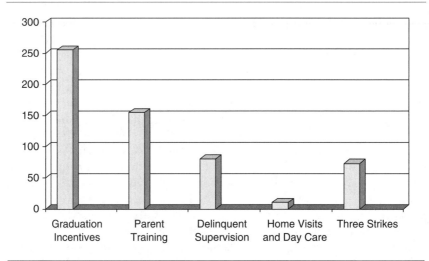

Figure 7.2   Cost-Effectiveness of Early Interventions, Compared With That of California's Three-Strikes Law

SOURCE: From Greenwood et al., *Three Strikes and You're Out: Estimated Benefits and Costs of California's New Mandatory Sentencing Law*. Reprinted with permission of RAND.

The Washington study found that programs for juvenile offenders could be quite cost-effective in terms of reducing future rates of adult criminality. Aos and his colleagues suggest that the research base of effective prevention strategies is still nascent and requires further development, including well-designed replications. Aos et al. (1999) summarize their findings across a wide variety of interventions. Cost savings were computed for both criminal justice system costs and costs to victims. Intensive home-based programs for juvenile offenders produce the greatest cost savings per dollar expended. One reason for this finding is that the juvenile justice programs are targeted at youths who are already showing extremely high probability of continued and serious offending. The early childhood education and family support programs appear to be less cost-effective. This result may be a direct by-product of policies that offer child development programs to all low-income families without identifying the small proportion of these families that will contain future serious and chronic offenders. More focused delivery of services to the highest risk families would likely increase the bottom line, or monetary benefit, for these programs. Of course, early-childhood programs are meant to accomplish multiple social objectives beyond crime control, and this must be factored into these economic calculations.

Is There a Science of Prevention?

There are still too many community prevention efforts that do appear to be pork—political payoffs by legislators for local constituency groups. The state-of-the-art in prevention needs further refinement. Sadly, like Gresham's Law of Currency, cheap and worthless prevention programs tend to drive out the "hard" or effective programs. Yet there is little doubt that a beginning science of prevention has emerged. Modern prevention programming is more likely to be guided by careful research on the etiology of youth crime and by rigorous evaluations of prevention programs. To the extent that political and public policy support grows for implementing knowledge-based prevention programming society may see smarter crime control investment strategies. Interestingly, some law enforcement groups—the National Crime Prevention Council and Fight Crime, Invest in Children—have joined in the conversation about the best prevention approaches to increase the safety of our communities.

Summary

Efforts to prevent juvenile delinquency have often been hotly debated in political venues. Liberals tend to like prevention programs, and conservatives often view them as useless social programs. The federal government's funding of delinquency prevention began during the Kennedy administration and continued to the passage of the JJDPA of 1974. The prevention programs supported by OJJDP were not well designed: Selecting appropriate clients was one issue, and documenting the services that were provided was another major concern. Traditionally prevention programs have taken the "cream," the most amenable youth, to work with, leaving out those needy youngsters from more difficult family backgrounds.

At the request of youth advocates and other groups, Congress amended the JJDPA in 1992 to include Title V, which directed some funding to localities to support prevention programs. OJJDP also provided high-quality training on the best practices in the prevention arena and funded a number of significant research studies and special study groups that expanded our understanding about the causes and correlates of serious delinquent behavior. The work of David Hawkins and Richard Catalano and their model approach to prevention, Communities That Care, greatly advanced the state-of-the-art in research-tested prevention programming.

Increasingly studies are showing the critical relationships between young people who are victims of or witnesses to violence in the home and involvement in serious and violent crime. A focus on the most vulnerable and maltreated young people could make better use of available prevention funding. There are many proven programs that can be helpful for these families including premarital counseling, visiting nurses for high-risk families, comprehensive early childhood education, and intensive family counseling programs.

Review Questions

1. What are risk and protective factors, and how can they be utilized to plan and organize prevention efforts?

2. What are the factors that have slowed the development of effective prevention programs?

3. What are the differences between the prevention models advocated by the administrations of Presidents Kennedy, Johnson, Reagan, and Clinton.

4. What are the characteristics of prevention programs that have been found to be the most effective?

Eight

What Works in Juvenile Justice

In the 1970s and 1980s it was common for academic observers and policy makers to conclude that "nothing works" in juvenile justice (Martinson, 1974). Conservative critics of juvenile justice argued that rehabilitation programs were not effective and that greater emphasis must be placed on deterrence and incapacitation (Murray & Cox, 1979; Wilson, 1983). Critics of juvenile justice from the left claimed that juvenile justice programs actually stigmatized youths, making them worse than if they had not been "helped" (Lemert, 1951; Schur, 1973). Conservatives claimed that the rehabilitative ideal of the juvenile court meant that its sanctions were too lenient, teaching youngsters that they could violate the law with impunity. Liberals felt that juvenile sanctions were often too harsh in relationship to the generally less serious crimes committed by young people. They pointed out that young women, the poor, children, and young people of color disproportionately felt the brunt of these overly harsh punishments.

Lack of confidence in the efficacy of juvenile court sanctions helped fuel a national movement to toughen penalties for juveniles, including new laws making it far easier to try minors in criminal courts (Torbet et al., 1996). The *get tough* lobby felt that the new laws would produce more punishment. At least some civil libertarians (Feld, 1984) argued that the criminal courts offered greater safeguards in terms of due process and equal protection of law.

Neither ideological side of this public policy debate paid much attention to a growing body of research suggesting that many juvenile justice sanctions were, in fact, effective. For example, careful studies of individual programs beginning in the 1960s showed many examples of very positive results. Research by Palmer (1971), employing a classic experimental design, demonstrated that intensive community treatment programs (in which parole officers had no more than 12 clients) produced a 1-year completion of parole success rate of 82%, compared to a 65% success rate for youths sent to the CYA. After 2 years, the intensive community treatment group had a 61% success rate, compared to 40% for the controls. A later reanalysis of Palmer's data by Lerman (1975) suggested that these results were a bit exaggerated but that the far less expensive community treatment produced no worse results than traditional youth incarceration policies. A second randomized experiment, conducted in Los Angeles, also found that community-based treatment was as effective as incarceration, but at less than half the cost (Empey and Lubeck, 1971). Other studies in Utah by Empey and Erickson (1972) and in Illinois by Murray and Cox (1979) demonstrated that very intensive probation or parole supervision could significantly reduce the incidence of reoffending. However, not all studies of intensive parole (or aftercare services) produced such positive results. A study in Pittsburgh, Pennsylvania, and Detroit, Michigan, found little difference in the results of youths receiving intensive aftercare services compared to a control group receiving traditional parole supervision (Greenwood & Turner, 1993). The authors of this study suggest that the lack of statistically reliable differences might be attributable to the low sample sizes in the experimental and control groups.

Besides a number of studies of discrete programs, there have been careful examinations of entire state systems that emphasize alternatives to traditional youth confinement policies. In the early 1970s the state of Massachusetts closed all of its traditional juvenile correctional facilities (these are often referred to as "state training schools"), moving nearly 1,000 youths to a varied network of small secure placements, community-based group homes, and intensive home-based services. This development was especially dramatic because it involved closing the first state training school in America, the Thomas Lyman School. For some, the Massachusetts juvenile correctional reforms constituted one of the most dramatic changes ever in juvenile justice policy (Miller, 1991).

Remarkably, the Massachusetts reform movement has been extremely durable. Since the early 1970s, the state has never opened a large juvenile correctional facility, despite a two-decade national policy debate that emphasized increasing use of incarceration for juveniles. Secure facilities are reserved for the most serious offenders, which comprise only about

15% of all commitments to the Massachusetts Department of Youth Services (DYS). The largest secure facility in Massachusetts holds only 20 youths, as compared to juvenile correctional facilities in other states that house hundreds of juvenile offenders. The basic philosophy and organizational structures that helped close the state facilities remain largely in place today. Interestingly, despite some periodic debates about juvenile justice policy in Massachusetts, most Bay State residents are not even aware of how radically different their system of youth corrections appears when compared to other jurisdictions.

The Massachusetts reforms were first studied by a team of Harvard University researchers, headed up by Professor Lloyd Ohlin (Coates, Miller, & Ohlin, 1978). The Harvard researchers compared the outcomes of youngsters released from the new network of community-based programs in 1974 to the results observed with those who were released from the state facilities in 1968, before the reforms were implemented. These initial research results were not encouraging. The recidivism rate after 12 months for the postreform cohort was actually higher than for the prereform group (74% versus 66%). One possible explanation for these negative results was that less serious offenders were being diverted from the state system during the postreform period, thus creating a cohort of youths who were likely to be more chronic and serious offenders compared to earlier cohorts. Ohlin and colleagues also noted that the recidivism data differed in various regions of Massachusetts. They noted that in areas of the state that had done a more thorough job of implementing the new community-based system of corrections, the recidivism rates were equal to or better than those of the prereform cohort (Coates et al., 1978).

With the support of the Edna McConnell Clark Foundation, NCCD completed a second research report on the Massachusetts community-based corrections system in 1989. One goal of this study was to see if a more mature and settled set of reforms was producing better outcomes. In fact, this *is* what NCCD found. The recidivism rate for those released in 1989 was 51%—much better than the results from either the prereform days or the early 1970s (Krisberg, Austin, & Steele, 1991). Further, multiple measures of postrelease failure showed that Massachusetts youths performed as well as, and often better than, youths from juvenile correctional systems in other states. The NCCD study of Massachusetts found a significant decline in the incidence and severity of DYS clients committing offenses when the 12 months prior to their admission to DYS was compared to the 12-month period after they returned to the community. These reductions in law-violating behavior were sustained over the next 2 years. NCCD also reported that the Massachusetts reforms were cost-effective, saving the state more than $11 million per year compared to more conventional juvenile correctional policies.

A related study by NCCD researchers of the juvenile corrections system in Utah produced equally encouraging results (Krisberg, Austin, Joe, & Steele, 1988). In the wake of serious scandals at the state training school, Utah had adopted many of the same reforms as Massachusetts in the late 1970s. Although the overall failure rates for Utah youths were higher than those for youngsters in Massachusetts, these youths showed a major decline in the severity and rate of offending after participation in community-based programs and detention in small, secure facilities. Other states such as Missouri, Maryland, New Jersey, Pennsylvania, and Vermont have attempted to implement some or all of the elements of the Massachusetts approach to juvenile corrections. Only Pennsylvania and Maryland conducted data-based evaluations of these efforts. The research by Goodstein and Sontheimer (1987), which covered 10 community-based residential programs in Pennsylvania, had reported outcomes that were equivalent to the NCCD study of Massachusetts. However, Gottfredson and Barton (1992) found less promising outcomes after the closing of a major state training school in Maryland. In their study, youths who were committed to the Maryland Division of Youth Services and placed in community-based programs were compared with youths who had been released from the Montrose State Training School before the reforms. The Montrose clients actually did better in terms of recidivism than those in the community programs. These Maryland results are reminiscent of the Harvard study in Massachusetts. It may well be the case that it takes time to implement effective systems of community-based corrections and that results measured in the early months of a reform will be disappointing.

The state of Ohio is another important locale for research on effective juvenile sanctioning programs. Under the title of Reclaim Ohio, the state youth corrections agency developed a strategy in which the most violent youths were housed in state-run correctional facilities, but Ohio counties were given funding to strengthen local programs for less serious offenders. A similar program had been attempted in California in the 1970s, producing mixed results (Lemert & Dill, 1978; Lerman, 1975; Palmer, 1992). Before the implementation of Reclaim Ohio, the state had one of the highest juvenile incarceration rates in the nation. Proponents of the new program observed that the counties were able to send unlimited numbers of juvenile offenders to state correctional facilities at no budgetary cost to local units of government.

Under the Reclaim program, counties were given funding that was proportionate to the number of juvenile felony adjudications, but they were now responsible for paying the incarceration costs associated with youths from their jurisdiction. Youthful offenders who were convicted of the most serious crimes would still be taken by the Ohio Department of Youth Services (ODYS) without costs to the localities. Counties could use the money to develop local programming options. Nine Ohio counties were pilot sites in 1994, with the program going statewide in 1996. Researchers at the University of Cincinnati evaluated the results of the original nine counties to determine if there had been a genuine reduction of commitments and if local juvenile justice officials were able to launch effective juvenile justice sanctions. The pilot jurisdictions were viewed next to a number of comparison counties. The initial evaluation results were very supportive of Reclaim Ohio. While the pilot and control counties began with very similar rates of commitment to state facilities, the pilot counties experienced a large decline in the number of youths sent to the ODYS (a 42% decline between 1993 and 1994). By contrast, the comparison counties witnessed a 42% increase in youths sent to ODYS during this same period. Further, the researchers noted that there was not a drop in felony adjudications, suggesting that the observed results were due to a declining commitment rate rather than there being fewer offenders in the system (Latessa, Turner, & Moon, 1998). The University of Cincinnati research team reported that the reduction in commitments to ODYS comprised less serious offenders—the group that was targeted for diversion by the Reclaim program. They also reported that the pilot counties were able to retain roughly 42% of their fiscal allocations under the Reclaim programs. Each pilot county began at least one new program, and there appeared to be stronger networks of juvenile sanctioning programs in most of the pilot sites contrasted with the comparison counties (Latessa et al., 1998).

Summaries of Program Evaluations and Meta-Analyses

Some researchers of juvenile justice sanctioning programs have gone beyond studies of individual programs, summarizing the results of dozens of studies through sophisticated research techniques known as meta-analyses (Lipsey & Wilson, 1998). The most prominent researcher in this group is Mark Lipsey. In his work, Lipsey combines multiple program evaluations and has identified intervention effects that have not been readily apparent in previous studies due to low numbers of subjects in the experimental and control groups. By statistically combining multiple studies, Lipsey has been able to document significant program results that did not emerge from single research efforts (Lipsey, 1992; Lipsey & Wilson,

1998, 2001). For example, in one of his earliest meta-analyses, Lipsey examined more than 400 studies of delinquency treatment programs that incorporated experimental designs since the year 1950. In contrast to claims that most delinquency treatment programs were not effective, Lipsey found that youth in treatment groups had recidivism rates that were, on average, 10% lower than those in control groups. According to Lipsey, the best juvenile justice treatment programs showed results that were 20%–37% better than for youths in control groups (Lipsey, 1992). The most effective programs typically involved structured training or behavioral modification programs to help youths change their ability to achieve in school, increase their job skills, and improve capacities for self-control. The most successful programs incorporated multiple therapeutic approaches and had higher levels of intensity in terms of the number of contact hours and the length of the treatment program. Lipsey found that close monitoring by researchers of the quality and integrity of the treatment programs was strongly related to positive outcomes. In general, programs that were located in the community were much more likely to show positive outcomes than programs that were operated in correctional facilities. For Lipsey, it is not a matter of "Does treatment of delinquency work?" but of defining the necessary conditions that maximize the effectiveness of various proven interventions.

Other researchers have reinforced and extended Lipsey's conclusions. Palmer (1996) looked at 23 literature reviews of juvenile justice and adult correctional programs, and 9 meta-analyses. He, as well, concluded that behavioral approaches that emphasized skill building seem to consistently produce positive results. Similarly, cognitive treatment programs that helped offenders sort out thinking patterns that led to criminal misconduct produced generally positive results. As with Lipsey's research, Palmer found multimodal approaches that combined behavior change, cognitive development, and skill acquisition to be consistently the most promising treatment models. Palmer also reported that programs that attempted to confront or threaten offenders (e.g., programs such as Scared Straight that used prisoners to frighten delinquents) were not at all effective. Traditional casework techniques were not found effective in multiple studies. Moreover, a variety of family interventions, vocational training, employment programs, or wilderness challenge programs met with, at best, mixed results (Palmer, 1996).

Several summative examinations of the most effective juvenile justice programs have highlighted the critical ingredients of these programs. For instance, Altschuler and Armstrong (1984) point to six critical components of successful programs for juvenile offenders. They argue that the best programs use "continuous case management" in which one staff person monitors a youth's progress toward certain well-defined treatment goals from the earliest stages of program entry into the period after program completion. Continuous case management also rests on the ability of staff to offer a broad range of highly individualized services that are closely tied to the young person's needs. Altschuler and Armstrong believe that good programs must pay special attention to community reentry and reintegration for youths who have been placed out of their homes. Also important are programmatic components that permit youths to participate in making program decisions and programs that offer clear opportunities for youths to demonstrate achievement of knowledge and skills. The best interventions offer enriched educational and vocational content. The reader may note that these latter program components are quite similar to the findings reported in Chapter 7 about the attributes of the most successful prevention programs. Altschuler and Armstrong (1984) make a strong case for the importance of juvenile justice sanctioning programs having clear and consistently applied consequences for youths who violate program rules.

Strikingly similar to the conclusions of Altschuler and Armstrong, Peter Greenwood and Franklin Zimring (1985) have offered their own list of core program ingredients based on an independent review of the delinquency treatment literature. They pointed to the value of providing young people with opportunities to develop positive self-images, reducing the influence of negative role models, and creating ways to bond youths to pro-social adults and social institutions. Greenwood and Zimring also emphasized the importance of allowing youths to discuss their childhood problems, especially their early exposure to violence and abuse. Similar to other program summaries and meta-analyses, Greenwood and Zimring echoed the value of cognitive programs that assisted youngsters in comprehending harmful thought patterns, particularly the ways in which criminal behavior was rationalized. For Greenwood and Zimring, effective programs must offer a range of services that are closely matched to particular youth needs. A broad review of delinquency programs completed for the National Institute of Justice by Lawrence Sherman and his colleagues at the University of Maryland (Sherman et al., 1997) and a comprehensive review by researchers Gendreau, Little, and Goggin (1996) further confirmed the key program ingredients cited by other researchers.

A Graduated System of Sanctions and Interventions

The studies discussed above have formed the foundation of modern thinking on how juvenile justice systems ought to be structured. OJJDP supported several research efforts that examined the elements of effective juvenile justice programs. The basic concepts supporting the new idea of a graduated system of sanctions and interventions were developed in connection with OJJDP's Comprehensive Strategy for Serious, Violent, and Chronic Offenders (Howell, 1995). In 2002 OJJDP commenced a multiyear training and technical assistance effort with NCCD and the National Council of Juvenile and Family Court Judges (NCJFCJ) to expand the implementation of model systems of graduated sanctions. Although there does not exist a perfect real-world model of the most effective system of graduated sanctions, many jurisdictions have made significant progress in this direction. Further, policy makers are increasingly demanding that practitioners incorporate this best thinking in new budget and program proposals.

Too often juvenile justice officials have put forward a single program as the panacea for curing juvenile offenders. Piled on this trash heap of failed juvenile justice wonder programs have been Scared Straight, reduced caseloads for probation and parole, wilderness challenge programs, and boot camps—all discredited based on careful and sound evaluations. Large-scale juvenile training schools have long been shown to be ineffective in reducing recidivism, yet advocates for institutions have constantly tried to repackage their programs using the latest psychological fads such as Tough Love, Reality Therapy, Victim Awareness, Transcendental Meditation, Positive Peer Culture, and so on. While there are clearly some program interventions with proven and research-based outcomes, it is not really plausible that one single therapeutic or programmatic approach will be effective for the wide range of needs of the young people who come into the juvenile justice system.

The concept of a graduated system of sanctions and interventions directs our attention toward an array of services and programs that should be available to troubled youths. Key to this notion is the idea of a continuum of responses that range from relatively unobtrusive and low-cost interventions for first-time or very minor offenders to more structured and comprehensive interventions for more serious and chronic juvenile offenders. The underlying theory of graduated sanctions is that the juvenile justice system needs to provide a flexible range of sanctions and interventions. As a youth's behavior gets worse, the system should be capable of increasing the level and intensity of supervision and services. If the youngster demonstrates appropriate and desired behavioral change, the juvenile justice system needs to be able to ratchet down the level of control so that the youth can move toward an independent and law-abiding life. Think of the analogy of a deep-sea diver. If the diver is at a very low depth under water and attempts to rise to the surface too quickly, he or she will suffer a severe and painful condition know as *the bends.* If, however, the diver comes to the surface in a more gradual manner (often remaining at certain depths for short periods of time), the effects of the changed levels of pressure are mitigated. Unfortunately, the current juvenile justice system ignores or fails to respond to many instances of youth misconduct, often because of perceived limits on existing correctional resources. Then, the juvenile court will impose very restrictive sanctions such as long-term placements in secure training schools. Youths may spend many months in a facility in which virtually every aspect of daily life (i.e., wake up times; meals; recreational hours; personal hygiene; drug, alcohol, and tobacco consumption; and bed times) is rigidly controlled by institutional rules. Upon release, these same youths are now required to reenter the real world in which they must confront many choices, some of which propel them back to criminal behavior. One way of explaining the very high rates of failure for young people who are released from secure facilities is that they suffer from a social and psychological equivalent of the bends. Legal scholar Franklin Zimring suggests that the juvenile justice system may be thought of as a "muscle-bound giant" (in press). The giant is very slow to move and when it moves, it does too much. Systems of graduated sanctions and interventions are designed to fix these major flaws in most juvenile justice systems.

The continuum of graduated sanctions should include immediate, intermediate, and secure sanctions (Wilson & Howell, 1993). Immediate sanctions are intended for youths who have committed relatively minor offenses or have come to the attention of the juvenile court for the first time. These interventions communicate to young people that there are clear consequences for misconduct. Immediate sanction programs are often targeted at juvenile status offenses such as running away, truancy, curfew violations, or chronic conflict with parents. These programs have been shown to be effective in preventing the escalation of youthful problem behavior to more serious law violations. Although immediate sanctions need not be expensive or of extended duration, these early juvenile justice interventions provide an opportunity to recognize risk factors that might lead to further problem behavior. One well-documented immediate sanction program is the Michigan State Diversion (MSD) Project. The Michigan effort has been subjected to rigorous experimental testing and has shown consistently lower recidivism rates for its clients compared to youths who were released with no services or supervision (Davidson et al., 1977; Davidson, Redner, Blakely, Mitchell, & Emshoff, 1987). The MSD project assumes that minor offenders are best handled outside the formal justice system by working with family and community resources. The program uses college students to work with the MSD clients. The college students receive eight weeks of training in behavioral change and client advocacy. The college students seek to direct youths to needed services as well as to provide one-on-one contacts in the community. Caseloads are very small, rarely exceeding 10 cases. Other immediate sanction programs that have demonstrated the value of intensive, non–justice system interventions include the Choice Program in Maryland (Maton, Seifert, & Zapert, 1991) and the North Carolina Intensive Protection Supervision project (Land, Land, & Williams, 1990).

Intermediate sanctions are designed for youths whose behavior has escalated to serious law violations. These youths engage in chronic misconduct, often involving drug use and property crimes. In some cases, intermediate sanctions can be used for youngsters who have committed very serious offenses but have never before come to the attention of legal authorities. These youths are not appropriate for placements in secure correctional facilities, although they are often sent there due to the lack of meaningful intermediate sanction programs. These programs provide a full range of very close supervision of the youth, intensive work with families, and a rich mixture of treatment services. These are costly programs, but they often cost less than one fifth of out-of-home placement or secure confinement (Henggeler, Melton, & Smith, 1992). One of the most well-researched intermediate sanction programs is multisystemic therapy (MST), which has demonstrated its effectiveness in treating serious and chronic offenders in a number of different settings (Borduin et al., 1995; Family Services Research Center, 1995). MST views troubled youths as "nested within a complex of interconnected systems that encompass individual, family, and extra familial (peer, school) factors; and interventions may be necessary in any one or a combination of these systems" (Family Services Research Center, 1995, p. 5).

MST works with youths in the context of their home and community environments. Based in part on the successes that Family Preservation services, in the child welfare arena, have had in avoiding foster care placements, MST offers very intensive home-based services. MST workers may spend as much as 60 contact hours over a 4-month period. The frequency of therapist contacts usually tapers off during the last few weeks. The MST therapist is very well trained and is assigned no more than four to six families at any given time. One should contrast this level of services with traditional juvenile probation programs in which the youth might see a probation officer once per month, and this meeting would typically occur in the probation office, not in the home. A typical probation officer might have a minimum of 50 clients, or as many as 100 youngsters, to monitor on a regular basis. Probation officers receive minimal or no training in working with families; they are primarily focused on ascertaining if the youth has obeyed the court's orders.

Other intervention programs that have proven their effectiveness include Functional Family Therapy (Alexander et al., 1998), and the Family and Neighborhood Services program, based on the principles of MST (Henggeler et al., 1992). A number of programs have successfully intensified probation services by increasing the frequency of client-probation officer contacts and enriching treatment services available to youths on probation. These include the Lucas County Intensive Supervision Unit (Wiebush, 1993) and the Wayne County Intensive Probation Program (Barton & Butts, 1988). Intermediate sanctions also include day treatment programs in which the youth spends the day at an educationally based treatment program and returns home at night. These latter programs are especially helpful for youngsters who are experiencing great difficulties in reentering traditional schools. At the upper end of intermediate sanctions are residential facilities that are nonsecure. These facilities may be located in both urban and rural areas, and youths may leave the facilities during the day to attend school or to perform community service. A small, nonsecure residential program, the Thomas O'Farrell Youth Center (TOYC), is located in a rural/suburban area outside of Baltimore, Maryland, and uses the *normative model* to reform its youthful wards. The normative model assumes that learning and helping others adhere to positive group values and expectations is crucial for teaching troubled adolescents how to make appropriate life choices. In addition to high-quality clinical and educational services, TOYC utilizes an intensive peer group process to achieve its goals. The average stay at TOYC is 9 months, with as many as 6 months of aftercare. Whereas previous research on positive peer culture has been mixed at best, studies show that TOYC has very impressive results in reducing recidivism (Krisberg, 1992). It is possible that other attempts at mobilizing peer influence as a rehabilitative tool have failed to achieve the appropriate level of intensity (at TOYC there are small groups and community meetings that occur throughout each day). Staff at TOYC are well trained in the normative model, operate under its rules, and actively participate in the group sessions.

Secure confinement programs are designed for the very small number of adolescents who have engaged in violent behavior or repetitive incidences of very serious criminal behavior. Yet, even for this very difficult group of youths, there are proven programs that reduce their criminal behavior. Research has shown that locked programs must be very small in capacity; otherwise a dangerous gang culture tends to dominate these secure facilities (Bartollas, Miller, & Dinitz, 1976; Feld, 1977). Further, secure correctional programs should be located where high-quality educational and treatment programs are available to all inmates.

In the mid-1980s, OJJDP sought to develop a treatment model for violent juvenile offenders. The Violent Juvenile Offender (VJO) program was tested in Boston, Massachusetts; Detroit, Michigan; Memphis, Tennessee; and Newark, New Jersey (Mathias, Demuro, & Allinson, 1984). Program clients were initially placed in small, locked facilities but were gradually phased into community-based residential facilities and then supervised very closely when they returned home. In VJO, youths had been adjudicated for a violent offense and had at least one prior adjudication for a very serious crime. The VJO clients received intensive treatment services and were subject to continuous case management from their initial entry to secure confinement until their release into the community. Youths were given tangible opportunities for pro-social achievements and were quickly sanctioned for violating program rules. Implementation of the VJO model was reasonably successful in Boston and Detroit but was never fully operational in Memphis or Newark. The VJO program evaluation employed a classic experimental design comparing the program to more traditional incarceration practices at the four test sites. The research found that there were no significant results in the sites that poorly implemented the VJO approach, but VJO youths were arrested less frequently and for less serious offenses than control groups in Boston and Detroit (Fagan, 1990).

The Florida Environmental Institute (FEI) is another example of an innovative secure sanction program. Operated by Associated Marine Institutes, the FEI is reserved for youngsters who would otherwise be sent to Florida's adult prisons. The average stay in FEI is 18 months, and almost all residents return to their home communities upon release. While FEI is not a locked facility, the remote location in the Florida Everglades, which is surrounded by swamps and dense vegetation, makes escape unlikely. Besides the desired attention to education and treatment needs, FEI engages its troubled clients in environmental reclamation work. There is a close staff-to-client ratio of no more than one to four. Despite small sample sizes and the need for more rigorous research designs, research to date has shown FEI to yield very promising results (Krisberg et al., 1995).

Perhaps the most impressive secure confinement program is the Capital Offender Program (COP) of the Texas Youth Commission (TYC), which is reserved for young people committed for homicide. Youths are sent to a state training school for an average incarceration period of up to 3 years. During this stay, the juvenile murderers are involved in a 16-week small group program with eight youths and two or three staff members who live together in a separate living unit for the duration of the intensive program. Youths in the COP have already been at the training school for

1 year and have at least 6 months left to serve. The COP is neither designed for youths with severe mental health problems nor designed for those with significant developmental disabilities.

Group psychotherapy and intensive role playing form the core of the COP intervention. Youths confront their own often-abuse-filled growing-up experiences. Role playing covers dramatic reenactment of the homicide from the perspective both of the offender and of the victim and asks the offender to imagine the experience of the crime from the point of view of the victim. The program is run by highly trained clinical staff with extensive experience in psychotherapy and small group work.

Research sponsored by the Texas Youth Commission has documented measurable personality changes in the COP youths. Program participants showed decreased levels of aggression and anger and increased ability to exert self-control and to accept personal responsibility for past actions. The COP clients showed improved ability to express empathy for the suffering of their victims. TYC researchers collected data on arrests and convictions of COP participants for up to 3 years after their release from the training school. These data were compared with a control group of capital offenders who did not experience the COP program. The treatment group showed a lower arrest rate than that for the controls (22% versus 40%) after a 1-year follow-up period. Longer term follow-up differences between COP and control youths were less impressive, suggesting that, to improve overall program outcomes, a longer period of more intensive and phased aftercare services should be considered.

The VJO, FEI, and COP outcome results are impressive in that they were accomplished with those youngsters for whom policy makers and the public-at-large are most likely to demand long-term confinement in adult prisons. Combined with the very positive results emerging from well-designed immediate and intermediate sanction programs, the foregoing research suggests that meaningful continua of graduated sanctions can be implemented at more reasonable costs and with no compromise of public safety. Moving juvenile justice systems in this direction can free up public funds to expand support for prevention programming.

Figure 8.1 summarizes what has been learned about the core components of highly effective graduated sanction programs. The lower right section of Figure 8.1 restates the basic notion that there must exist a full continuum of interventions with a range of immediate, intermediate, and secure sanctioning options, with aftercare services needed to support each discrete sanctioning program.

The lower left side of Figure 8.1 lists treatment and services that have proven to be effective with seriously delinquent youths. These programs can exist as part of the various components of the continuum of sanctions.

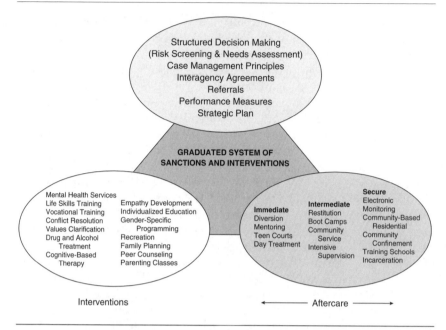

Figure 8.1   Components of a Model System of Graduated Sanctions

SOURCE: Derived from the Comprehensive Strategy Curriculum.

The top of Figure 8.1 refers to knowledge, skills, tools, and practices that form the infrastructure of a fully effective graduated system.

There is no more important part of this continuum of sanctions than the use of structured decision-making tools. These consist of research based assessment or screening instruments to permit juvenile justice decisions to be made on objective criteria that are directly related to protecting public safety. Typically, objective risk screening tools utilize a small number of factors that are given numerical weights. See Form 8.1 for an example of such an instrument.

The higher the score, the more likely that the individual will reoffend. These instruments do not claim to provide perfect predictions of future behavior, which is nearly impossible. The instruments place youths into distinct risk pools that possess very different probabilities of further criminal conduct. Once the juvenile justice worker scores the individual case, there are presumptive expectations about how the youth will be assigned to a range of graduated sanctions. The worker may override the presumed action, but this generally requires that an immediate supervisor also reviews the case.

By utilizing objective decision-making tools, the juvenile justice system can better ensure that the most dangerous cases, and those with the greatest treatment needs, are getting priority attention and supervision. Structured decision-making facilitates a better allocation of scarce justice resources. On average, objective screening and assessment lead to lower levels of incarceration and appears to be fairer to minority youths (Wiebush et al., 1995). Most current juvenile justice systems rely almost exclusively on the very subjective judgments of police, detention intake workers, and probation officers. These unfettered subjective judgments mean that personal biases color how the juvenile justice system decides who will be confined and under what levels of control (Bridges & Steen, 1998). In this book we also examine in more detail the toll of injustice that subjective decision-making systems exact on minority children and young women.

Case management refers to a process of identifying clear expectations for behavioral change that should occur within a specific sanctioning option. The case manager is required to frequently monitor the youth's progress and to make programmatic adjustments as needed. If at all possible, the youth should have the same case manager from entry into the juvenile justice system through release from the program. Case plans need to consider the whole child, addressing health, educational, vocational, and family issues as well as the youth's criminal conduct. The best case management plans are well documented and updated regularly. The youth and his family should participate in the formulation of the case plan.

Effective sanctioning systems make extensive use of referrals to other agencies to provide the full range of services that youngsters may require. These referral systems need to be formalized via interagency memoranda of understanding (MOU). Too often juvenile justice systems depend on very informal mechanisms through which other agencies accept and provide help to delinquent youths. Unfortunately when funds are tight, these informal agreements, which rest on worker relationships, may fall apart. Finally, sanctioning programs need to have clear rules and defined responses when youths break these rules. Young people do best when adults set well-defined and consistent boundaries and the adults are prepared to respond with proportionate and fair restrictions to adolescents who test those limits.

Research on effective graduated sanctions programs has taken us far from superficial polarities, which conclude that every program works or that nothing works with serious and chronic juvenile offenders. We have learned that "small is beautiful"—that the best juvenile programs are of a human dimension in which staff and youths can interact in a constructive manner. The best juvenile justice programs treat the whole child and customize services and

Form 8.1   Sample Risk Assessment Scale

		Score
1. Age at first adjudication		
11 or under	3	
12–14	1	
16 or over	0	
2. Number of prior arrests		
None	0	
One or two	1	
Three or more	2	
3. Current offense		
Nonassaultive offense (e.g., property, drug, etc.)	2	
All others	0	
4. Number of prior out-of-home placements		
One or fewer	0	
Two or more	1	
5. History of drug usage		
No known use or experimentation only	0	
Regular use, serious disruption of functioning	1	
6. Current school status		
Attending regularly, occasional truancy only, or graduated/GED	0	
Dropped out of school	1	
Expelled/suspended or habitually truant	2	

supervision to the needs of the individual youth. Moreover, effective responses to youth crime must be capable of de-escalating or escalating formal controls as a youngster's behavior improves or deteriorates. The best juvenile justice programs take advantage of the same social development process that has been proven valuable in prevention programs. Put simply, good sanctioning programs attempt to bond youths to pro-social adults by giving the youths new skills, opportunities to demonstrate those skills, and positive recognition for successful achievement. At the

7. Youth was on probation at time of commitment to DSS

No	0	_____
Yes	1	_____

8. Number of runaways from prior placements

None	0	_____
One or more	1	_____

9. Number of grades behind in school

One or fewer	0	_____
Two or three	1	_____
Four or more	2	_____

10. Level of parental/caretaker control

Generally effective	0	_____
Inconsistent and/or ineffective	1	_____
Little or no supervision provided	2	_____

11. Peer relationships

Good support and influence; associates with nondelinquent friends	0	_____
Not peer-oriented or some companions with delinquent orientations	2	_____
Most companions involved in delinquent behavior or gang involvement/membership	3	_____

Total Score   _____

Risk Assessment	0–8	Low Risk
	9–13	Moderate Risk
	14–18	High Risk

SOURCE: Howell (1995, p. 220).

same time, sanctioning programs must attempt to reduce the risk factors that propel youths further into criminal conduct.

Summary

The successful experiences of states such as Massachusetts, Missouri, and others have shown the elements of effective juvenile justice interventions. One core concept is the idea of a system of graduated sanctions that allows more flexibility in response to problems or behavior of young people under court supervision. What is needed is a continuum of care that offers a full range of immediate, intermediate, and secure program options. Further, the success of any placements can be enhanced with intensive and high-quality reentry services.

Placement in graduated sanctions should be guided by objective tools that measure risks of future recidivism as well as treatment needs. Juvenile justice sanctions work best if they are closely matched to youths needs. Several studies have demonstrated the cost-effectiveness of home-based care models such as multi-systemic therapy, functional family therapy, and wrap-around services. For more chronic and serious offenders, cognitive and behavioral therapies have shown very promising results.

On a systemic basis, states such as Ohio have reduced their dependence on training schools by providing more resources to communities to treat youngsters locally. Good juvenile justice programs require strong linkages between the juvenile justice system and community agencies, especially the schools. Job training and other skill-building programs have shown great promise in reducing recidivism.

Review Questions

1. What were the initial research results (by the Harvard Law School) of the Massachusetts juvenile justice reforms of the 1970s? How did these results change over time and why?

2. What are the key elements of structured decision making, and why is SDM so important in building and maintaining a model system of graduated sanctions?

3. How do the ideas of risk and protective factors and of social development theory help define the core principles of the most effective juvenile justice interventions?

Nine

The Gang Busters: Does Getting Tough Reduce Youth Crime?[1]

M ost reviews of juvenile justice interventions have focused on the effectiveness of prevention and alternatives to incarceration. Examinations of correctional programs have primarily covered treatment-oriented approaches. Yet the bulk of funding that is aimed at reducing juvenile crime has been devoted to programs designed to get tough with juvenile offenders. These programs are premised on several interrelated ideas, including, first, the belief that taking serious offenders off the streets will lead to crime reductions. The second underlying concept is that harsh penalties will deter other potential offenders from serious law-breaking behaviors. Third, there is the assumption that the juvenile justice system is too lenient and that minors who commit adult-type crimes should receive adult penalties. Given that get-tough strategies are

---

[1]An earlier version of this chapter appeared as Barry Krisberg (1997). *The Impact of the Justice System on Serious, Violent, and Chronic Juvenile Offenders.* Oakland, CA: NCCD.

expensive compared to community-based alternatives, it is reasonable to question whether research has demonstrated the efficacy of these approaches.

The move to institute more get-tough programs in the juvenile justice system rests on some research indicating that there is a small core of serious and violent offenders who account for the vast majority of serious crime committed by youth (Elliott, 1994; Wolfgang et al., 1972). By contrast, the available data show that the caseloads of the juvenile justice system are dominated by troubled teenagers who are generally not very violent offenders. For example, about 5% of juvenile arrests are for violent crimes. There are nearly twice as many youths arrested for liquor law violations as for robbery. In 1995, 104,000 young people were arrested for vandalism compared to 2,560 who were arrested for homicide (Federal Bureau of Investigation, 1996). Approximately 8% of juvenile court referrals are for murder, robbery, assault, or forcible rape. The vast majority of the court's caseload consists of youths charged with violations of probation, minor property crimes, and status offenses such as truancy, curfew violations, running away, and incorrigibility. The juvenile justice system is awash with troubled but minor offenders. However, the public policy debate on youth crime has been preoccupied with the "dangerous few" (Hamparian, 1982).

The Gang Busters

The principal target of tough law enforcement and prosecution of juvenile offenders has been members of juvenile gangs. The research on these gang suppression programs has been limited, and the findings have been inconclusive at best. A review of some of these antigang programs is instructive.

During the Reagan and Bush administrations there was ample federal funding for gang control programs operated by police departments or prosecutors. A virtual cottage industry of gang experts emerged to offer training and assistance to law enforcement agencies. Longtime gang researcher Malcolm Klein noted that, somewhat ironically, Los Angeles was set forth as a model of gang suppression programs. However, few cities have suffered more from the violence connected with gangs than the City of Angels, despite substantial public investments in antigang programs.

Los Angeles gang control efforts have involved all aspects of the criminal and juvenile justice systems. City and county officials have tried saturation patrols, intensified surveillance, special police tactical units, and even a "ninja-style unit, complete with black clothing" (Klein, 1995). The most widely known of these programs, called Operation Hammer, involved military-type police sweeps in the South Central area of Los Angeles. During one weekend in 1988, the Los Angeles Police Department (LAPD) sent more than 1,000 additional officers into South Central. The police assault teams made numerous arrests for traffic violations, outstanding court warrants, curfew violations, and other gang-related behavior. In all, there were more than 1,450 arrests made in one weekend. The volume of young suspects taken into custody was so great that the LAPD set up a temporary booking operation in the University of Southern California (USC) football stadium.

Of those arrested, all but 103 defendants were released by the police with no charges being filed. Only 32 persons were charged with felonies. The vast majority of those arrested were not gang members. The director of the CYA noted that not one youth was sent to the state's youth corrections system as a result of the enforcement activities during Operation Hammer.

Over the next several weekends, Operation Hammer continued, although the number of police officers assigned to the antigang crusade decreased dramatically. The large volume of arrests continued, and most of these defendants were charged with outstanding warrants. There was little or no evidence that gang violence decreased in South Central or other sections of the city. The large commitment of police resources netted little in terms of the capture of illegal drugs or weapons. Operation Hammer was subjected to a careful research analysis. Few similar programs have been rigorously evaluated. An empirical review by Lawrence Sherman (1990), conducted for the National Institute of Justice, suggested that some enforcement sweeps did show short-term crime suppression results followed by a rapid decline in effectiveness. Sherman found that targeted enforcement crusades were somewhat useful in reducing parking violations, prostitution, street drug sales, and drunk driving. There is no evidence that targeted crackdowns on gangs have any effect in reducing the more serious crimes associated with these criminal groups.

Proponents of intensive police efforts such as Operation Hammer argue that these campaigns exert a deterrent effect for would-be offenders. However, research on deterrence indicates that the swiftness and certainty of punishment is at least as important as the severity of those penalties (Zimring & Hawkins, 1973). When one evaluates Operation Hammer in light of the theory and views the research on deterrence, it seems apparent that the program was bound to fail. The sanctions were not swift because they were tied to outstanding warrants for offenses that had occurred well in the past. Certainty of punishment was almost nonexistent. Few if any defendants that were swept up in the police raids were punished at all. Most defendants had their charges dropped immediately. Very few alleged gang members suffered anything worse than a brief, involuntary visit to the USC football stadium. Penalties were not a core component of Operation Hammer. Indeed, many gang members and residents of South Central Los Angeles viewed the weekend police invasions as little more than a cynical "made for television" public relations campaign by the LAPD.

Other gang suppression programs have dispatched roaming patrol cars to "saturate" alleged gang turfs with the goal of increasing the surveillance of gang activities and of harassing gang members. Such saturation patrols most often produced arrests for minor offenses such as loitering, disorderly conduct, or wearing gang paraphernalia. Typically, the overtaxed Los Angeles County court system dropped these minor charges almost immediately. Some LAPD officers were actually dispatched to disrupt truce or peace-making meetings among gangs because they feared the formulation of mega-gang alliances.

The Chicago police added their own special touch to gang suppression activities. They arrested youngsters and then released them on the territories of rival gangs (Klein, 1995). In many cities, police crackdown campaigns against gangs have led to repeated complaints of police misconduct, illegal searches, and even planting of illegal evidence.

Several well-known gang researchers such as Matthew Klein and Irving Spergel have noted that aggressive law enforcement tactics that are divorced from community-organizing efforts may actually make the gang problem worse. According to these scholars, police antigang crackdowns reinforce the reputation of gangs and promote greater cohesiveness among gang members (Klein, 1995; Spergel & Grossman, 1996). Greater gang cohesion is generally associated with gang members engaging in more violent crimes (Klein, 1995).

Gang suppression efforts have also involved targeted prosecution programs, often in tandem with increased police pressure on gangs. Prosecutors have sought out innovative legal strategies to widen the range of tools that could be used against gangs. For example, the Los Angeles County District Attorney asked for a court order declaring gangs to be "quasi-corporate" entities, thus permitting legal actions against any member based on the activities of the group. One such program required those identified as gang members to participate in a graffiti removal program. Other prosecution efforts tried to declare parks and other public places as gang-free zones. In theory, this permitted the police to arrest gang members simply because they were present at some location, not because they were actually engaging in violations of the law. There have also been efforts to declare juvenile gangs as a new form of organized crime, permitting the use of state and federal racketeering charges to be used to suppress gang activity. More recently, law enforcement officials have been exploring the application of the label "terrorist organization" to some gangs, in the hopes that the broad provisions of homeland security legislation that was enacted after the attacks on the World Trade Towers in New York on September 11, 2001, could be used to fight urban street gangs. During the 1980s and 1990s, federal crime legislation attempted to authorize the FBI, the Drug Enforcement Administration (DEA), the Bureau of Alcohol, Tobacco, Firearms and Explosives (ATF), and other federal law enforcement agencies to attack juvenile gangs.

There is little evidence that any of these approaches actually reduced gang activities. However, it is reasonable to assume that young gang members took great pride in how "bad" they were that their activities required the attention of federal law enforcement officers. This fueled their teenage fantasies about being "real Gs" (gangsters). In the youth culture the word *federal* came to be a compliment—one was truly worthy if the "feds" were after you.

One of the best known gang prosecution programs was known as Operation Hardcore. This was the prototype for many subsequent, specialized, career-criminal prosecution units. Operation Hardcore involved enhanced training of police and prosecutors in gathering evidence and in the use of expert testimony. Prosecutors were given greatly reduced caseloads so that they could focus their attention on the most notorious gang members. There were provisions for witness protection programs that gave new identities to effective snitches. Operation Hardcore claimed to not engage in plea bargaining and to request very high amounts of bail. The main strategy was vertical prosecution in which one district attorney carried the case forward from beginning to end.

The Mitre Corporation was hired to conduct an evaluation of Operation Hardcore and reported that the program achieved a 95% rate of convictions and longer prison terms for convicted gang members (Dahmann, 1982/1995). The evaluators noted that the intensive staff commitment required by the program and the related high costs meant that Operation Hardcore was applied to just a few gang members. The Mitre Corporation noted that Operation Hardcore achieved a marginal increase in the incapacitation of targeted offenders, but it was far more difficult to prove that a larger deterrent effect was accomplished with other gang members. There was little evidence that Operation Hardcore exerted an impact on the gang problem of Los Angeles that grew throughout the decade of the 1980s (Dahmann, 1982/1995). Operation Hardcore still exists today, but the caseloads of prosecutors assigned to the special unit have grown tremendously, and both conviction rates and average prison terms have gone down.

A variation on the Operation Hardcore model was funded by OJJDP and designed as a national model. Renamed the Habitual, Serious, and Violent Juvenile Offender Program (HSVJOP), this get-tough approach was tested by OJJDP in a number of cities. Cronin and her colleagues conducted a detailed process evaluation of the program, concluding that the targeted prosecution approach was able to overcome the initial resistance of the traditionally treatment-oriented leaders of the juvenile justice system (Cronin, Bourque, Gragg, Mell, & McGrady, 1988). Further iterations of the model, known as Serious, Habitual Offender Directed Intervention Program (SHODIP) and Serious, Habitual Offender Comprehensive Action Program (SHOCAP), were funded by OJJDP in several additional locales. These later versions attempted to add treatment components to the core of focused prosecution. These later versions received much less research than the original HSVJOP.

The research found that more experienced prosecutors and more time for case preparation and work with witnesses and victims led to speedier adjudications in some locations. Serious and chronic offenders were more likely to be convicted because of these programs, and there were increases in the numbers of youths who were transferred to criminal courts. It was less clear whether sentences in the juvenile corrections system were toughened. Moreover, OJJDP hoped to implement comprehensive treatment programs that would complement the prosecution approach, but these rehabilitative resources rarely were put in place. Cronin and her colleagues also noted that the case-screening criteria for HSVJOP were overly broad, producing caseloads that were well beyond the program resources (Cronin et al., 1988).

The researchers for HSVJOP could not answer a number of crucial public policy concerns. The selective prosecution programs were able to identify offenders with many prior arrests, but it was less clear how well the project's screening criteria would predict future criminal behavior. Cronin and her colleagues (1988) could not demonstrate what case-screening criteria would be optimal in averting future serious youth crime. Chaiken and Chaiken (1987) reached similar conclusions in their study of career criminal prosecutions in Los Angeles, California, and Middlesex, Massachusetts. The information contained in the case files of the prosecution units was not very useful in discriminating the future between very frequent and less frequent offenders. An analysis of data from the Wolfgang Philadelphia cohort study could not produce a screening tool useful to prosecutors to correctly identify high-rate offenders (Weiner, 1996). The factors that could predict those youths who committed multiple minor crimes were quite different from the factors that isolated those who committed the most serious violent crimes. Weiner concluded, "There is little reason to believe that warning signs, early or otherwise, can soon be developed that will provide a firm basis for identifying serious or habitual offenders" (Weiner, 1996). Further, Delbert Elliott's research suggests that many offenses committed by juvenile offenders do not result in arrests and that the duration of the careers of high-rate offenders is usually less than one year. Thus, by the time we catch the chronic and serious offenders, their criminal behavior is diminishing in frequency and severity (Elliott, 1994). The sum of these studies suggests that career criminal prosecution programs are of very limited utility in suppressing the future incidence of serious juvenile crime.

Another question that remains unresolved about targeted youth prosecution programs is the impact of the penalties that these programs seek to achieve. A key question is whether traditional juvenile corrections programs or adult-style punishments exert a positive, negative, or neutral impact on criminal careers. If, as some critics have suggested, correctional experiences are criminogenic, then the short-term incapacitation effects may be outweighed by longer term escalation in offending. Getting youthful offenders more quickly into "schools for crime" may be self-defeating. We will take up this issue a little later in this chapter.

Not surprisingly, targeted law enforcement and prosecution programs have been very popular among politicians and justice system professionals. However, the sizeable financial investments in these labor-intensive programs have not been matched with serious investments of research dollars to measure their results or refine the state of the art. We know little more today about how to target career offenders than we knew two decades ago. Since crackdowns on gangs and other perceived dangerous offenders are likely to remain popular and to absorb large amounts of funding, it is imperative that these efforts be subjected to far more intensive research efforts than they have been thus far.

The Impact of Juvenile Corrections

Measuring the impact of placing youths in juvenile correctional facilities is no simple task. Juvenile corrections encompasses a very wide range of settings that vary tremendously in terms of security level, size, location, and staffing patterns. The extremes can be represented by 15-bed secure facilities in Massachusetts to institutions of the California Youth Authority that each hold more than 600 young people. Juvenile correctional facilities may closely resemble adult prisons and jails, or they may include wagon trains, correctional sailing ships, military-style boot camps, environmental or wilderness programs, group homes, foster homes, chemical dependency residential programs, and independent living arrangements. Most juvenile correctional programs are operated by government agencies, but an increasing number of programs are run by nonprofit organizations and for-profit companies. Most serious and violent juvenile offenders are held in facilities operated by state juvenile correctional agencies, but there is a growing trend to remove the most dangerous youthful offenders and place them in special institutions that are run by adult departments of corrections.

The states differ in their juvenile correctional policies (Krisberg, Litsky, & Schwartz, 1984). Age boundaries between the adult and juvenile correctional systems vary from state to state, and the laws defining these boundaries are changing rapidly (Torbet et al., 1996). There are states such as Ohio, Pennsylvania, and California in which juvenile facilities are operated by both state and local government agencies. There are other states such as Georgia, Florida, and Louisiana in which all juvenile corrections facilities are managed at the state level. Moreover, states such as Maryland, Utah, Rhode Island, and Massachusetts rely very heavily on nongovernmental programs to run their youth corrections programs. States also vary considerably in how commitment and release decisions are made. In some locales, judges choose the location of incarceration and specify the length of confinement. In other states, institutional placements are determined by the juvenile correctional agencies, sometimes in concert with a juvenile parole board (Dedel, 1998). The nature and extent of aftercare or reentry services that are available to youths upon release is not uniform across jurisdictions.

The general status of juvenile corrections is not good. A national study of juvenile corrections reported that many facilities do not meet even minimal professional standards (Parent et al., 1994). Other data suggest that juvenile facilities are becoming more crowded, especially urban juvenile detention centers. Prisons have fared much better in the competition for public funding. There has been little funding available to juvenile facilities for repairs or replacements of dangerous and dilapidated buildings. Reports of institutional violence and escapes that plagued the early 19th century houses of refuge continue to the present day (Krisberg & Breed, 1986).

The argument over whether juvenile confinement reduces or increases juvenile offending goes back to the founding of the first juvenile institutions. Advocates of alternatives to incarceration from Charles Loring Brace to Jane Addams to Jerome Miller have asserted that incarceration breeds crime (Krisberg & Austin, 1993). Defenders of juvenile corrections have argued that confinement, even in terrible conditions, exerts a deterrent effect on offenders (DiIulio, 1995b; Murray & Cox, 1979). Some have claimed that institutional treatment programs can be an effective response to youth crime (Rhine, 1996). This debate has rarely been enlightened by sound empirical data.

While there are many complex issues involved in measuring the recidivism rates of youths who exit juvenile correctional programs, it is more troubling that few states even bother to collect and report these data. Given the great public interest in reducing youth crime and the sizeable investments of tax dollars in these programs, the absence of routine outcome data is puzzling.

There is a handful of intriguing research studies looking at postrelease outcomes of various youth corrections programs. Each of these studies suffers from some limitations such as the absence of experimental designs, inadequate control groups, or rudimentary outcome measures. However, there are many useful insights that can be gleaned from this body of research.

A Florida study by Tollett (1987) looked at a cohort of almost 1,700 youths released from a range of correctional programs. Recidivism was defined as being placed on probation or being returned to a juvenile or adult correctional facility within one year of release from the original correctional placement. Tollett found that approximately 44% of this cohort was convicted for new juvenile or adult charges. However, about 30% of the group was returned to a correctional institution during the follow-up period. Recidivism rates were highest for nonwhites, males, and for those who were principally property offenders. Interestingly, those youth who had prior juvenile institutional placements possessed the highest recidivism rate of almost 59%. This finding suggests, but does not prove, that Florida's juvenile correctional programs had a limited effect in reducing future rates of offending. Tollett also reported that the lowest recidivism rates were from youths who exited nonresidential programs; the worst failure rates came from youths released from the most secure juvenile facilities. Obviously, this research could not properly control for the different risks posed by youths in different types of correctional programs. Tollett tried to partially answer this concern by computing each program's rate of failure compared to the proportion of youths with prior commitments. He also attempted to factor in the costs of each program. These methods revealed that the less secure programs still produced better results and were cost-effective when compared to the more secure Florida programs (Tollett, 1987).

A study of 10 residential juvenile corrections programs in Pennsylvania reported a rearrest rate of 55% within 18 months; 48% were arrested again in the first year after their release. Of the random sample of 527 youths, 31% were convicted of a new offense within 18 months (Goodstein & Sontheimer, 1987). Similar to the Florida research discussed above, the Pennsylvania research found that the failure rates were highest for youths with extensive prior records and prior histories of institutionalization. In fact, one of the strongest predictors of recidivism was the age at which youths were first incarcerated—those youths who were incarcerated at the youngest ages had the highest recidivism rates after their most recent period of confinement. Youths who had the most troubled histories of institutional placement, such as disciplinary infractions and running away, were the most likely to continue patterns of offending. Goodstein and Sontheimer (1987) also reported that youths with poor school performance were at risk of continued offending. Like the Florida study, this review of Pennsylvania residential programs lent little support to the idea that juvenile corrections programs could head off future offending once the youths returned home.

Two NCCD studies of juvenile correctional systems concluded that the vast majority of the youths that were released continued to reoffend. For example, a study of a random sample of youths released from the CYA observed a rearrest rate of 70% within one year. NCCD found a rearrest rate of almost 79% from Utah's youth corrections programs (Austin, Krisberg, Joe, & Steele, 1988). A Harvard University study of Massachusetts training schools in the late 1960s found a failure rate of 66% (Coates et al., 1978). However, a later study by NCCD that looked at the Massachusetts juvenile corrections system after it had abandoned large facilities in favor of smaller and more community-based programs, reported a failure rate of 51% (Austin, Elms, Krisberg, & Steele, 1991). The reformed Massachusetts system also used much shorter periods of confinement than the older system. NCCD also assembled data from 35 states and examined the proportion of youths who were readmitted to youth corrections systems after release. This is a conservative measure of recidivism that does not count those youths who are confined in local juvenile facilities or those who "graduate" to confinement in adult jails and prisons. These data show that 27% of the youths are returned to state custody in less than 12 months (Krisberg, DeComo, Wordes, & Del Rosario, 1996). These national-level data also show that histories of prior incarceration were one of the strongest predictors of recidivism.

Finally, the most extensive follow-up of youths released from youth corrections systems was conducted in California by Rudy Haapanen (1988). He traced the subsequent criminal behavior of samples of youths released from CYA programs in the 1960s and found a rearrest rate of 96% as these youths entered adulthood. Although Haapanen did find a tendency for these youths to slow their frequency of offending over time, his research reinforces the general finding that incarceration of young people is not a very effective long-term crime control strategy. Haapanen further showed that increasing the length of incarceration for selected high-rate offenders would be a very costly policy that would potentially produce little in the way of overall crime reductions (Haapanen, 1988).

The Boot Camp Frenzy

Almost 100 years after Zebulon Brockway introduced the concept of military drill and regimen at the Elmira Reformatory in New York, America fell back in love with the idea that military discipline could reform offenders. Maybe it the was the popularity of the movie, *An Officer and a Gentleman* in which the hard-nosed marine drill sergeant played by Louis Gossett rescued the miscreant naval officer played by Richard Gere. The tough but secretly sympathetic drill sergeant helped the wayward young officer to overcome his unsavory past (he was raised in a brothel) to find the meaning of honor. Perhaps it was the nostalgia of many elected officials for their boot camp experiences in the military, whether real or imagined, that led them to support funding boot camps in virtually every community. Whatever the immediate catalyst, correctional boot camps became a national obsession. The U.S. Congress and many state legislatures appropriated hundreds of millions of dollars to set up correctional boot camps across the nation. Some advocates believed that boot camps could exert a strong rehabilitative effect, combining improved physical conditioning with an ethic of hard work. Some believed that boot camps delivered real punishment when compared to other correctional settings in which inmates spent most of the day in idleness, watching television, lifting weights, or engaging in professional networking with other criminals. Others claimed that short-term intensive military-like experiences would be cheaper than conventional corrections programs and help reduce prison and jail overcrowding. Boot camps were instituted for a wide range of offenders, both adults and juveniles.

The boot camps started by government agencies were soon joined by private nonprofit and for-profit agencies. The private sector boot camps took some referrals for criminal and juvenile courts, but they soon found a more lucrative market in middle-class parents who wanted some options to deal with their troublesome teenaged children. Boot camps were marketed through school counselors, physicians, the Internet, and advertising in prominent magazines. Parents were told that boot camps could help children who had drug problems or those who were engaging in risky behavior. Boot camps were a cure for problems as diverse as underachievement in school to sexual promiscuity.

Boot camps were made for TV. Almost every week, one of the afternoon talk shows would feature a topic such as "Your Teenage Daughter Is Out of Control." These shows were remarkably similar to one another. The viewer would meet a provocatively dressed young girl who rejected all forms of authority and loved using profanities. The other guest on the show was the distraught mom (somehow dad was not around) who pleaded for help in controlling her wayward child. The solution was always a big man in a military uniform who would come on the show and yell at the young girl. These first confrontations did not seem to produce much behavior change, but later in the show there would be film clips of the child who was sent to the boot camp. The final segment of the show typically involved the erstwhile devil-child reappearing as an angelic persona, reunited with her family and back on track. The pretend drill sergeant would reappear for a round of hugs and tears. It was almost too good to be true.

The problem was that boot camps produced few if any of these alleged miracle cures. Most boot camps were never evaluated, but of those that did receive an objective review, the results were not impressive. For example, a comprehensive review of delinquency reduction programs conducted by the University of Maryland (Sherman et al., 1997) pointed to boot camps as a category of programs that was generally ineffective. Many studies suggested that boot camp graduates performed no better, and sometimes worse, than comparable youths who went to conventional correctional programs. A national juvenile boot camp demonstration project funded by OJJDP produced no positive results (Peters, Thomas, & Zamberlan, 1997). Other studies suggested that boot camps were often used for offenders who were already receiving lesser penalties, not those headed for long-term confinement. Thus, boot camps were often more expensive than traditional correctional interventions. Though wayward youths playing soldier was an appealing image for the politicians, it was largely ineffective as a rehabilitative or deterrent program.

Even more troubling was the fact that boot camps seemed to produce a series of deaths for their young inmates. Although there are no comprehensive data on deaths that take place in juvenile corrections programs, especially the private sector programs, there have been many media reports of the lethal consequences of juvenile boot camps. Typically youths died from excessive physical exertion, inadequate medical attention, or exposure to the elements. In one Florida case, a 300-pound staff member was physically restraining a frail youth who died of compression asphyxiation—his chest was crushed. The staff member later testified that he thought that the youth's lack of movement was a sign that the youngster was "playing possum." An overweight young girl was forced to run 5 miles to "boost her self esteem." As she collapsed and died of dehydration, two staff members watched her demise while drinking soft drinks. The staff assumed that she was faking her illness. These tragic scenes have been repeated all too frequently. Untrained staff, who rarely possess the requisite clinical skills, force youths to engage in dangerous activities. If a youth refuses to participate, the staff conclude that the young person is faking illness or is malingering, providing the staff member the justification for further punitive actions. A few of these deaths have resulted in criminal indictments, but the courts have been reluctant to sanction the offending staff. Parents, who often lack the resources to file lawsuits against these programs, are devastated and often feel partly responsible for their child being in the program. Further, many of the private programs are unregulated by state agencies. Even if a state decides not to permit any of its children to be placed in a suspect program, the boot camp can receive youngsters from other states. The federal government, which in theory could oversee the interstate placement of court-involved youths, has taken a hands-off position.

As the 1990s came to a close, the boot camp frenzy was beginning to wane. Federal funding to start up new boot camps was shrinking. Public officials were becoming more aware of the potential legal exposure from lawsuits about injuries and wrongful deaths. Moreover, the research studies continued to report negative results. Although the boot camp movement still has its committed adherents, it now seems clear that some of our efforts to scare youths away from delinquency were scaring some young people to their deaths.

Transferring Juveniles to the Criminal Justice System

Since the mid-1970s, a substantial amount of media and political attention has been focused on the policy of moving juvenile offenders out of the juvenile and family courts and into adult criminal courts. There is very little empirical evidence suggesting that this approach can produce public safety benefits. There are many mechanisms through which the transfer can occur. Legislatures have lowered the age threshold at which adult court jurisdiction begins. Some states allow prosecutors to select certain cases to file in the criminal courts (a practice known as direct file); other states permit a sort of concurrent jurisdiction in which cases can be tried in either the adult or juvenile system for certain offenses and certain age categories. One of the most common forms of transfer involves decisions that are made by juvenile court judges, usually after a hearing, to determine if a youngster could benefit from the more rehabilitative programs of the juvenile justice system. Whereas the norm for these judicial hearings used to be that the prosecution had the burden to prove that the youth was unfit for the juvenile court, increasingly it is the defense that must convince the judge to retain a case in the juvenile justice system.

There are few precise counts of the number of young people who are transferred, or waived, to adult court proceedings. In 1978 one research team estimated that at least 9,000 youths were waived to the adult courts by juvenile court judges, another 2,000 cases were transferred via the discretion of prosecutors, and more than 1,300 youths were tried as adults because of statutes that automatically placed them in criminal courts based on the alleged offense (Hamparian, 1982). This study did not cover the number of youths who were being tried as adults due to the lowered age of criminal court jurisdiction. More recent estimates place these numbers at much higher levels. For example, Snyder and Sickmund (1999) contend that there are as many as 176,000 youths below age 18 that are tried as adults in states that set the upper age of juvenile court jurisdiction at ages 16 or 17. Butts and Poe-Yamagata (1993) reported that there are approximately 11,800 cases waived from the juvenile court to the adult system nationally. While there are no national data on the extent of direct file cases, there were 7,000 such cases in 1991 in Florida alone (Snyder & Sickmund, 1999).

Howell's excellent review of the literature on juvenile transfers makes it clear how little is known about this dramatic public policy decision (Howell, 1997). Most studies cover the practice of waiver decisions made by juvenile court judges. There are very few analyses of direct file or statutory transfer laws. The research literature is primarily centered on how discretion is exercised by juvenile courts in making the transfer decision. There is a scarcity of careful studies comparing the differential treatment by adult authorities of those juveniles who are transferred. There are even less data on the comparative outcomes upon release of those young people tried in the adult system.

An early study by White (1985) compared samples of juveniles charged with very serious crimes in the juvenile court with similar cases tried in criminal courts. White reported that the criminal courts were slightly more likely to convict and incarcerate youthful offenders. He found that youths were likely to spend considerably more time in adult correctional facilities than juveniles that were sent to state juvenile facilities. Krisberg and his colleagues (in an unpublished reanalysis of data from the National Correctional Reporting Program) found that the average stay for minors sent to prison was almost three times that of youths charged with very serious offenses who were sent to juvenile facilities. The youths sent to adult prisons had much higher recidivism rates than their juvenile-corrections counterparts (Perkins, 1994). At least one study by Forst and his associates suggests that these longer stays are due to the fact that the youngest inmates commit many institutional infractions, thus losing their "good time" release credits and lengthening their period of confinement (Forst et al., 1989). These researchers also reported that juveniles in adult facilities were less likely to receive treatment services than youths in juvenile corrections. Young people in prison are also less likely to receive education and vocational services. Juveniles in adult facilities more often report being victimized while incarcerated than those in juvenile facilities. Much of this victimization is at the hands of the prison guards (Forst et al., 1989).

A Minnesota study compared youths who were waived to the adult court to those retained in the juvenile justice system. The transferred youths were much more likely to be incarcerated, and for longer periods, than the juvenile court sample. The transferred youths had a rearrest rate of 58% compared to 42% for the nontransferred juvenile offenders over the 2-year period that each group was back on the streets (Podkopacz & Feld, 1996). The researchers could not say for sure if the higher recidivism rates for the transfer cases were due to this group's containing more chronic serious offenders, the superior rehabilitative services of the juvenile justice system, or the general failure of severe adult penalties to deter adolescents from committing future crimes.

In another innovative research effort, Fagan (1995) examined the differential methods that New York and New Jersey used to deal with serious and violent juvenile offenders. Due to state laws, juvenile offenders in New York are more likely to be processed in adult courts, whereas comparable New Jersey youngsters would be handled in the juvenile justice system. Fagan looked at nearly 1,200 felony offenders who were ages 15 and 16 and arrested for robbery or burglary in matched New York and New Jersey counties. Interestingly, Fagan found that penalties were both more certain and severe for the New Jersey sample, compared with the New York youths. However, he also reported that the New York youths had higher recidivism rates, committed more new crimes, and were crime-free for a shorter time than the New Jersey youths (Fagan, 1995). These results, while intriguing, are difficult to interpret. Were the higher New York recidivism rates due to lesser penalties experienced by the New York youths, the adverse consequences of the adult correctional interventions, or the inability to perfectly match offenders from the two samples?

A far more compelling study by Bishop and her research team produced a more conclusive look at the outcomes of transferred youths in Florida (Bishop, Frazier, Lanza-Kaduce, & Winner, 1996). Nearly 5,500 youths who were transferred and retained in the juvenile justice system were matched on social and demographic factors, as well as a number of legal variables such as the seriousness of the instant charge, the number of current charges, and nature and extent of the youth's prior record. During the follow-up period, the transferred youths had higher failure rates, committed more serious new offenses, and passed less time until the next criminal activity. Bishop and her colleagues conclude that there was little evidence that Florida's aggressive legal policy of trying youngsters in criminal courts had any positive effect on deterring future offending (Bishop et al., 1996). These researchers concluded that the short-term effects of incapacitating youths for a longer period of time in adult facilities was negated quickly as the youths returned to their home communities and committed many more new offenses than their juvenile court counterparts.

OJJDP funded additional studies of waiver that included a more detailed study in Florida, an analysis of transfer in Utah, and another study in Arizona. Although the results of these studies are still to be published, it seems clear that the findings of the earlier research are confirmed. At best, transfer has no positive deterrent value and may indeed accelerate the criminal conduct of youthful offenders.

Summary

The vast majority of new juvenile justice dollars have gone toward get-tough policies rather than to more treatment services. These policies were designed to get the most serious juvenile offenders off the street and to deter potential offenders through the threat of very harsh penalties. Many of the get-tough programs were aimed at juvenile gangs.

Research has consistently shown that deterrence is best accomplished when sanctions are swift and certain. By contrast, the harsher penalties often are applied in an arbitrary and capricious manner. Overall, the research on these programs does not support the argument that they are effective. Strong criminal and juvenile justice sanctions possess a natural, intuitive appeal. They permit politicians to talk with macho bravado without being held accountable for the poor results of these programs. Given the enormous fiscal and human investments and human consequences of these approaches, it is scandalous that our research base is so slender. It is as if contemporary policies have adopted a "hear no evil, speak no evil, see no evil" strategy. In particular, policies to increase the use of secure confinement or to place more youths in prison are not supported by scientific evidence, but are informed by anecdotes, jingoes (Do the Crime, Do the Time), and media popularized fads. Our elected officials go from Tough Love to Scared Straight, from boot camps to chain gangs. It is not surprising that many of our young people have become very cynical about a public policy process that squanders so much money on unproven policies and programs.

Review Questions

1. What was Operation Hardcore, and what factors made it so ineffective?

2. What are the principles of the most effective programs to reduce gang behavior?

3. What are the principles of deterrence theory that should guide juvenile justice sanctions?

4. What led to the rise of juvenile boot camps? What were the results of boot camp programs?

Ten

Redeeming
Our Children

Evolving Standards of Juvenile Justice

For most of recorded history the standard of justice was based on a harsh regimen of social revenge (Foucault, 1977; Rusche & Kirchheimer, 1939). Stark punishments were designed to instill fear in the hearts and minds of the lower classes. This fear was designed to deter potential lawbreakers and to head off any possibilities of social revolt. Frequent use of the death penalty, especially public executions, was part of the ceremony of justice. Torture of defendants and extreme physical brutality were part of the penal practice of Europe and the New World until well into the 19th century. Thorsten Sellin, in his extraordinary book, *Slavery and the Penal System,* demonstrates the similarity in the treatment of slaves and convicts going back to Greek and Roman civilizations (Sellin, 1976). Sellin points out that soldiers captured in wars were quickly converted to slave status and that emerging state authorities used the customs and practices surrounding slavery to establish standards for penal practice. Not surprisingly, the growth of the slave trade to Virginia and other southern colonies came close on the heels of transporting convicts to perform hard labor in America and Australia. The practice of transporting convicts to colonial territories provided European nations with a cheap source of labor and a safety valve to reduce the threats posed by crowded jails (Hughes, 1987).

During this time there were few distinctions made between children and adults. It was very common for young people to be housed in the same jails and workhouses as adults. English common law set age 7 as a bottom threshold for treating children as criminally culpable. Beyond that principle of culpability, there were few practical differences between children and adults in penal practice until well into the 19th century. Childhood as a concept was not well developed.

Efforts to reform the brutal penal practices of the 18th century were spearheaded primarily by religious groups. The efforts of the Quakers of Pennsylvania to install a new penal philosophy based on religious conceptions of penitence and expiation of sins resulted in the establishment of the first penitentiary in America in the early part of the 19th century (Barnes, 1926). There were also a few isolated attempts to replace the cruelty of penal practice with more reformative methods that were tied to some Catholic orders in France and Belgium. Coincident with the Quaker reforms in Pennsylvania were the efforts of the religiously motivated reformers who created the first houses of refuge and training schools (Mennel, 1973). Other voices joined in the movement to humanize the punishment system. These advocates relied on enlightenment philosophy to construct a theory of proportionate penalties that they argued were more productive in maintaining social order (Beccaria, 1963; Bentham, 1830). The noted British penal reformer John Howard used both religious arguments and enlightened self-interest to propose massive improvements in the British jail system. Howard noted how diseases such as smallpox, plague, and yellow fever, which were incubating in penal facilities, led to horrendous epidemics that infected free society—an argument that we are hearing again today concerning rates of HIV and hepatitis C among prisoners. The advocates for separating children from adult prisoners suggested that younger offenders were being schooled in criminal behavior by their older inmates. It was also argued that juries would acquit guilty youths because they did not want them housed with adults. Very slowly and inconsistently, in different locales in Europe and America, the regime of penal terror was replaced with other standards of justice.

The most important standard of juvenile justice was the ideal of rehabilitation. The concepts of individualized treatment and personal reform were the cornerstones of the American juvenile court. Interestingly, the ideal of rehabilitation is a relatively recent intellectual development, dating back to the Progressive Era at the beginning of the 20th century. Let us recall that the founders of the houses of refuge placed most of their faith in religious instruction, a very regimented daily routine, and hard work. The Elmira Reformatory of the last decade of the 19th century added military drill and physical exercise as part of the reform program. However, it was the advocates for the new juvenile court, such as Julia Lathrop and Jane Addams, who sought to harness the power of the emerging sciences of biology, psychology, sociology, and psychoanalysis to reform wayward youths. Addams and her associates raised funds to support the work of William Healy to study the cases of thousands of delinquent youths and to create child guidance clinics that were to support the work of juvenile court judges. The core of this approach was in-depth testing and data collection about individual young people. A range of medical, psychological, and social facts were then crafted into a diagnosis and specific treatment plan for each lawbreaker. The goal was to uncover the causes of the delinquent behavior and to alleviate some of those negative forces. Scientific knowledge was to be utilized by the emerging cadre of social workers who would connect with families and youths and provide the needed interventions and services. The rehabilitative ideal rested on a far more optimistic conception of human nature than the punishment model. It assumed that young people were malleable due to their tender ages and developmental potential. It is also important to note that traditional Anglo-American criminal law rests on a crucial assumption that human behavior is guided by free will and that offenders are thus accountable for their actions. The rehabilitative ideal is corrosive of the concept of free will. Under the precepts of the rehabilitation ideal, the offender's free will has been partially or fully impeded by internal and environmental factors. If human behavior can be explained, diagnosed, and treated, then the conventional ideology of free will is called into question. Moreover, our emerging scientific knowledge has made it clear that free will is particularly problematic for young people who have yet to develop fully formed cognitive, emotional, and evaluative abilities.

Unfortunately, the reality of rehabilitation rarely matched its rhetoric. Juvenile courts were never afforded the resources that were actually required to diagnose and treat their young clients. Neither were judges or probation staff given the appropriate training to implement rehabilitative programs. Further, the tragic patterns of abuse in the treatment of incarcerated young people continued despite the incorporation of benign treatment language that masked traditional practices. However, the rehabilitation ideal linked the juvenile court with the broader pursuit of child welfare and contributed to many positive system reforms.

America's most famous legal philosopher Roscoe Pound went so far as to describe the juvenile court as the greatest step forward in Anglo-American law since the Magna Charta. He meant to highlight the unique commitment of the juvenile court to individualized and compassionate responses to youthful offenders. How remarkable to have a legal system that was principally guided by the best interests of the child and not primarily grounded in the nature of the offense. However, the primacy of treating the child might also result in very intrusive interventions by the court in cases in which the legal infractions were fairly minor. Pound was keenly aware that individualized justice, the private nature of juvenile court proceedings, and the lack of emphasis on due process considerations could turn the court into a *star chamber*. Contemporary proponents of a separate judicial system for children continue to struggle with this dilemma (Pound, 1957).

Other early observers of the juvenile court remarked at the internal contradictions that plagued it. For example, sociologist George Hebert Mead (1961) noted that crime control is sought via the "hostile procedures of law and . . . through comprehension of social and psychological conditions" (p. 882). He wryly observed, "The social worker in court is the sentimentalist, and the legalist in the social settlement, in spite of his learned doctrine, is the ignoramus" (p. 882). Mead did not believe that these two alternative approaches ever harmonized. There were also concerns expressed that the broad discretion that was central to the rehabilitative ideal could result in discriminatory practices toward children of color and immigrant children. As we noted earlier, there remain serious concerns that young women are accorded overly harsh and intrusive treatment by the juvenile justice system under the rubric of the concept of rehabilitation.

Beginning in the mid-1960s, the rehabilitative ideal was challenged by legal thinkers, social scientists, and politicians. Court decisions required that the juvenile court be guided by due process and equal protection. In the classic words of U.S. Supreme Court Justice Abe Fortis, "Under our Constitution the condition of being a boy does not justify a kangaroo court" (*In re Gault*, 1967). Juvenile courts and legislatures reluctantly moved to accommodate these constitutional requirements. Simultaneously, social scientists reported a range of research findings that questioned the efficacy of many rehabilitative programs. Robert Martinson and others raised the specter that few interventions with chronic delinquents actually worked. Another powerful social science paradigm, *Labeling Theory*, suggested that apparently well-meaning societal interventions actually stigmatized young clients and made them worse. The growing skepticism of the rehabilitative idea was met with law and order advocates that had always decried the coddling of young criminals by the juvenile court.

The rehabilitative ideal was being attacked on many fronts. On the left, the critics urged policy makers to divert youthful offenders away from the court and to increase the legal assistance available to young defendants. On the right, the call was for harsher punishments and expanded processes to transfer youths to criminal courts and to sentence youth criminals to adult correctional facilities. The emerging standard of justice was a mixture of older notions of deterrence and social revenge, mixed with limited rehabilitative services for "worthy" youngsters. Some called for the juvenile justice system to give out "adult time for adult crime." Treatment services, if offered, were to be backstopped by harsh penalties if young offenders failed to take advantage of these second chances. The media-fueled hysteria over rising juvenile crime rates in the first few years of the 1990s and the political rhetoric demanding tough new measures to control a new generation of supposed super predators led to the ascendancy of the updated punishment model at all levels of government. It began to look like the juvenile court would soon be abolished. Some of us wondered if the children's court would survive until its centennial celebration in 1999, or if it was already dead.

Contemporary Standards of Juvenile Justice

Just when the juvenile court seemed doomed, two new models of juvenile justice emerged and exerted a profound impact on laws and practice throughout the nation. The first of these approaches was known as Balanced and Restorative Justice (BARJ); the second approach was known as the Comprehensive Strategy for Serious, Violent, and Chronic Offenders (CS). Both models were critiques of the deterrence-focused punishment philosophy that was advocated by more conservative policy makers and practitioners during the Reagan and Bush administrations.

There are several ways in which BARJ and CS could be utilized as complementary standards of juvenile justice. As we will see, BARJ is primarily a way of thinking about the official response to youthful lawbreakers, whereas CS places major emphasis on preventive measures and encompasses a wider range of community institutions. The two models also differ on a number of other dimensions. For example, BARJ is largely a philosophic statement that is not particularly rooted in the research literature, whereas the core of CS is derived from a careful examination of research on the causes and correlates of youth crime, as well as rigorous research on promising prevention and intervention programs. The BARJ model established a central role in the justice process for the victims of juvenile crimes; CS pays scant attention to victims as a key aspect of the reform process. Whereas CS is basically a community-level response to youthful criminality, BARJ concentrates its attention on the individual offender and his or her victim.

Seeking Balance and Restorative Justice

Gordon Bazemore and Dennis Maloney (1994) have been the most strenuous advocates of BARJ. Their work began as an attempt to reformulate and strengthen the theory and practice of juvenile probation, but it has enjoyed an excellent reception among legislators, judges, and a broad range of juvenile justice practitioners. Bazemore and Maloney began with the articulation of a set of values and principles that could provide a guiding vision for juvenile justice agencies. This vision was intended to create organizational missions that would determine operational policies and practices.

The big idea underlying BARJ is the notion that crime is injury. BARJ seeks to highlight the hurtful nature of juvenile offending and to define the harm to victims, to the community at large, and to the young lawbreakers. Under the BARJ philosophy, these harms create an obligation to make things right. The traditional paradigm of the juvenile court was guided by considerations of the best interests of the child—there was no particular role in this jurisprudence for discussions about victims' rights or obligations of the child offender to the victims. This is not to say that many juvenile justice agencies paid little attention to victims. Indeed, many of the diversionary programs created by the juvenile justice system made extensive use of monetary compensation to victims or community service as part of their repertoire of sanctions. Moreover, it has become more common for juvenile courts to require monetary payments to victims as a routine part of probation orders even for youths placed in juvenile correctional facilities.

BARJ created an explicit role for victims and other community representatives in the justice process. It is assumed that the victim's point of view is crucial in fashioning a plan to repair the harm created by the offender. BARJ defines *accountability* as the offender accepting personal responsibility for the harm caused by his or her actions, and the offender is required to actively assist in mitigating that damage. The concept of *restoration* is a core component of BARJ. Restoration implies a process that both repairs the hurt to victims and seeks to rebuild relationships in the community. Advocates of BARJ measure the results of juvenile justice sanctions by how much damage is repaired and how much community relationships are strengthened. Proponents of BARJ are less concerned with the amount of punishment that is exacted. They are also less focused on preventing recidivism, although it is assumed that more effective crime control will emerge from the community involvement and victim restoration.

Figure 10.1 illustrates the three components of BARJ. It is referred to as Balanced and Restorative Justice because it seeks to give equivalent emphasis to offender restoration, public safety, and improving the competency of youthful offenders that enter the juvenile justice system. Operationally, BARJ means the creation of more services for victims, as

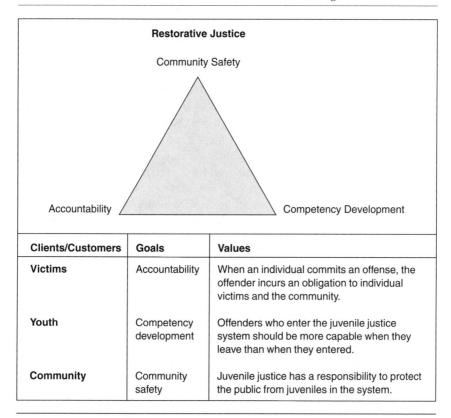

Figure 10.1   The Balanced Approach

SOURCE: Office of Juvenile Justice and Delinquency Prevention (1998, p. 6).

well as making existing victim services available to all segments of the community. As noted above, BARJ envisions giving victims greater opportunity for their voices to be heard and for them to participate in the juvenile justice system. Increasing community connections requires involving community members directly in the juvenile justice process. This is a radical departure from traditional notions that keep the community out of juvenile court to protect the confidentiality of young offenders. There is also the implication that ordinary citizens have an important role to play as equal partners with highly professionalized judges, prosecutors, defense attorneys, and probation staff. Offenders are encouraged and given chances to repair the harm that they created. The advocates of BARJ assert that offenders need opportunities to build their skills and abilities so that they can adequately participate in the BARJ process. Core competencies for offenders include educational and vocational advancements and resources to deal with existing family issues, substance abuse problems, or other health issues.

The BARJ movement offers few blueprints for local communities. While many jurisdictions have embraced BARJ in law and agency missions, there is no fully developed implementation to guide replication. BARJ is a value-driven and philosophical approach to establishing a new standard of juvenile justice. Communities are encouraged to use the broad-value framework of BARJ to craft their own approaches.

The open-ended nature of BARJ poses some important concerns. First and foremost, how do you know that BARJ is really being implemented? For example, it is not uncommon for juvenile justice practitioners to assert that they are "already doing BARJ." It remains to be seen how much real innovation will be driven by BARJ. Another concern is the appropriate target population for BARJ approaches: Does it equally apply to juvenile murderers, sex offenders, graffiti artists, drug dealers, and car thieves? BARJ is not rooted in an extensive body of research literature. Indeed, earlier evaluations of victim restitution and community service sanctions for juveniles have produced few positive results in terms of reducing future offending behavior (Krisberg & Austin, 1981). Typically, restorative sanctions have been utilized for minor crimes and as a diversionary option for first-time lawbreakers. There is a large need to fund and complete research on the more recent advances in restorative programming, such as victim–offender reconciliation, community sanctioning panels, and sentencing circles.

Another concern is the definition of community that seems so central to BARJ. One can easily imagine how BARJ might be implemented in small, close-knit communities, but the translation of BARJ concepts to highly urbanized areas or the bedroom communities of the suburbs is much more challenging. Moreover, it is not clear that BARJ will be readily accepted in disenfranchised communities that have often been victimized by overly aggressive law enforcement. The social disorganization that plagues many urban areas seems a major hurdle for the implementation of BARJ. Nor is it clear that BARJ will be equally effective in ethnically and culturally differing communities. There seems a real danger that BARJ will advance as the new juvenile justice paradigm for white, middle-class offenders, leaving children of color and poor whites to be relegated to the traditional punishment-oriented incarceration system. Also, there have been concerns expressed that the implementation of BARJ has advanced mostly in the areas of offender accountability and restorative programs. There has been far less attention and funding provided to improving competencies and skills of young offenders.

The future of BARJ is uncertain. The early enthusiasm for its adoption by policy makers and practitioners was supported by OJJDP through conferences, training sessions, and high-quality publications. Expanded juvenile justice funding during the late 1990s provided opportunities for many communities to experiment with BARJ-inspired programs. But, hard times in terms of disappearing OJJDP funding and severe fiscal crises at the state and local levels have descended on the nation's juvenile courts. OJJDP is no longer actively encouraging communities to adopt the BARJ model. How well BARJ will fare in this difficult environment remains to be seen.

The Comprehensive Strategy for Serious, Violent, and Chronic Juvenile Offenders

In the closing days of the administration of George H. W. Bush, two top OJJDP officials, John W. Wilson and James C. Howell, began circulating a policy statement on how to deal with serious, chronic, and violent juvenile offenders. They sought to summarize available research on the topic and to extrapolate principles for improved programming. After significant input from a broad range of researchers and practitioners, they published their conclusions to the field. Wilson and Howell presented a policy statement that was sharply at odds with the views of U.S. Attorney General William Barr. Had President Bush been reelected, this publication would not have been a great career move for them. However, their policy statement was embraced by Attorney General Janet Reno and came to be the official policy view of the Department of Justice. The Comprehensive Strategy on Serious, Violent, and Chronic Juvenile Offenders was subsequently implemented in nearly 50 communities and emerged as an influential paradigm on juvenile justice (Wilson & Howell, 1993).

As compared with BARJ, which rested on a philosophical foundation, the CS was explicitly linked to research on the causes and correlates of delinquent behavior as well as rigorous program evaluations. The core assumptions of the CS were far more oriented toward prevention than BARJ. Indeed, the CS asserted that prevention was the most cost-effective response to youth crime and that strengthening families was the top priority for prevention programs. The CS also asserted that the core social institutions of the community such as schools, youth-serving organizations, faith-based groups, recreational services, and cultural organizations were key to effective prevention strategies. The CS argued that there was a very small number of serious, violent, and chronic juvenile offenders

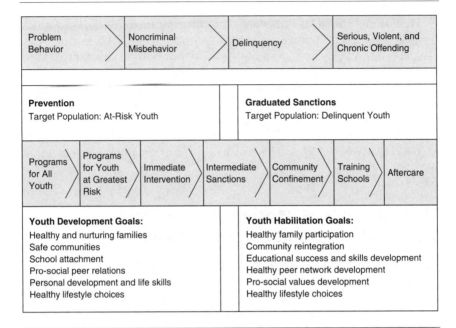

Figure 10.2   Overview of Comprehensive Strategy
SOURCE: Howell (1995, p. 8).

that needed to be identified and controlled through a range of graduated sanctions. Each community needed to assess its current inventory of prevention and juvenile justice services and to plan to fill gaps in these services. The CS envisioned a continuum of programs and services linking prevention and early intervention programming with juvenile justice responses. The core idea of the CS was to have the right service available to individual youngsters at the appropriate point in their psychosocial developmental stage. Juvenile justice systems needed a mix of immediate sanctions when youths first broke the law, intermediate sanctions for repeat offenders, and secure confinement options for violent youths. Ideal juvenile sanction systems also needed appropriate reentry services for youths who had to be placed out of home. Wilson and Howell urged communities to develop and implement research-based risk and needs assessment tools to guide juvenile justice decision making.

OJJDP issued a request for proposals to take the basic contours of the CS and flesh out the details. The NCCD and Developmental Research and Programs (DRP) were selected to conduct assessments of the best research-tested prevention and sanctioning programs, to offer communities guidance on planning strategies, and to inventory existing risk and needs assessment instruments. The resulting product was *The Guide for Implementing the Comprehensive Strategy for Serious, Violent, and Chronic Juvenile Offenders* (Howell, 1995), which was released at a national conference jointly keynoted by Attorney General Janet Reno and Marion Wright Edelman, president of the Children's Defense Fund. The CS guide was later distributed by OJJDP to more than 70,000 juvenile justice professionals and policy makers and was embraced by influential groups such as the National Conference of State Legislatures.

OJJDP and the Jessie Ball duPont Fund provided funding to pilot the implementation of the CS in two Florida communities, Ft. Meyers and Jacksonville, and in San Diego, California. Based on very promising results in the pilot sites, OJJDP selected eight states (Florida, Texas, Wisconsin, Maryland, Ohio, Oregon, Iowa, and Rhode Island) to implement the CS in up to six communities in those states. Michigan, Kansas, and Hawaii used their own funds to bring the CS to multiple jurisdictions in those states.

The prevention component of the CS was based on the model of Communities that Care discussed in Chapter 7. The focus was on community-wide planning that identified risk factors that propel youths toward delinquency and protective factors that partially neutralize these risk factors. The graduated sanctions or juvenile justice part of the CS was also based on a risk-focused model that considered factors indicative of serious and repetitive offending. The research suggested that the same protective factors that were effective as prevention resources were also crucial to helping offenders desist from law breaking. One of the key insights of the CS was that prevention and intervention strategies should be part of a seamless continuum of youth and family services. The CS implementation attempted to keep the prevention practitioners and the juvenile justice professionals together to conduct joint planning and program development. The CS also relied on empirical data showing that expensive incarceration options were being used for youngsters who could be better managed in less expensive community-based care. Instituting smarter juvenile justice policies and practices could actually free up scarce public dollars to increase investments in prevention services.

The underlying assumption of the CS was that the juvenile justice system should be guided by research and should stress those sanctions shown through research to be most effective. The CS placed a very high priority on public safety as the foremost goal of the juvenile justice system. Research suggested that sanctioning programs that genuinely focused on public protection would rely less on incarceration than current policies that often confined youngsters "for their own protection" or for "treatment." The emphasis on public safety might also go far to reduce the subjective decision making that results in disproportionate minority confinement. Not all adherents of the CS explicitly took this position, however. The logic of the CS required that the first set of justice system decisions had to do with the severity of the current offense (just deserts) and the odds that the youth would recidivate in the future (social defense). After the appropriate level of juvenile justice was determined, based on the above considerations, the CS implied that all youths are entitled to educational, vocational, health care, and counseling services regardless of the gravity of their crimes. Because the criminal court system was ill equipped to provide the appropriate services to young people, this position virtually precluded policies of trying youths as adults or placing them in prisons or jails. In fact, the *Guide for Implementing the Comprehensive Strategy for Serious, Violent, and Chronic Offenders* (Howell, 1995) contained almost no reference to waiver or transfer policies except to say that these practices should be severely limited. The CS offered a range of proven juvenile justice graduated sanctions programs that were effective with the most serious and violent youthful offenders. The CS attempted to sort out the mélange of purposes that were being used by juvenile justice practitioners to explain their actions. These multiple purposes were confusing to workers within the system, to youths and families, and to the public at large. The CS sought to provide a simple rationale for systems of graduated sanctions for juvenile offenders—a rationale that was grounded in solid research.

The CS was met with a very positive reception in virtually all of the communities in which it was implemented. At the local level there were far fewer shrill voices calling for harsher punishments for young people. Almost all the communities that embraced the CS placed significant attention on expanding prevention and early intervention services. Home-based and family strengthening services generally received the highest priority in local CS plans. Communities set out to fill key gaps in their local continuum of services. For many localities, it was the first time that they had conceptualized these continua or had applied data-driven comprehensive planning to juvenile crime issues. These communities employed the CS to commence a number of new programs and were able to attract substantial funding for these efforts (Krisberg et al., 2004).

In 2003 OJJDP decided to scrap the CS despite ample evidence that it was helpful to juvenile justice practitioners. OJJDP chose to substitute a more traditional topical approach to providing technical assistance to communities. At this writing, the new model has not been successfully implemented in any location. Many communities are still interested in the CS, but further implementation may be frustrated by current severe budget crises within state and local governments. The current federal administration has proposed substantial cutbacks in federal funding for juvenile justice programs. In the wake of the tragic loss of lives on September 11, 2001, Attorney General John Ashcroft directed the Department of Justice to place the highest priority on fighting international and domestic terrorism. Juvenile justice reform is no longer on the radar screen of the federal administration. Congressional leaders who have traditionally supported a strong federal role in juvenile justice seem to be supporting the position of the executive branch. Similar to BARJ, the future of the CS as an evolving standard of juvenile justice remains very much in doubt.

Our Children and Other People's Children

Jerome Miller, whose vision led to the closing of the Massachusetts training schools in the early 1970s, often asks his audiences to define the kind of justice system that they would want to encounter if their own child, grandchild, or sibling was in trouble. His assertion is that most people would choose the ideal of the juvenile justice system with its focus on compassion, individualized care, and rehabilitation. Few of us would select an inflexible system of punishments, with little regard for the possibility of personal redemption. Miller asks his listeners to consider that what they want for their own children is what should be available to all children. His point is that only when we delude ourselves into thinking that other people's children deserve a lesser standard of justice can we tolerate the sort of juvenile justice system that we currently have. Elsewhere I have argued that only racism, class biases, and our unconscious antagonism to troubled young people permit us to consider as rational such draconian juvenile justice polices as trying very young children in criminal courts, sending children to adult jails and prisons, or allowing horrid conditions of confinement to exist in juvenile facilities (Krisberg, 2003).

Much has been made in political debate about the demands of justice. Advocates for dismantling the juvenile justice system have urged us to embrace a single standard of justice for adults and for youths, "Do the Crime, Do the Time." They have advanced arguments that a return to a purely punishment-oriented model will scare young people, deterring them from law breaking. Anyone who has taken an introductory psychology course has heard that rewards and reinforcements are a much more powerful method of changing behavior than the calculus of punishments. There is little evidence supporting the claims of the advocates of get-tough policies; moreover, there are important moral reasons why we should not follow this course.

As the horrors of totalitarianism and genocidal hatred descended on Europe, the noted English philosopher Aldous Huxley wrote that real progress in human societies involved progress in charity.

> In the course of recorded history real progress has been made by fits and starts. Periods of advance in charity have alternated with periods of regression. The eighteenth century was an epoch of real progress. So was most of the nineteenth, in spite of the horrors of industrialism, or rather because of the energetic way in which its men of goodwill tried to put a stop to those horrors. The present age is still humanitarian in spots; but where major political issues are concerned it has witnessed a definite regression in charity. (Huxley, 1937, p. 7)

He reminded us that bad means can never be justified by good ends—justice is not an absolute destination that is unrelated to the road traveled to get there.

Huxley urged consideration of a quality of mind that he called being "nonattached." This meant being able to free oneself from angry prejudices, emotional responses to immediate events and to class prerogatives. For Huxley, the higher ideal meant the application of intelligence to human affairs and the practice of generosity. The nonattached person in Huxley's terms "puts an end to pain; and he puts an end to pain not only in himself, but also, by refraining from malicious and stupid activity, to such pain as he may inflict on others" (Huxley, 1937, p. 6). A generation earlier, the founders of the juvenile court such as Jane Addams and Ben Lindsey grasped this wisdom. They sought to establish a new standard of juvenile justice that was redemptive. For these reformers, a redemptive system of justice was the only one that was consistent with democracy.

Can a redemptive standard of justice reemerge in a political climate dominated by fear of outsiders and the genuine sense of personal vulnerability that followed the attacks on the World Trade Center and the Pentagon? There are some hopeful signs in many communities that the original ideal of the juvenile court can be attained, at least partially. We noted that many communities have tried to implement the philosophy of BARJ and that this development may lead to more connectedness among neighbors on behalf of troubled youngsters. In other locales, juvenile court judges have attempted to put into operation ideas of therapeutic justice through the creation of specialized courts that are tailored for drug-involved youths, victims of domestic violence, and young people with serious mental health issues. The Comprehensive Strategy illustrated that communities can coalesce around a common agenda of prevention and improved youth development services.

At present, the topic of juvenile crime is not on media or political agendas. The fear over relatively rare instances of internationally inspired terrorism is getting more attention than the everyday terror experienced by the abused child, by the frightened teen who lacks parental support, by the challenged student who is neglected in school. Some public officials seem lulled into a false sense of security that youth violence rates will continue to fall without our needing to improve the juvenile justice system and the lives of young people. This is probably not a good bet as the decline in public funding forces major cutbacks in vital educational and social services or as rising unemployment rates put increased pressure on our most vulnerable citizens. Each era creates its own challenges and opportunities. For all of us, especially the politically active and concerned young people whose voices are beginning to be heard, the advancement of Huxley's ideal of charity as the standard of juvenile justice is an important quest. A good place to start is to expose the pernicious fallacy that there are our children and other people's children. Only when communities embrace all children as our children and work actively for their positive social development can real progress in charity be achieved in the modern age.

Summary

Throughout most of human history, justice has been synonymous with extreme and harsh punishments. These brutal actions were justified based on the theory that draconian penalties would instill fear in the minds of potential law breakers. Until the 19th century, there was little distinction in the handling of children by the punishment system. Religious groups, most notably the Quakers, attempted to reduce the severity of the penal system. Others, such as the English reformer John Howard, argued that prisons were the breeding grounds for diseases such as smallpox, yellow fever, and plague that were impacting the free society.

In the 19th century, the founders of the houses of refuge, and later, child advocates such as Jane Addams and Julia Lathrop, furthered the call for enlightened justice by demanding a separate way of dealing with delinquent youths. The ideal of juvenile justice that was established in the first juvenile court laws in America envisioned a model of justice that was individualized, humane, and believed in the possibility of redemption.

By the end of the 20th century, it appeared that the ideal of juvenile justice was in retreat. The dominant political rhetoric favored abolishing the juvenile court and trying children as if they were merely small adults. Just when it looked like the juvenile court was breathing its last sighs, two models emerged to strengthen and reinforce the value of the American juvenile court. The Comprehensive Strategy for Serious, Violent, and Chronic Juvenile Offenders and the paradigm of Balanced and Restorative Justice are two approaches that return to the core principles of Jane Addams and her colleagues, while building on the best available research. The Comprehensive Strategy and BARJ have been embraced in hundreds of communities as the appropriate direction for reforming the juvenile justice system.

Although many thinkers such as Roscoe Pound and George Herbert Mead have pointed out how difficult it is to actualize the visions of redemptive justice that were championed by the founders of the juvenile court, the accumulated weight of scientific data supports the efficacy of this approach. Moreover, it is patently clear that most of us would seek a justice system that is founded on core principles of charity and redemption if it were our own children who were in trouble. This, of course, is the key issue. If we recognize the truth that all children are our children, the search for the juvenile justice ideal is our only moral choice.

Review Questions

1. Why do you think Roscoe Pound described the American Juvenile Court as "the greatest step forward in Anglo-American law since the Magna Charta"?

2. How did the Gault case fundamentally change juvenile justice in America?

3. Compare and contrast the Comprehensive Strategy and BARJ.

4. Who was Jane Addams, and what are the core components of her redemptive ideal of juvenile justice?

References

Acoca, L. (1998). Outside/inside: The violation of American girls at home, on the streets, and in the juvenile justice system. *Crime and Delinquency, 44*(4), 561–589.

Acoca, L. (1999). Investing in girls: A 21st century strategy. *Juvenile Justice Journal, 6*(1), 3–13.

Acoca, L. (2000). *Educate don't incarcerate: Girls in the Florida and Duval County juvenile justice systems.* San Francisco: National Council on Crime and Delinquency.

Acoca, L., & Austin, J. (1996). *The crisis: Women in prison.* Unpublished manuscript. (Report submitted to the Charles E. Culpeper Foundation, available from the National Council on Crime and Delinquency)

Acoca, L., & Dedel, K. (1998). *No place to hide: Understanding and meeting the needs of girls in the California juvenile justice system.* San Francisco: National Council on Crime and Delinquency.

Addams, J. (1911). *Twenty years at Hull-House.* New York: Macmillan.

Adler, F. (1975). *Sisters in crime.* New York: McGraw-Hill.

Alexander, J. F., Pugh, C., & Parsons, B. (1998). Functional family therapy. In D. S. Elliott (Series Ed.), *Blueprints for violence prevention. Book Three.* Golden, CO: Venture; Denver, CO: Can M Press.

Alinsky, S. (1946). *Reveille for radicals.* Chicago: University of Chicago Press.

Altschuler, D., & Armstrong, T. (1984). Intervening with serious juvenile offenders. In R. Mathias, P. Demuro, & R. Allinson (Eds.), *Violent juvenile offenders* (pp. 187–206). San Francisco: National Council on Crime and Delinquency.

American Association of University Women. (1991). *Shortchanging girls, shortchanging America: A nationwide poll that assesses self-esteem, educational experiences, interest in math and science, and career aspirations of girls and boys ages 9–15.* Washington, DC: Author.

American Bar Association, & National Bar Association. (2001). *Justice by gender: The lack of appropriate prevention, diversion and treatment alternatives for girls in the justice system.* Washington, DC: Author.

Amnesty International. (1998, November 20). Betraying the young: Human rights violations against children in the US justice system. *United States of America: Rights for all.* Author.

Aos, S., Phipps, P., & Korinek, K. (1999). *Research findings on adult corrections' programs: A review.* Olympia: Washington State Institute for Public Policy.

Asian/Pacific Islander Youth Violence Prevention Center. (2001). *Asian/Pacific Islander communities: An agenda for positive action.* Oakland, CA: National Council on Crime and Delinquency.

Asian/Pacific Islander Youth Violence Prevention Center. (in press). *Under the microscope: Asian and Pacific Islander Youth in Oakland, Needs–Issues–Solutions.* Oakland, CA: National Council on Crime and Delinquency.

Austin, J., Elms, W., Krisberg, B., & Steel, B. (1991). *Unlocking juvenile corrections: Evaluating the Massachusetts Department of Youth Service.* San Francisco: National Council on Crime and Delinquency.

Austin, J., Krisberg, B., & DeComo, R. (1995). *Juveniles taken into custody: Fiscal year 1993. Statistics report.* San Francisco: National Council on Crime and Delinquency.

Austin, J., Krisberg, B., Joe, K., & Steele, P. (1988). *The impact of juvenile court sanctions.* San Francisco: National Council on Crime and Delinquency.

Baerger, D. R., Lyons, J. S., Quigley, P., & Griffin, E. (2001). Mental health service needs of male and female juvenile detainees. *Journal of the Center for Families, Children, & the Courts* (Judicial Council of California), *3*, 21–29.

Baird, S. C., Ereth, J., & Wagner, D. (1999). *Research-based risk assessment: Adding equity to CPS decision making.* Madison, WI: National Council on Crime and Delinquency, Children's Research Center.

Baird, S. C., Wagner, D., Caskey, R., & Neuenfeldt, D. (1995). *The Michigan Department of Social Services structured decision making system: An evaluation of its impact on child protective services.* Madison, WI: National Council on Crime and Delinquency, Children's Research Center.

Baird, S. C., Wagner, D., Healy, T., & Johnson, K. (1999). Risk assessment in child protective services: Consensus and actuarial model reliability. *Child Welfare, 78*(6), 723–748.

Bakal, Y. (1973). *Closing correctional institutions.* Lexington, MA: Lexington Books.

Barnard, D. E., Booth, C. L., Mitchell, S. K., & Telzrow, R. W. (1988). Newborn nursing models: A test of early intervention to high-risk infants and families. In E. Hibbs (Ed.), *Children and families: Studies in prevention and intervention* (pp. 63–81). Madison, CT: International Universities Press.

Barnes, H. E. (1926). *The repression of crime.* New York: George H. Doran.

Bartollas, C., Miller, S., & Dinitz, S. (1976). *Juvenile victimization: The institutional paradox.* New York: Wiley.

Barton, W. H., & Butts, J. A. (1988). *Intensive supervision in Wayne County: An alternative to state commitment for juvenile delinquents. Final report.* Ann Arbor: University of Michigan, Institute for Social Research.

Bazemore, G., & Maloney, D. (1994). Rehabilitating community service: Toward restorative service in a balanced justice system. *Federal Probation, 58,* 24–35.

Beccaria, C. (1963). *On crimes and punishments.* (H. Paolucci, Trans.). New York: Botts-Merrill. (Original work published 1764)

Beck, A., Kline, S., & Greenfeld, L. (1988). *Survey of youth in custody.* Washington, DC: U.S. Department of Justice, Bureau of Justice Statistics.

Benson, P. L. (1997). *All kids are our kids: What communities must do to raise caring and responsible children and adolescents.* San Francisco: Jossey-Bass.

Bentham, J. (1830). *The rationale of punishment*. London: R. Heward.

Bishop, D. M., & Frazier, C. E. (1992). Gender bias in juvenile justice processing: Implications of the JJDP act. *Journal of Criminal Law and Criminology, 82,* 1162–1186.

Bishop, D. M., Frazier, C., Lanza-Kaduce, L., & Winner, L. (1996). The transfer of juveniles to criminal court: Does it make a difference? *Crime and Delinquency, 42*(2), 171–191.

Blumstein, A. (1996). *Youth violence, guns, and illicit drug markets: A summary of a presentation*. Washington DC: U.S. Department of Justice, Office of Justice Programs, National Institute of Justice.

Borduin, C. M., Mann, B. J., Cone, L. T., Henggeler, S. W., Fucci, B. R., Blaske, D. M., & Williams, R. A. (1995). Multisystemic treatment of serious juvenile offenders: Long-term prevention of criminality and violence. *Journal of Consulting and Clinical Psychology, 63,* 569–578.

Brace, C. L. (1872). *The dangerous classes of New York*. New York: Wynkoop & Hallenbeck.

Brager, G., & Purcell, F. (1967). *Community action against poverty*. New Haven, CT: College and University Press.

Bremner, R., Barnard, J., Hareven, T. K., & Mennel, R. M. (1970). *Children and youth in America: A documentary history* (Vol. 1.). Cambridge, MA: Harvard University Press.

Bridges, G. S., & Steen, S. (1998). Racial disparities in official assessments of juvenile offenders: Attributional stereotypes as mediating mechanisms. *American Sociological Review, 63*(4), 554–570.

Brown, C. (1966). *Manchild in the promised land*. London: Cape.

Brown, L., & Gilligan, C. (1992). *Meeting at the crossroads*. New York: Ballantine.

Butts, J. A., & Connors-Beatty, D. J. (1993). The juvenile court's response to violent crime: 1985–1989. Washington, DC: U.S. Department of Justice, Office of Justice Programs, Office of Juvenile Justice and Delinquency Prevention.

Butts, J. A., & Poe-Yamagata, E. (1993). *Offenders in juvenile court, 1990.* Washington, DC: U.S. Department of Justice, Office of Justice Programs, Office of Juvenile Justice and Delinquency Prevention.

Chaiken, M. R., & Chaiken, J. M. (1987). *Selecting "career criminals" for priority prosecution*. Cambridge, MA: ABT.

Chesney-Lind, M. (1974, July). Juvenile delinquency: The sexualization of female crime. *Psychology Today,* 43–46.

Chesney-Lind, M. (1997). *The female offender: Girls, women, and crime*. Thousand Oaks, CA: Sage.

Chesney-Lind, M., & Shelden, R. G. (1992). *Girls: delinquency and juvenile justice*. Pacific Grove, CA: Brooks/Cole.

Chibnall, S. (2001, November). *National evaluation of the Title V Community Prevention Grants Program*. FS 200137. Washington, DC: U.S. Department of Justice, Office of Justice Programs, Office of Juvenile Justice and Delinquency Prevention.

Cicourel, A. V. (1968). *The social organization of juvenile justice*. New York: Wiley.

Clark, K. B., & Myrdal, G. (1965). *Dark ghetto: Dilemmas of social power*. Middletown, CT: Wesleyan University Press.

Cloward, R., & Piven, F. (1971). *Regulating the poor.* New York: Pantheon.

Coalition for Juvenile Justice. (2000). *Enlarging the healing circle: Ensuring justice for American Indian children.* Washington, DC: Author.

Coates, R. B., Miller, A. D., & Ohlin, L. E. (1978). *Diversity in a youth correctional system: Handling delinquents in Massachusetts.* Cambridge, MA: Ballinger.

Coben, S., & Ratner, L. (Eds.). (1970). *The development of an American culture.* Englewood Cliffs, NJ: Prentice Hall.

Coles, R. (1967). *Children of crisis: A study of courage and fear.* Boston: Little, Brown.

Commonwealth v. Fisher, 213 Pennsylvania 48 (1905).

Commonwealth v. M'Keagy (1831).

Community Research Associates. (1997). *Juvenile female offenders: A status of the states report.* Northglenn, CO: Author.

Crawford, R., Malamud, D., & Dumpson, J. R. (1970). Working with teenage gangs. In N. Johnson (Ed.), *The sociology of crime and delinquency.* New York: John Wiley.

Cronin, R., Bourque, B., Gragg, F., Mell, J., & McGrady, A. (1988). *Evaluation of the habitual, serious, and violent juvenile offender program: Executive summary.* Washington, DC: U.S. Department of Justice, Office of Juvenile Justice and Delinquency Prevention.

Dahmann, J. (1982). *Operation Hardcore, a prosecutorial response to violent gang criminality: Interim evaluation report.* Washington, DC: Mitre. (Reprinted from *The Modern Gang Reader,* by M. A. Klein, C. L. Maxson, & J. Miller, Eds., 1995, Los Angeles: Roxbury)

Davidson, W. S., Redner, R., Blakely, C. H., Mitchell, C. M., & Emshoff, J. G. (1987). Diversion of juvenile offenders: An experimental comparison. *Journal of Consulting and Clinical Psychology, 55*(1), 68–75.

Davidson, W. S., Seidman, E., Rappaport, J., Berck, P., Rhodes, W., & Herring, J. (1977). Diversion programs for juvenile offenders. *Social Work Research and Abstracts, 13,* 40–49.

DeComo, R., Tunis, S., Krisberg, B., & Herrera, N. (1993). *Juveniles taken into custody research program: FY 1992 annual report.* Washington, DC: U.S. Department of Justice, Office of Justice Programs, Office of Juvenile Justice and Delinquency Prevention.

Dedel, K. (1998). National profile of the organization of state juvenile corrections systems. *Crime and Delinquency, 44*(4), 507–525.

Developmental Research and Programs. (2000). *Communities that care: Prevention strategies: A research guide to what works.* Seattle, WA: Author.

Devoe, E. (1848). *The refuge system, or prison discipline applied to delinquency.* Sprague Pamphlet Collection. Cambridge, MA: Harvard Divinity School.

DiIulio, J. J. (1995a). Crime in America: It's going to get worse. *Reader's Digest,* 55–60.

DiIulio, J. J. (1995b). Arresting ideas. *Policy Review, 74*(5), 12.

DiIulio, J. J. (1996). They're coming: Florida's youth crime bomb. *Impact,* 25–27.

Dorfman, L., & Schiraldi, V. (2001). *Off balance: Youth, race & crime in the news.* Washington, DC: Building Blocks for Youth.

Dryfoos, J. G. (1990). *Adolescents at risk: Prevalence and prevention.* New York: Oxford University Press.

Du Bois, W. E. B. (1903). *The souls of black folk*. New York: Library of America.

Duxbury, E. (1972). *Youth bureaus in California: Progress report #3*. Sacramento: California Youth Authority.

Eigen, J. (1972). Punishing youth homicide offenders in Philadelphia. *Journal of Criminology and Criminal Law, 72*, 1072–1093.

Elikann, P. (1999). *Superpredators: The demonization of our children by the law*. New York: Insight.

Ellingston, J. (1955). *Protecting our children from criminal careers*. Englewood Cliffs, NJ: Prentice-Hall.

Elliott, D. S. (1994). Serious violent offenders: Onset, developmental course, and termination. *Criminology, 32*(1), 1–21.

Elliott, D. S., & Ageton, S. S. (1980). Reconciling race and class differences in self-reported and official estimates of delinquency. *American Sociological Review, 45*(1), 95–110.

Elliott, D. S., Huizinga, D., & Ageton, S. S. (1985). *Explaining delinquency and drug use*. Beverly Hills, CA: Sage.

Emerson, R. M. (1969). *Judging delinquents; context and process in juvenile court*. Chicago: Aldine.

Empey, L. T., & Erickson, M. L. (1972). *The Provo experiment: Evaluating community control of delinquency*. Lexington, MA: Lexington Books.

Empey, L. T., & Lubeck, S. G. (1971). *The Silverlake experiment; testing delinquency theory and community intervention*. Chicago: Aldine.

English, D. J. (1997). Current knowledge about CPS decision making. In T. D. Morton & W. Holder (Eds.), *Decision making in children's protective services: Advancing the state of the art*. Atlanta, GA: National Resource Center on Child Maltreatment.

Espiritu, Y. L. (1992). *Asian American panethnicity: Bridging institutions and identities*. Philadelphia: Temple University Press.

Ex parte Becknell, 51 California 692 (1897).

Ex parte Crouse, 4 Wharton (PA) 9 (1838).

Fagan, J. A. (1990). Treatment and reintegration of violent juvenile offenders: Experimental results. *Justice Quarterly, 7*(2), 233–263.

Fagan, J. A. (1991). *The comparative impacts of juvenile and criminal court sanctions on adolescent felony offenders: Final report*. Washington, DC: U.S. Department of Justice.

Fagan, J. A. (1995). Separating the men from the boys: The comparative advantage of juvenile versus criminal court sanctions on recidivism among adolescent felony offenders. In J. C. Howell, B. Krisberg, J. D. Hawkins, & J. J Wilson (Eds.), *Serious, violent, and chronic juvenile offenders: A sourcebook* (pp. 238–260). Thousand Oaks, CA: Sage.

Family Services Research Center. (1995). *Multisystemic therapy using home-based services: A clinically effective and cost effective strategy for treating serious clinical problems in youth*. Unpublished manuscript, Medical University of South Carolina, Department of Psychiatry and Behavioral Sciences, Charleston.

Federal Bureau of Investigation. (1996). *Uniform crime reports: Crime in the United States 1995*. Washington, DC: Criminal Justice Information Services Division.

Federal Bureau of Investigation. (1997). *Uniform crime reports 1993–1997.* Washington, DC: Criminal Justice Information Services Division.

Federal Bureau of Investigation. (1999). *Crime in the United States, 1998.* Washington, DC: Criminal Justice Information Services Division

Feld, B. C. (1977). *Neutralizing inmate violence: Juvenile offenders in institutions.* Cambridge, MA: Ballinger.

Feld, B. C. (1984). Criminalizing juvenile justice: Rules of procedure for the juvenile court. *Minnesota Law Review, 69*(2), 141–276.

Finckenauer, J. O., Gavin, P. W., Hovland, A., & Storvoll, E. (1999). *Scared straight: The panacea phenomenon revisited.* Prospect Heights, IL: Waveland Press.

Forer, L. G. (1970). *No one will lessen. How our legal system brutalizes the youthful poor.* New York: John Day.

Forst, M., Fagan, J., & Vivona, T. S. (1989). Youth in prisons and state training schools: Perceptions and consequences of the treatment-custody dichotomy. *Juvenile and Family Court Journal, 81,* 314–347.

Foucault, M. (1977). *Discipline and punish: The birth of the prison.* New York: Pantheon.

Fox, J. A. (1996). *Trends in juvenile violence: A report to the United States attorney general on current and future rates of juvenile offending.* Washington, DC: U.S. Department of Justice, Bureau of Justice Statistics.

Frazier, C. E. (1991). *Deep end juvenile justice placements or transfer to adult court by direct file?* Tallahassee: Florida Commission on Juvenile Justice.

Freitag, R., & Wordes, M. (2001). Improved decision making in child maltreatment cases. *Journal of the Center for Families, Children & the Courts, 3,* 75–85.

Gendreau, P., Little, T., & Goggin, C. (1996). A meta-analysis of the predictors of adult offender recidivism: What works. *Criminology, 34*(4), 575–607.

Gendreau, P., & Ross, R. (1987). Revivification of rehabilitation: Evidence from the 1980s. *Justice Quarterly, 4,* 349–407.

Glueck, S., & Glueck, E. T. (1934). *One thousand juvenile delinquents: Their treatment by court and clinic.* Cambridge, MA: Harvard University Press.

Goodstein, L., & Sontheimer, H. (1987). *A study of the impact of ten Pennsylvania residential placements on juvenile recidivism.* Shippensberg, PA: The Center for Juvenile Justice Training and Research.

Gossett, T. (1963). *Race: The history of an idea in America.* Dallas, TX: Southern Methodist University Press.

Gottfredson, D. C., & Barton, W. H. (1992). *Deinstitutionalization of juvenile offenders.* College Park: University of Maryland.

Greene, Peters, & Associates. (1998). *Guiding principles for promising female programming: An inventory of best practices.* Washington, DC: U.S. Department of Justice, Office of Justice Programs, Office of Juvenile Justice and Delinquency Prevention.

Greenwood, P. W., Model, K. E., Rydell, C. P., & Chiesa, J. (1996). *Diverting children from a life of crime: Measuring costs and benefits* (Rev. ed.). Santa Monica, CA: Rand.

Greenwood, P. W., Rydell, C. P., Abrahamse, A. F., Caulkins, J. P., Chiesa, J. P., Model, K. E., et al. (1994). *Three strikes and you're out: Estimated benefits and costs of California's new mandatory sentencing law.* Santa Monica, CA: Rand.

Greenwood, P. W., & Turner, S. (1993). Evaluation of the Paint Creek Youth Center: A residential program for serious delinquents. *Criminology, 31*(2), 263–279.

Greenwood, P. W., & Zimring, F. (1985). *One more chance: The pursuit of promising intervention strategies for chronic juvenile offenders.* Santa Monica, CA: Rand.

Haapanen, R. A. (1988). *Selective incapacitation and the serious offender: A longitudinal study of criminal career patterns.* Sacramento: California Department of the Youth Authority, Program Research and Review Division.

Hagedorn, J. M. (1988). *People & folks: Gangs, crime, and the underclass in a rustbelt city.* Chicago: Lakeview Press.

Hahlweg, D., Markman, H. J., Thurmaier, F., Engl, J., Eckert, V. (1998). Prevention of marital distress: Results of a German prospective longitudinal study. *Journal of Family Psychology, 12*(4), 543.

Haley, A. (1965). *The autobiography of Malcolm X, with assistance from Alex Haley.* New York: Grove Press.

Hammond, W. R., & Yung, B. R. (1993). *Evaluation and activity report: Positive adolescents choices training program (PACT).* Dayton, OH: Wright State University, School of Professional Psychology.

Hamparian, D. (1982). *Major issues in juvenile justice information and training. Youth in adult courts: Between two worlds.* Washington, DC: U.S. Government Printing Office.

Hamparian, D., & Leiber, M. (1997). *Disproportionate confinement of minority juveniles in secure facilities: 1996 national report.* Champaign, IL: Community Research Associates.

Handlin, O. (1959). *The newcomers.* New York: Doubleday.

Hartney, C., Wordes, M., & Krisberg, B. (2002). *Health care for our troubled youth: Provision of services in the foster care and juvenile justice systems of California.* Commissioned by the California Endowment. Oakland, CA: National Council on Crime and Delinquency.

Hawes, J. (1971). *Children in urban society: Juvenile delinquency in nineteenth century America.* New York: Oxford University Press.

Hawkins, J. D., & Catalano, R. F. (1992). *Communities that care: Action for drug abuse prevention.* San Francisco: Jossey-Bass.

Hawkins, J. D., & Weis, J. G. (1985). The social development model: An integrated approach to delinquency prevention. *Journal of Primary Prevention, 6*(2), 73–97.

Healy, W. (1915). *The individual delinquent: A textbook of diagnosis and prognosis for all concerned in understanding offenders.* Boston: Little, Brown.

Healy, W. (1917). *Mental conflicts and misconduct.* Boston: Little, Brown.

Healy, W., Bronner, A., & Shimberg, M. (1935). The close of another chapter in criminology. *Mental Hygiene, 19,* 208–222.

Henggeler, S. W., Melton, G. B., & Smith, L. A. (1992). Family preservation using multisystem therapy: An effective alternative to incarcerating serious juvenile offenders. *Journal of Consulting and Clinical Psychology, 60,* 953–961.

Henry, B., Moffitt, T. E., Robins, L., Earls, F., & Silva, P. A. (1993). Early family predictors of child and adolescent antisocial behavior: Who are the mothers of delinquents? *Criminal Behavior & Mental Health, 3,* 97–118.

Herrnstein, R. J., & Murray, C. (1994). *The bell curve: Intelligence and class structure in American life.* New York: Free Press.

Higham, J. (1971). *Strangers in the land.* New York: Atheneum.

Horachek, H. J., Ramey, C. T., Campell, F. A., Hoffman, K. P., & Fletcher, R. H. (1987). Predicting school failure and assessing early intervention with high risk children. *Journal of the American Academy of Child and Adolescent Psychiatry, 26*(5), 758–763.

Howell, J. C. (Ed.). (1995). *Guide for implementing the comprehensive strategy for serious, violent, and chronic juvenile offenders.* Washington, DC: Office of Justice Programs, Office of Juvenile Justice and Delinquency Prevention.

Howell, J. C. (1997). *Juvenile justice and youth violence.* Thousand Oaks, CA: Sage.

Howell, J. C. (1998). *Youth gangs: An overview.* Washington, DC: U.S. Department of Justice, Office of Justice Programs, Office of Juvenile Justice and Delinquency Prevention.

Howell, J. C. (2003). *Preventing & reducing juvenile delinquency: A comprehensive framework.* Thousand Oaks, CA: Sage.

Howell, J. C., Krisberg, B., Hawkins, J. D., & Wilson, J. J. (Eds.). (1995). *Serious, violent, & chronic juvenile offenders: A sourcebook.* Thousand Oaks, CA: Sage.

Hoyt, S., & Scherer, D. G. (1998). Female juvenile delinquency: Misunderstood by the juvenile justice system, neglected by social science. *Law and Human Behavior, 22*(1), 81–107.

Hoytt, E. H., Schiraldi, V., Smith, B. V., & Ziedenberg, J. (2001). *Reducing racial disparities in juvenile detention.* Baltimore: Annie E. Casey Foundation.

Hsia, H. M. (2001, May). *An overview of the Title V community prevention grants program.* Washington, DC: U.S. Department of Justice, Office of Justice Programs, Office of Juvenile Justice and Delinquency Prevention.

Hubner, J., & Wolfson, J. (1996). *Somebody else's children: The courts, the kids, and the struggle to save America's troubled families.* New York: Crown.

Hughes, R. (1987). *The fatal shore.* New York: Knopf.

Huizinga, D., & Elliott, D. S. (1987). Juvenile offenders: Prevalence, offender incidence, and arrest rates by race. *Crime and Delinquency, 33*(2), 206–223.

Huxley, A. (1937). *Ends and means.* New York: Harper & Brothers.

In re Gault, 387 U.S. 1 (1967).

In re Winship, 397 U.S. 358 (1970).

Johnson, L. D., & Bechman, J. G. (1981). *Highlights from student drug use in America 1975–1980.* Washington, DC: U.S. National Institute on Drug Abuse, U.S. Government Printing Office.

Jones, M. A., & Krisberg, B. (1994). *Images and reality: Juvenile crime, youth violence, and public policy.* San Francisco: National Council on Crime and Delinquency.

Jordan, W. (1974). *The white man's burden.* New York: Oxford University Press.

Juszkiewicz, J. (2000). *Youth crime/adult time: Is justice served?* Washington, DC: Building Blocks for Youth.

Katz, J. (1988). *Seductions of crime: Moral and sensual attractions in doing evil.* New York: Basic Books.

Kelley, B. T., Thornberry, T. P., & Smith, C. A. (1997). *In the wake of childhood maltreatment.* Washington, DC: U.S. Department of Justice, Office of Justice Programs, Office of Juvenile Justice and Delinquency Prevention.

Kent v. United States, 383 U.S. 541 (1966).

Kittrie, N. (1971). *The right to be different: Deviance and enforced therapy.* Baltimore: Johns Hopkins Press.

Klein, M. (1969, July). Gang cohesiveness, delinquency, and a street-work program. *Journal of Research on Crime and Delinquency,* 143.

Klein, M. W. (1995). *The American street gang: Its nature, prevalence, and control.* New York: Oxford University Press.

Kobrin, S. (1970). The Chicago area project: A twenty-five year assessment. In N. Johnson (Ed.), *The sociology of crime and delinquency.* New York: Wiley.

Kolbo, J. R., Blakely, E. H., & Engleman, D. (1996). Children who witness domestic violence: A review of empirical literature. *Journal of Interpersonal Violence,* 11(2), 281–293.

Krisberg, B. (1971). *Urban leadership training: An ethnographic study of 22 gang leaders.* Unpublished doctoral dissertation, University of Pennsylvania, Philadelphia.

Krisberg, B. (1975). *Crime and privilege.* Englewood Cliffs, NJ: Prentice Hall.

Krisberg, B. (1981). *National evaluation of prevention: Final report.* San Francisco: National Council on Crime and Delinquency.

Krisberg, B. (1992). *Excellence in adolescent care: The Thomas O'Farrell Youth Center (TOYC) Marriottsville, MD.* Oakland, CA: National Council on Crime and Delinquency.

Krisberg, B. (1997). *The impact of the justice system on serious, violent, and chronic juvenile offenders.* San Francisco: National Council on Crime and Delinquency.

Krisberg, B. (2003). The end of the juvenile court: Prospects for our children. In D. Hawkins, S. Meyers, & R. Stone (Eds.), *Crime control and social justice: The delicate balance.* Westport, CT: Greenwood Press.

Krisberg, B., & Austin, J. (1981). Wider, stronger and different nets: The dialectics of criminal justice reform. *Journal of Research on Crime and Delinquency, 18,* 165–196.

Krisberg, B., & Austin, J. (1993). *Reinventing juvenile justice.* Thousand Oaks, CA: Sage.

Krisberg, B., Austin, J., Joe, K., & Steel, P. (1988). *A court that works: The impact of juvenile court sanction.* San Francisco: National Council on Crime and Delinquency.

Krisberg, B., Austin, J., & Steele, P. (1991). *Unlocking juvenile corrections.* San Francisco: National Council on Crime and Delinquency.

Krisberg, B., Barry, G., & Sharrock, E. (2004). *Reforming juvenile justice through comprehensive community planning.* Oakland, CA: National Council on Crime and Delinquency.

Krisberg, B., & Breed, A. (1986, December). Juvenile corrections: Is there a future? *Corrections Today, 48*(8), 14–20.

Krisberg, B., Currie, E., Onek, D., & Wiebush, R. G. (1995). Graduated sanctions for serious, violent, and chronic juvenile offenders. In J. C. Howell, B. Krisberg, J. D. Hawkins, and J. J. Wilson (Eds.), *Serious, violent, & chronic juvenile offenders: A sourcebook* (pp. 142–170). Thousand Oaks, CA: Sage.

Krisberg, B., DeComo, R., Wordes, M., & Del Rosario, D. (1995). *Juveniles taken into custody research program: FY 1995 annual report.* San Francisco: National Council on Crime and Delinquency.

Krisberg, B., Litsky, P., & Schwartz, I. (1984). Youth in confinement: Justice by geography. *Journal of Research in Crime and Delinquency, 21*(2), 153–181.

Krisberg, B., Noya, M., Jones, M., & Wallen, J. (2001). *Juvenile detention alternatives initiative: Evaluation Report.* Unpublished manuscript.

Krisberg, B., Schwartz, I., Fishman, G., Eisikovits, Z., Guttman, E., & Joe, K. (1987). The incarceration of minority youth. *Crime and Delinquency, 33*(2), 173–205.

Land, K. C., Land, P. L., & Williams, J. R. (1990). Something that works in juvenile justice. *Evaluation Review, 14*(6), 574–606.

Langan, P. A., & Solari, R. (1993). *National judicial reporting program, 1990.* Washington, DC: U.S. Department of Justice, Office of Justice Programs, Bureau of Justice Statistics.

Latessa, E. J., Turner, M. G., Moon, M. M. (1998). *A statewide evaluation of the RECLAIM Ohio Initiative: Executive summary.* Columbus: Ohio Department of Youth Services.

Lawrence, C. (1987). The id, the ego and equal protection: Reckoning with unconscious racism. *Stanford Law Review, 39*, 317–388.

Le, T., Arifuku, I., Louie, C., & Krisberg, M. (2001). *Not invisible: Asian Pacific Islander juvenile arrests in San Francisco County.* Oakland, CA: National Council on Crime and Delinquency, Asian/Pacific Islander Youth Violence Prevention Center.

Le, T., Arifuku, I., Louie, C., Krisberg, M., & Tang, E. (2001). *Not invisible: Asian Pacific Islander juvenile arrests in Alameda County.* Oakland, CA: National Council on Crime and Delinquency, Asian/Pacific Islander Youth Violence Prevention Center.

Lee, L. C., & Zahn, G. (1998). Psychological status of children and youths. In L. C. Lee, & N. Zane (Eds.), *Handbook of Asian American psychology.* Thousand Oaks, CA: Sage.

Lee, V. E., & Croninger, R. G. (1996). The social organization of safe high schools. In K. M. Borman, P. W. Cookson, Jr., & J. Z. Spade (Eds.), *Implementing educational reform: Sociological perspectives on educational policy* (pp. 359–392). Norwood, NJ: Ablex.

Leffert, N., Benson, P. L., Scales, P. C., Sharma, A. R., Drake, D. R., & Blyth, D. A. (1998). Developmental assets: Measurement and prediction of risk behaviors among adolescents. *Applied Developmental Science, 2*(4), 209–230.

Lejins, P. P. (1967). The field of prevention. In W. E. Amos & C. E. Wellford (Eds.), *Delinquency prevention: Theory and practice* (pp. 1–21). Englewood Cliffs, NJ: Prentice-Hall.

Lemert, E. M. (1951). *Social pathology: A systematic approach to the theory of sociopathic behavior.* New York: McGraw Hill.

Lemert, E. M., & Dill, F. (1978). *Offenders in the community: The probation subsidy in California.* Lexington, MA: Lexington Books.

Lemert, E. M., & Rosenberg, J. (1948). *The administration of justice to minority groups in Los Angeles County.* Berkeley: University of California Press.

Leonard, K. K., Pope, C. E., & Feyerherm, W. H. (Eds.). (1995). *Minorities in juvenile justice.* Thousand Oaks, CA: Sage.

Lerman, P. (1975). *Community treatment and social control: A critical analysis of juvenile correctional policy.* Chicago: University of Chicago Press.

Lerner, G. (1973). *Black women in white America.* New York: Random House Vintage.

Liazos, A. (1974). Class oppression and the juvenile justice system. *Insurgent Sociologist, 1,* 2–22.

Lindsey, B. B., & Borough, R. (1931). *The dangerous life.* New York: Arno.

Lipsey, M. W. (1992). The effect of treatment on juvenile delinquents: Results from meta-analysis. In F. Loesel, D. Bender, & T. Bliesener (Eds.), *Psychology and law: International perspectives.* (pp. 131–143). Berlin, NY: Walter de Gruyter.

Lipsey, M. W., & Wilson, D. B. (1998). Effective interventions with serious juvenile offenders: A synthesis of research. In R. Loeber & D.P. Farrington (Eds.), *Serious and violent juvenile offenders: Risk factors and successful interventions* (pp. 313–345). Thousand Oaks, CA: Sage.

Lipsey, M. W., & Wilson, D. B. (2001). *Practical meta-analysis.* Thousand Oaks, CA: Sage.

Loeber, R., & Farrington, D. P. (Eds.). (1998). *Serious and violent juvenile offenders: Risk factors and successful interventions.* Thousand Oaks, CA: Sage.

Loeber, R., & Farrington, D. P. (Eds.). (2001). *Child delinquents: Development, intervention, and service needs.* Thousand Oaks, CA: Sage.

Loeber, R., & Hay, D. F. (1997). Key issues in the development of aggression and violence from early childhood to early adulthood. *Annual Review of Psychology, 48,* 371–410.

Lubove, R. (1965). *The professional altruist: The emergence of social work as a career, 1880–1930.* Cambridge, MA: Harvard University Press.

MacKenzie, D. L. (2000). Evidence-based corrections: Identifying what works. *Crime & Delinquency, 46,* 457–471.

MacKenzie, D. L., Grover, A. R., Armstrong, G. S., & Mitchell, O. (2001). *National study comparing the environments of boot camps with traditional facilities for juvenile offender.* Washington, DC: U.S. Department of Justice, Office of Justice Programs, National Institute of Justice.

Maguire, K., & Pastore, A. (Eds.). (2000). *Sourcebook of criminal justice statistics.* Washington, DC: U.S. Department of Justice, Bureau of Justice Statistics.

Males, M. A., & Macallair, D. (2000). *The color of justice: An analysis of juvenile adult court transfers in California.* San Francisco: Justice Policy Institute.

Mann, C. R. (1984). *Female crime and delinquency.* Tuscaloosa: University of Alabama Press.

Marans, S., Adnopoz, J., Berkman, M., Esserman, D., MacDonald, D., Nagler, S., et al. (1995). *The police-mental health partnership: A community-based response to urban violence.* New Haven, CT: Yale University Press.

Markman, H. J., Renick, M. J., Floyd, F. J., Stanley, S. M., & Clements, M. (1993). Preventing marital distress through effective communication and conflict management: A 4- and 5-year follow-up. *Journal of Consulting and Clinical Psychology, 61*(1), 70–77.

Marris, P., & Rein, M. (1967). *Dilemmas of social reform: Poverty and community action in the United States.* New York: Atherton.

Martinson, R. (1974). What works? Questions and answers about prison reform. *Public Interest, 35,* 22–54.

Mathias, R. A., DeMuro, P., & Allinson, R. S. (Eds.). (1984). *Violent juvenile offenders: An anthology.* San Francisco: National Council on Crime and Delinquency.

Mathieson, T. (1965). *The defences of the weak.* London: Travistock.

Maton, K., Seifert, K., & Zapert, K. (1991). *Choice program evaluation: Preliminary findings.* Catonsville: University of Maryland, Department of Psychology.

Mattick, H., & Caplan, W. S. (1967). Stake animals, loud-talking and leadership in do-nothing and do-something situations. In M. Klein (Ed.), *Juvenile gangs in context* (pp. 121–135). Englewood Cliffs, NJ: Prentice Hall.

Mayer, J. (1994). *Girls in the Maryland juvenile justice system: Findings of the female population taskforce.* Presentation to the Gender Specific Services Training, Minneapolis, MN.

McKelvey, B. (1972). *American prisons.* Montclair, NJ: Patterson Smith.

McKiever v. Pennsylvania, 403 U.S. 528 (1971).

Mead, G. H. (1961). The psychology of punitive justice. In T. Parsons (Ed.), *Theories of society* (pp. 878–894). Glencoe, IL: Free Press.

Melton, A. P. (1998). American Indians: Traditional and contemporary tribal justice. In C. R. Mann & M. S. Zatz (Eds.), *Images of color, images of crime: Readings* (pp. 58–71). Los Angeles: Roxbury.

Mennel, R. (1973). *Thorns and thistles.* Hanover: The University of New Hampshire Press.

Miller, J. G. (1991). *Last one over the wall: The Massachusetts experiment in closing reform schools.* Columbus: Ohio State University Press.

Moone, J. (1997). *Counting what counts: The census of juveniles in residential placement.* Washington, DC: U.S. Department of Justice, Office of Justice Programs, Office of Juvenile Justice and Delinquency Prevention.

Moore, J. W., & Hagedorn, J. (1988). Youth gangs: Milwaukee and Los Angeles compared. *Research and Opinion, 5*(1).

Moore, J. W., & Hagedorn, J. (2001). *Female gangs: A focus on research.* Washington, DC: U.S. Department of Justice, Office of Justice Programs, Office of Juvenile Justice and Delinquency Prevention.

Morris, M. W. (2002, June). Black girls on lockdown. *Essence, 33*(2), 186.

Moynihan, D. (1969). *Maximum feasible misunderstanding.* New York: Free Press.

Murray, C. A., & Cox, L. (1979). *Beyond probation: Juvenile corrections and the chronic delinquent.* Beverly Hills, CA: Sage.

National Advisory Committee on Criminal Justice Standards and Goals. (1976). *Juvenile justice and delinquency prevention: Report of the task force on juvenile justice and delinquency prevention.* Washington, DC: Author.

National Commission on the Causes and Prevention of Violence. (1969). *To establish justice, to ensure domestic tranquility.* Washington, DC: Government Printing Office.

National Council on Crime and Delinquency. (1997). *Reducing crime in America.* San Francisco: Author.

National Council on Crime and Delinquency. (2000). *Promising approaches for graduated sanctions.* Oakland, CA: Author.

National Council on Crime and Delinquency. (2001). *What works?: The R.Y.S.E. program, Alameda County Probation Department.* Oakland, CA: Author.

National Council on Crime and Delinquency. (in press). *An analysis of Asian and Pacific Islander youth in the California Youth Authority.* Oakland, CA: Author.

Norman, S. (1972). *The youth service bureau: A key to delinquency prevention.* Hackensack, NJ: National Council on Crime and Delinquency.

Obeidallah, D. A., & Earls, F. J. (1999, July). *Adolescent girls: The role of depression in the development of delinquency* [Research Preview]. Washington, DC: U.S. Department of Justice, Office of Justice Programs, National Institute of Justice.

O'Connor, J. (1973). *The fiscal crisis of the state.* New York: St. Martin's Press.

Office of Juvenile Justice and Delinquency Prevention. (1998, December). *Guide for implementing the balanced and restorative justice model.* Washington, DC: U.S. Department of Justice.

Office of Juvenile Justice and Delinquency Prevention. (1999). *Juvenile arrests 1998.* Washington, DC: U.S. Department of Justice.

Olds, D. L., Henderson, C. R., Chamberlin, R., & Tatelbaum, R. (1986). Preventing child abuse and neglect: A randomized trial of nurse home visitation. *Pediatrics, 78,* 65–78.

Olds, D. L., Hill, P., & Rumsey, E. (1998). *Prenatal and early childhood nurse home visitation.* Washington, DC: U.S. Department of Justice, Office of Justice Programs, Office of Juvenile Justice and Delinquency Prevention.

Olds, D. L., & Kitzman, H. (1993). Review of research on home visiting for pregnant women and parents of young children. *The Future of Children, 3*(3), 53–92.

Ong, P., & Miller, D. (2002). *Economic needs of Asian Americans and Pacific Islanders in distressed areas: Establishing baseline information.* Washington, DC: U.S Department of Commerce, Research and National Technical Assistance, Economic Development Administration.

Osofsky, J. D. (2001). *Addressing youth victimization: Action plan update.* Washington, DC: U.S. Department of Justice, Office of Justice Programs, Office of Juvenile Justice and Delinquency Prevention, Coordinating Council on Juvenile Justice and Delinquency Prevention.

Palmer, T. (1971). California's community treatment program for delinquency adolescents. *Journal of Research in Crime and Delinquency, 8*(1), 74–82.

Palmer, T. (1992). *The re-emergence of correctional interventions.* Newbury Park, CA: Sage.

Palmer, T. (1996). Programmatic and nonprogrammatic aspects of successful intervention. In A. T. Harland (Ed.), *Choosing correctional options that work: Defining the demand and evaluating the supply* (pp. 131–182). Thousand Oaks, CA: Sage.

Parent, D. G., Lieter, V., Kennedy, S., Livens, L., Wentworth, D., & Wilcox, S. (1994). *Conditions of confinement: Juvenile detention and corrections facilities: Research report.* Washington, DC: U.S. Department of Justice, Office of Justice Programs, Office of Juvenile Justice and Delinquency Prevention.

Parry, D. (1996). Race and community in juvenile justice decision making: Native Americans and the convergence of minority status and rural residence. *Social Pathology, 2*(2), 120–153.

Pasawerat, J. (1991). *Identifying Milwaukee youth in critical need of intervention: Lessons from the past, measure for the future.* Milwaukee: University of Wisconsin, Employment and Training Institute.

The People v. Turner, 55 Illinois 280 (1870).

Perkins, C. (1994). *National corrections reporting program, 1992.* Washington, DC: U.S. Department of Justice, Office of Justice Programs, Office of Juvenile Justice and Delinquency Prevention.

Peters, M., Thomas, D., & Zamberlan, C. (1997). *Boot camps for juvenile offenders: Program summary.* Washington, DC: U.S. Department of Justice, Office of Justice Programs, Office of Juvenile Justice and Delinquency Prevention.

Peterson, D. M., & Truzzi, M. (Eds.). (1972). *Criminal life: Views from the inside.* Englewood Cliffs, NJ: Prentice-Hall.

Pickett, R. (1969). *House of refuge: Origins of juvenile justice reform in New York, 1815–1857.* Syracuse, NY: Syracuse University Press.

Piliavin, I., & Briar, S. (1964). Police encounters with juveniles. *American Journal of Sociology, 70*(2), 206–214.

Platt, A. (1968). *The child savers: The invention of delinquency.* Chicago: Chicago University Press.

Podkopacz, M. R., & Feld, B. C. (1996). The end of the line: An empirical study of judicial waiver. *Journal of Criminal Law and Criminology. 86*(2), 449–492.

Poe-Yamagata, E., & Butts, J. A. (1996). *Female offenders in the juvenile justice system.* Pittsburgh, PA: National Center for Juvenile Justice.

Poe-Yamagata, E., & Jones, M. (2000). *And justice for some.* New York: National Council on Crime and Delinquency.

Poe-Yamagata, E., Wordes, M., & Krisberg, B. (2002). *Young women and delinquency: Refining the research agenda.* A concept paper submitted to the MacArthur Foundation. Available from the National Council on Crime and Delinquency.

Pope, C. E., Lovell, R., & Hsia, H. M. (2002). *Disproportionate minority confinement: A review of the literature from 1989 through 2001.* Washington, DC: U.S. Department of Justice, Office of Justice Programs, Office of Juvenile Justice and Delinquency Prevention.

Pound, R. (1957). *Guide to juvenile court judges.* New York: National Probation and Parole Association.

President's Advisory Commission on Asian Americans and Pacific Islanders. (2001). *A people looking forward: Action for access and partnerships in the 21st century.* Rockville, MD: White House Initiative on Asian Americans and Pacific Islanders.

President's Commission on Law Enforcement and the Administration of Justice. (1967). *The challenge of crime in a free society.* Washington, DC: Government Publishing Office.

Puzzanchera, C., Stahl, A. L., Finnegan, T. A., Snyder, H. N., Poole, R. S., & Tierney, N. (2000). *Juvenile court statistics 1997.* Pittsburgh, PA: National Center for Juvenile Justice.

Rhine, E. (1996). Something works: Recent research on effective correctional programming. *The State of Corrections: Proceedings of the American Correctional Association Annual Conferences, 1995.*

Richette, L. A. (1969). *The throwaway children.* Philadelphia: Lippincott.

Rothman, D. (1971). *The discovery of the asylum.* Boston: Little, Brown.

Rusche, G., & Kirchheimer, O. (1939). *Punishment and social structure.* New York: Columbia University Press.

Ryan, W. (1971). *Blaming the victim.* New York: Random House.

Sanchez-Jankowski, M. S. (1991). *Islands in the street: Gangs & American urban society.* Berkeley: University of California Press.

Sanders, W. B. (1970). *Juvenile offenders for a thousand years.* Chapel Hill: University of North Carolina.

Scahill, M. C. (2000). Female delinquency cases, 1997. *OJJDP Fact Sheet #16.* Washington, DC: U.S. Department of Justice, Office of Justice Programs, Office of Juvenile Justice and Delinquency Prevention.

Schall v. Martin, 467 U.S. 253 (1984).

Schur, E. M. (1973). *Radical nonintervention: Rethinking the delinquency problem.* Englewood Cliffs, NJ: Prentice-Hall.

Schwartz, I. M., & Barton, W. H. (Eds.). (1994). *Reforming juvenile detention: No more hidden closets.* Columbus: Ohio State University Press.

Sechrest, D. (1970). *The community approach.* Berkeley: University of California, School of Criminology.

Sellin, J. T. (1976). *Slavery and the penal system.* New York: Elsevier.

Sellin, T. (1944). *Pioneering in penology.* Philadelphia: University of Pennsylvania Press.

Shaffer, A. (1971). The Cincinnati social unity experiment. *Social Service Review, 45,* 159–171.

Shakur, S. (1993). *Monster: The autobiography of an L.A. gang member.* New York: Atlantic Monthly Press.

Shaw, C. R. (1930). *The jack-roller, a delinquent boy's own story* [Series title: Behavior research fund monographs]. Chicago: The University of Chicago Press.

Shaw, C. R. (1938). *Brothers in crime* [Series title: Behavior research fund monographs]. Chicago: University of Chicago Press.

Shaw, R., & McKay, L. (Eds.). (1942). *Juvenile delinquency and urban areas.* Chicago: University of Chicago Press.

Sherman, L. (1990). Police crackdowns. *National Institute of Justice Reports, 219,* 2–6.

Sherman, L. W., Gottfredson, D., McKenzie, D. L., Eck, J., Reuter, P., & Bushway, S. (1997). *Preventing crime: What works, what doesn't, what's promising. Report to the U.S. Congress.* Washington, DC: U.S. Department of Justice, Office of Justice Programs, National Institute of Justice.

Singer, S., & McDowall, D. (1988). Criminalizing delinquency: The deterrent effects of the New York juvenile offender law. *Law and Society Review, 22,* 521–535.

Smith, B. (1998). Children in custody: 20-year trends in juvenile detention, correctional, and shelter facilities. *Crime and Delinquency, 44*(4), 526–543.

Snyder, H. (1999). *Juvenile arrests 1998.* Washington, DC: U.S. Department of Justice, Office of Justice Programs, Office of Juvenile Justice and Delinquency Prevention.

Snyder, H., Finnegan, T., Stahl, A., & Poole, R. (1999). *Easy access to juvenile court statistics: 1988–1997* [data presentation and analysis package]. Pittsburgh, PA: National Center for Juvenile Justice (producer); Washington, DC: Office of Juvenile Justice and Delinquency Prevention (distributor).

Snyder, H., & Sickmund, M. (1999). *Juvenile offenders and victims: 1999 national report.* Washington, DC: U.S. Department of Justice, Office of Justice Programs, Office of Juvenile Justice and Delinquency Prevention.

Sok, C. W. (2001). Southeast Asian Americans and education. *The Bridge, 19,* 1–2.

Spergel, I. A., & Grossman, S. F. (1996). *Evaluation of a gang violence reduction project: A comprehensive and integrated approach.* Chicago: University of Chicago, School of Social Service Administration.

Stahl, A. (1998). *Delinquency cases in juvenile courts: Fact sheet #79, 1995.* Washington, DC: U.S. Department of Justice, Office of Justice Programs, Office of Juvenile Justice and Delinquency Prevention.

Stamp, K. M. (1956). *The peculiar institution.* New York: Random House.

State of California, Department of the Youth Authority. (n.d.). *A comparison of first commitment characteristics 1990–2001.* Sacramento, CA: Administrative Services Branch, Research Division, Ward Information, and Parole Research Bureau.

State v. Ray, 63 New Hampshire 405 (1886).

Steinhart, D. (1988). California legislature ends the jailing of children: The story of a policy reversal. *Crime and Delinquency, 32*(2), 169–189.

Steinhart, D. (1994, August). Assessing the need for secure detention: A planning approach. *NCCD Focus.* San Francisco: The National Council on Crime and Delinquency.

Streib, V. L. (1987). *Death penalty for juveniles.* Indianapolis: Indiana University Press.

Strom, K. (2000). *Profile of state prisoners under age 18.* Washington, DC: U.S. Department of Justice, Office of Justice Programs, Bureau of Justice Statistics.

Sue, S., & Kitano, H. L. (Issue Eds.). (1973). Asian Americans: A success story? *Journal of Social Issues, 29*(2).

Takagi, P. (1974). The correctional system. *Crime and Social Justice, 2,* 82–87.

Takagi, R. T. (1989). *Strangers from a different shore: A history of Asian Americans.* Boston: Little Brown.

Thomas, P. (1967). *Down these mean streets.* New York: Vintage.

Thornberry, T. P. (1994). *Violent families and youth violence: Fact sheet #21.* Washington, DC: U.S. Department of Justice, Office of Justice Programs, Office of Juvenile Justice and Delinquency Prevention.

Thornberry, T. P., Huizinga, D., & Loeber, R. (1995). The prevention of serious delinquency and violence: Implications from the program of research on the causes and correlates of delinquency. In J. C. Howell, B. Krisberg, D. Hawkins, & J. J. Wilson (Eds.), *Serious, violent, & chronic juvenile offenders: A sourcebook* (pp. 213–237). Thousand Oaks, CA: Sage.

Thrasher, F. M. (1927). *The gang.* Chicago: University of Chicago Press.

Tollett, T. (1987). *A comparative study of Florida delinquency commitment programs.* Tallahassee: Florida Department of Health and Rehabilitative Services.

Torbet, P., Gable, R., Hurst, I., IV, Montgomery, L., Szymanski, L., & Thomas, D. (1996). *State responses to serious and violent juvenile crime.* Washington, DC: U.S. Department of Justice, Office of Justice Programs, Office of Juvenile Justice and Delinquency Prevention.

U.S. Department of Health and Human Services, Administration of Children, Youth and Families. (1999). *Child maltreatment 1997: Reports from the states to the National Child Abuse and Neglect Data System.* Washington, DC: U.S. Government Printing Office.

U.S. Department of Health, Education, and Welfare. (1973). *National study of youth service bureaus—Final report.* Washington, DC: California Youth Authority.

Villarruel, F. A., Walker N. E. (with Minifee, P., Rivera-Vazquez, O., Peterson, S., & Perry, K.). (2002). ¿Dónde está la justicia? A call to action on behalf of Latino and Latina youth in the U.S. justice system. Lansing: Michigan State University Institute for Children, Youth, & Families.

Walker, J., Albert, P., Cardarelli, P., & Billingsley, D. (1976). The theory and practice of delinquency prevention in the United States: Review, synthesis and assessment. Columbus: Ohio State University, Center for Vocational Education.

Walker, M. (1969). Jubilee. New York: Bantam.

Weiner, N. A. (1996). The priority prosecution of the serious habitual juvenile offender: Roadblocks to early warning, early intervention, and maximum effectiveness—the Philadelphia study. Philadelphia: University of Pennsylvania, School of Social Work, Center for the Study of Youth Policy.

Weinstein, J. (1968). The corporate ideal in the liberal state. Boston: Beacon Press.

Weiss, F. L., Nicholson, H. J., & Cretella, M. M. (1996). Prevention and parity: Girls in juvenile justice. New York: Girls Incorporated Nation Resource Center.

Weissman, J. (1969). Community development in the mobilization for youth. New York: Association Press.

White, J. (1985). The comparative dispositions study: A report. Washington, DC: U.S. Department of Justice, Office of Justice Programs, Office of Juvenile Justice and Delinquency Prevention.

Widom, C. S. (1989). Does violence beget violence? A critical examination of the literature. Psychological Bulletin, 106, 3–28.

Widom, C. S. (1992). The cycle of violence. Washington, DC: U.S. Department of Justice, Office of Justice Programs, National Institute of Justice.

Widom, C. S. (1995). Victims of childhood sexual abuse: Later criminal consequences. Washington, DC: U.S. Department of Justice, Office of Justice Programs, National Institute of Justice.

Wiebush, R. G. (1993). Juvenile intensive supervision: The impact on felony offenders diverted from institutional placement. Crime and Delinquency. 39(1), 68–89.

Wiebush, R. G., Baird, C., Krisberg, B., & Onek, D. (1995). Risk assessment and classification for serious, violent, and chronic juvenile offenders. In J. C. Howell, B. Krisberg, J. D. Hawkins, & J. J. Wilson (Eds.), Serious, violent, & chronic juvenile offenders: A sourcebook (pp. 171–212). Thousand Oaks, CA: Sage.

Wilhelm, S. (1970). Who needs the Negro? Cambridge, MA: Schenkman.

Williams, W. A. (1973). The contours of American history. New York: New Viewpoints.

Wilson, J. Q. (1968). Varieties of police behavior: The management of law and order in eight communities. Cambridge, MA: Harvard University Press.

Wilson, J. Q. (1983). Thinking about crime (Rev. ed.). New York: Basic.

Wilson, J. Q. (1995). Crime and public policy. In J. Q. Wilson & J. Petersilia (Eds.), Crime (pp. 489–507). San Francisco: Institute for Contemporary Studies Press.

Wilson, J. Q., & Herrnstein, R. J. (1985). Crime and human nature. New York: Simon & Schuster.

Wilson, J. Q., & Howell, J. C. (1993). A comprehensive strategy for serious, violent, and chronic juvenile offenders. Washington, DC: U.S. Department of Justice, Office of Justice Programs, Office of Juvenile Justice and Delinquency Prevention.

Wines, E. C. (1880). *The state of prisons and child-saving institutions in the civilized world*. Cambridge, UK: J. S. Wilson and Son.

Witmer, J., & Tufts, E. (1954). *The effectiveness of delinquency prevention programs*. Washington, DC: Government Printing Office.

Wolfgang, M. E., Figlio, R. M., & Sellin, T. (1972). *Delinquency in a birth cohort*. Chicago: University of Chicago Press.

Wolfgang, M. E., Thornberry, T. P., & Figlio, R. M. (1987). *From boy to man, from delinquency to crime*. Chicago: University of Chicago Press.

Wordes, M., & Nuñez, M., (2002). *Our vulnerable teenagers: Their victimization, its consequences, and directions for prevention and intervention*. Oakland, CA: National Council on Crime and Delinquency.

Wright, W. E., & Dixon, M. C. (1977). Community prevention and treatment of juvenile delinquency: A review of evaluation studies. *Journal of Research in Crime and Delinquency, 14*(1), 35–67.

Yetman, N. R. (1970). *Voices from slavery*. New York: Holt, Rinehart and Winston.

Yoshikawa, H. (1994). Prevention as cumulative protection: Effects of early family support and education on chronic delinquency and its risks. *Psychological Bulletin, 115,* 1–27.

Yoshikawa, H. (1995). Long-term effects of early childhood programs on social outcomes and delinquency. *The Future of Children, 5*(3), 51–75.

Zimring, F. (in press). Minimizing harm from minority disproportion in American juvenile justice. In D. Hawkins & K. Kempf-Leonard (Eds.), *Our children, their children: Confronting racial and ethnic differences in American juvenile justice*. Chicago: University of Chicago Press.

Zimring, F. E., & Hawkins, G. J. (1973). *Deterrence: The legal threat in crime control*. Chicago: University of Chicago Press.

Index

Page numbers in *italics* are for tables and figures.

and juvenile delinquents, serious,
    violent, and chronic, 58
and laws for juvenile court, 39, 57–58
and leniency issues, 3–4
and longer, mandatory sentences, 5
minorities, 81–111
    and arrest statistics for, 85–90
    and bilingual staff, 98
    and diversity training, 98–99,
        108–109
    and DMC, 81–82, 90, 110–111
    and federal statistics, 95–97
    and immigration issues, 99–100
    and prisoner statistics, 93–95
    and probation statistics, 90
    and state correctional facility
        statistics, 90–93
and myths, policies based on, 1–7
and processing stages for cases,
    78–79, 84–90
and process of selection for transfer
    to criminal justice system,
    78–79, 80
and racism, 105–110
and RAIs, 75
referrals to, 79
and rehabilitation, 182–185
and sanctions, graduated system of,
    161–162
and standards, 181–185
statistics, 12
Juvenile Protective League, 41, 42
Juvenile Psychopathic Institute, 42

Katz, J., 16
Kelley, B. T., 128, 136, *136*
Kennedy, John F., 126, 143
Kennedy, Robert F., 126
Kennedy, S., 170
Kent v. United States, 57
Kirchheimer, O., 21, 181
Kitano, H. L., 102
Kittrie, N., 57
Kitzman, H., 138
Klein, M., 49
Klein, M. W., 164, 166

Kline, S., 13
Kobrin, S., 45, 46
Kolbo, J. R., 137
Korinek, K., 141, 142
Krisberg, B., 4, *4*, 5, 6, 11, 13, 16, 59, 75,
    76, 77, 78, 82, 93, 107, 108, 117, 118,
    128, 133, 135, 147, 163, 170, 172,
    192, 193
Krisberg, M., 101

Labeling theory, 184
Land, K. C., 154
Land, P. L., 154
Langan, P. A., 3
Lanza-Kaduce, L., 178
The Last One Over the Wall (Miller), 17
Latessa, E. J., 149
Lathrop, Julia, 39, 183, 195
Latino youths
    and arrest statistics for, 85
    and gang stereotypes, 100–101
    and immigrant issues, 99–100
    and institutionalization statistics
        for, 91–92
    and juvenile justice system, 97–100
    and prisoner statistics, 93–95
    and processing in criminal justice
        system, 89
Lawrence, C., 108
Laws
    Anglo-American law, 19–22, 181,
        183, 185
    Jim Crow laws, 38
    and jury trials, 57
    for juvenile court, 39, 57–58
    and legal status in criminal justice
        system, 79
    and rights of juveniles, 57–58, 71
Le, T., 101
Lee, L. C., 103
Lee, V. E., 102
Leffert, N., 133
Legal representation issues, 109
Leiber, M., 84, 90
Lejins, P. P., 126
Lemert, E. M., 55, 145, 148

and meta-analyses of programs,
149–151
and Native American youths, 105
and recidivism, 6, 162
residential programs, 123
secure confinement programs,
155, 156
and shelter programs,
nonsecure, 76
and stereotypical programs, 115
Progressive Era, 36–41
Psychologically oriented treatments,
55–56
Puerto Rican immigrants, and Chicago
Area Project, 47
Pugh, C., 138, 139
Punishments
capital punishment, 24, 79, 80, 125
corporal punishment, 24, 29
and juvenile justice system, 58
Purcell, F., 51
Puritans, 21
Puzzanchera, C., 113

Quakers, 182, 195
Quigley, P., 116

Race, concept of, 82–84
Racism. *See also* Immigrant issues;
Minorities
and African American youths,
29, 36
and API youths, 103
and immigrants, 29, 47, 59
and Irish immigrants, 29
and juvenile delinquency, 49
and juvenile justice system, 105–110
and police department policies,
73, 87–88
and reform schools, 38
Ramey, C. T., 138
RAND Corporation, 140, 141
Rappaport, J., 153
Ratner, L., 26
Reagan, Ronald, 58, 126
Rebel Without a Cause (film), 16

Recidivism
and boot camp programs, 6
and child guidance clinic
movement, 44
and D.A.R.E. program, 6
and institutionalization, 170–173
and intervention programs, 6
and prevention programs, 6
and psychologically oriented
treatments, 55
and skill-building programs, 162
and Tough Love program, 6
Redemptive justice, x
Redner, R., 153
Reform schools, 33–34, 38
Rehabilitation issues, 182–185
Rein, M., 51
Renick, M. J., 138
Reno, Janet, 189, 191
Residential programs, 123
Reuter, P., 69, 135, 174
Rhine, E., 171
Rhode Island, and history of juvenile
justice system, 25
Rhodes, W., 153
Richette, L. A., 17
Rights of juveniles, 57–58, 71
Riots, urban, 27, 47, 48, 52
Risk assessment scale, 160–161
Robins, L., 2
Rosenberg, J., 55
Ross, R., 5
Rothman, D., 23, 30
Rumsey, E., 138
Rural areas, 34, 77
Rusche, G., 21, 181
Ryan, W., 48
Rydell, C. P., 6, 141
RYSE (Reaffirming Young Sisters'
Excellence) program,
118–121, 123

Salvation Army, 127
Samuel Slater factory, 25
Sanborn, Franklin, 35
Sanchez-Jankowski, M. S., 16